To Nancy

SECONDARY EDUCATION IN IRELAND
1870-1921

This comprehensive study deals with a period of great significance in the educational history of Ireland. In it the author assesses the role and contribution of the two chief forces, Church (both Catholic and Protestant) and State, which shaped policy and development in Irish secondary education from 1870 to the founding of the Irish Free State in 1921; he also chronicles the slow advance of a third force, the teachers, who grew from a lowly, underpaid workforce into a body whose status and influence as a profession were assured.

The story of the emergence of the second-level system is a complex and fascinating one, and it is seen to echo the larger struggle between rival forces seeking control, not of education but of the State.

Political and literary movements of the time have tended to eclipse other issues in posterity's eyes; educational development, central to the struggle for the minds of a people, while not so dramatic, is shown nonetheless to be just as vital in its underlying effects.

T. J. McElligott was born in Cork in August 1914 and graduated from University College, Cork, in 1935. After some years teaching at Glenstal Abbey and Ballymena Academy, he joined Aer Lingus as a traffic officer, resuming teaching in 1945. Dr McElligott is author of *Education in Ireland* (1966), a detailed contemporary survey, and was editor of *The European Teacher* from 1962 to 1977. In 1977 he left his teaching post in Mountjoy School and joined the staff of the Lester B. Pearson College in British Columbia, retiring in 1980.

T. J. McELLIGOTT

SECONDARY EDUCATION IN IRELAND 1870-1921

IRISH ACADEMIC PRESS

This book was printed in the
Republic of Ireland by
The Leinster Leader Limited, Naas,
County Kildare, for
Irish Academic Press Limited,
Kill Lane, Kill-o'-the-Grange, Blackrock,
County Dublin.

ISBN 0 7165 0074 4

CONTENTS

Preface *ix*

1 Schools in Existence before 1878 *1*

2 Rising Demand for Government Aid
for Secondary Education *16*

3 The Bill of 1878 Presented to Parliament *30*

4 The Working of the Act of
Intermediate Education *41*

5 The Educational Endowments' Commission *56*

6 The Work of the Intermediate
Education Commission *64*

7 The Struggle to Introduce Inspection *79*

8 The Report of Dale and Stephens *87*

9 The Irish Councils Bill *98*

10 Moves to Form a Teaching Profession *105*

11 The Commissioners Criticise the System *117*

12 The Vice-Regal Committee of 1918 *125*

13 The Catholic Church Asserts Control *131*

14 The Last Years *139*

15 An Analysis of the System *146*

16 The Commissioners: Their Power
and Limitations *160*

17 Church and State Defend their Positions *168*

Appendixes *72*

Notes *183*

Sources and Bibliography *191*

Index *197*

PREFACE

L'Irlande est une petite contrée sur laquelle se débattent les plus grandes questions de la politique, de la morale et de l'humanité.
Gustave de Beaumont, *L'Irelande Sociale, Politique et Religieuse,* Vol. 1, p. ii.

The period under review covers half a century which was one of formative changes in the structure of Irish secondary education. In the background was the growing political threat to British power in Ireland: in the foreground, the problems posed by increasing numbers in the schools, falling revenue and a militant Church. Throughout, the treatment of my theme is roughly chronological and I have used as a link the activities of the Commissioners of Intermediate Education. Where I have thought it necessary to do so, I have slowed down to fill out the picture by a detailed account of the work of some Commission or the contents of some Report. (Certain matters 1 considered marginal to my main theme and summaries are given only as appendixes.)

The problem of what to put in and what to leave out, where to begin and where to end, compelled me to make decisions which every student must make if he is ever to complete his work. Some of the gaps are due to my own ignorance, others to definite policy, as when I glide rather lightly over the financial scarcities suffered by the Commissioners. Education is my concern but it was economic and not educational imperatives which dictated government policy, particularly in the early years of this century.

The period 1870-1921 was marked by intermittent conflicts that pitted administration against government and Church against State, and these conflicts prevented the emergence of any coherent objectives for the Irish system of education. The evolution of educational policy was thus faltering and fitful, but it is not I think an exaggeration to say that by 1921 education had become a matter of general interest as one of the main problems of democratic government.

As anyone who has embarked on a work of research comes to realise, history is theoretically boundless and educational history is no exception. There is abundant material for further debate in the period I have dealt with, as future students come to assess the subject-matter in accordance with their interests and the demands of society. I may remark that the absence of systematic archives is everywhere apparent and nowhere is this more noticeable than in dealing with diocesan records, vital for an understanding of the place of seminaries as well as other secondary schools in second-level education.

N.B. The terms 'intermediate' and 'secondary' are used interchangeably throughout.

T. J. McElligott
February, 1981

CHAPTER 1

SCHOOLS IN EXISTENCE BEFORE 1878

A traveller in Ireland in the middle of the last century could have found, in nearly every county through which he passed, a small but varied collection of schools for those who wanted a 'superior' education. 'Superior', as distinct from 'primary', had a particular significance for the Census officials of the time who defined a superior school as one in which a foreign language was taught, 'Upon the assumed likelihood that the presence of a foreign language on the school course argues a higher standard of general instruction than is to be found when such an element is wanting.'[1] Some were in the hands of Catholic religious, others were supported by endowments from Protestant Societies or established by royal decree, and not a few were privately owned grinding schools. Of those that loosely might be called 'Protestant', there were Diocesan Free Schools, Royal Schools and the schools of the Incorporated Society for the Promotion of the Protestant Faith in Ireland. A French writer of the time has well summed up the position: *'Les seuls établissements destinés à l'instruction secondaire en Irlande sont ou exclusivement protestants et largement dotés par l'État, ou exclusivement Catholiques, mais uniquement soutenus par les dons volontaires des fidèles.'*[2] *Dotés par l'État,* i.e. endowed by the State, they may well have been but they were in no sense State institutions. In all of them, the management, whether vested in a board of governors or in the head of a religious congregation, was entirely independent of control by the State.

Some secondary education was also given in the national schools. In the 1871 *Census Report,* two training colleges and two ordinary national schools were returned as 'affording higher instruction to 261 pupils (237 males and 24 females), of whom 159 were Catholics, 61 Episcopal Protestants and 41 non-Episcopal Protestants'.[3] It is, however, true to say that in general the founding of the national schools had the effect of killing a great number of small schools where a single teacher often taught a wide range of subjects. Keenan, then Resident Commissioner for Education in Ireland, refers in his evidence to the Powis Report to the National School of Ratoath, Co. Meath, where the Master 'belonged to the old class of teachers' reared in schools which commonly taught classics, and the Report goes on to say: 'The evidence before us proves conclusively that this class of school has been destroyed by the competition of State-aided National Schools.'[4] The closure of these schools was to some extent offset by the opening of the schools of the Christian Brothers which, though classed as 'Primary' in the Reports of the Commissioners of National Education, were in fact often much more than that. The Christian Brothers concentrated on a vocational system of education and whether that education was technical and scientific, as it largely was before the passing of the Act of 1878, or classical and literary, as it later became, they were entirely consistent in continuing to consult the needs of their pupils. A note attached to their roll-books

> gives a very practical direction to the Brothers on how the system was to be adapted to suit the individual boy: The order of subjects here laid down is not intended to be invariably followed. The requirements and tastes of the pupil should be consulted, and his studies directed accordingly. A boy, for example who is preparing for mercantile business, and whose time at school will not admit of his completing the full course, should study bookkeeping rather than astronomy or the use of the globe; a boy destined for the building trades should learn geometry, mensuration and drawing in preference to algebra, navigation, etc.[5]

Schools of the Sisters of Mercy, which may be said to have done for girls what the schools of the Christian Brothers did for boys, i.e. provide cheap education, were established in every diocese between the year 1836 when the head house in Dublin sent out the first 'colony' of nuns and 1861 when the school in Longford was opened. Many of these were Pension Schools or High Schools which, again, like the schools of the Christian Brothers, often combined primary and secondary departments in the one building.

The motives that lay behind the founding of many of these schools were complex, but one thing is certain, that proselytism was no longer the great driving force it once had been in the setting up of schools. It looked as though the rival religious denominations had accepted the existence of certain spheres of influence and were prepared to respect their borders. But the new schools were undeniably serving separate sects, emphasising what F. S. L. Lyons called 'the inexorably denominational character of Irish education'.[6] Each Church held out for what it wanted and, in the absence of government aid and an upper class possessed of sufficient wealth to endow schools, only a clerical system was possible. If integrated education never became a reality in the Ireland of the time, it was because none of the Churches wanted it and also because Catholicism asserted itself early on as the dominant ecclesiastical authority. The authority was recognised by successive British governments throughout the last half of the nineteenth century and, with it, recognition of the fact that education must inevitably reflect the outlook of the religious majority. As Akenson remarks when writing of primary education, 'as the hierarchy grew stronger, and as the government's position throughout Ireland grew less secure',[7] concession after concession was made to the Catholic Church. What was at the outset in 1831 a State system of non-denominational education had been made into a State system of denominational education, and it was this triumph of the denominational principle in the national system which made certain its acceptance in the secondary system.

The complexity of the situation was increased by the fact that endowments, dependent as they often were on the generosity of some local benefactor, were unevenly distributed over the country, and there was no way of making necessary changes except by dealing with individual trusts by applications to Chancery or Charity Commissions or to Parliament itself for a special Act. There were many bodies whose schools were not subject to any inspection and in which the headmaster was permitted to exercise almost absolute control, and Mahaffy describes one headmaster who was in charge of the school at Carrickmacross as living, presumably quite happily, as a sort of pensioner on the endowment.[8] The decline in the value of the endowments themselves, together with the falling Protestant population, must have caused a good deal of uncertainty among Protestants already concerned by the disestablishment of the Church of Ireland in 1869.

The question of secondary education for Catholics had not become a matter for serious discussion until the second half of the nineteenth century and, even then, there were not many Catholics whose social and financial standing was such as to make them feel the want of facilities for such an education. Those who aspired to a fuller education for their children were chiefly of two classes. There were tenant-farmers fortunate enough to enjoy good holdings and favourable leases, and, in the towns, small merchants, shopkeepers and general traders. Sending their children to a secondary school, particularly to a boarding school, gave them confidence in their new position and helped to further their social aspirations.

This new power base was made use of not only by bishops anxious to establish diocesan seminaries but also by religious communities entering the field of education because of their desire to attract vocations. There was one barrier, and a rather formidable one, which, in some dioceses, religious orders had to surmount. Many bishops, in order to assure a sufficiency of pupils for the diocesan college, refused permission to those who would establish boys' schools. As the bishop saw the situation, he had a duty to safeguard the diocesan college which was, in fact, a junior seminary and, because of this, he made known his opposition to schools run by laymen and, to a lesser extent, those in orders. To this arbitrary factor is to be attributed one of the distinguishing characteristics of Irish education, i.e. a wide regional difference between participation rates in different counties.

The Christian Brothers, despite their growing reputation as educationists, were not always welcomed and, when they were, they had to submit to certain irksome restrictions on their liberty. Exception was taken by them to a statute passed by the Synod of Maynooth in 1875 'for the good governance of the Irish Church' and they appealed against it in a Memorial to Rome, asking that their houses and internal affairs be exempt from episcopal visitation. The bishops wished to retain the power of inspection and it was widely felt that, if denied this right, they would expel the Brothers from their schools which, in many cases, were parochial property.[9] The coadjutor to the Archbishop of Tuam, John McEvilly, added that if the Brothers were successful, they were doomed as 'neither the Bishops or P.P.['s] will have collections for them'.[10] In the event a rescript was received from Propaganda upholding the appeal of the Brothers and they retained, and still retain, a considerable degree of autonomy in the governance of their houses. In fact the only internal control exercised by a bishop is in a supervisory capacity over the arrangements for the conservation of the Blessed Sacrament.

It is not without interest that where there had been the greatest concentration of hedge schools, in the counties of Clare, Kerry and Cork, the provision of intermediate schools was usually adequate. The hedge schools had come into existence as an underground form of education at a time in Irish history when education was proscribed and when wandering scholars set up school in the open or in some barn or cabin. They increased very rapidly during the second half of the eighteenth century when the laws against education began to be relaxed. There is evidence to show that in many of the hedge schools instruction of a high quality was given in the classics, in mathematics and in other branches of learning. No single academic or religious factor could, however, account for the uneven distribution of schools which, in the absence of any State grants, continued to depend on the initiative of private individuals or groups of individuals who opened schools only 'wherever there was any possibility of commercial success'.[11] There was also of course the uneven distribution of population which scarcely encouraged the opening of schools in, for instance, isolated rural districts. This imbalance in educational provision was to continue when industrial activity in the east attracted people from the western seaboard.

The diocesan colleges had one immediate advantage: bishops could, through parish priests, 'recruit' suitable pupils and wealthy Catholics were also invited to provide bourses for the education of necessitous pupils. These colleges always accepted students other than those intended for the priesthood and the continental type of seminary which restricts entry to those studying for the priesthood has never flourished in Ireland. For instance, after the founding in 1782 of Carlow College, St Mary's College, Knockbeg, was set up a few miles away and given the status of a 'Minor Diocesan Seminary' where lay students were accepted.[12] Side by side with the diocesan colleges, the schools of the different religious orders developed their own programmes of education and training. In some cases the juniorates became secondary schools, in others philosophy and theology were taken outside the country, usually in Louvain or Rome, but even where, as in St Kieran's College, Kilkenny, the scholastics and the lay students were kept rigidly apart, a secondary school always existed as a common base.

The eagerness with which the religious orders undertook the work of teaching had one paradoxical effect: it both lessened and increased the need for government intervention. On the one hand, the orders were in effect beginning to build a system of education which was eventually to supply the needs of over 90 per cent of the island's inhabitants. Hence the government could argue that it need do nothing. On the other hand, these same schools were soon to find the burden of providing money for building and maintenance, as well as paying lay staff, altogether too much for them and so *had* to seek government aid. As the Bishop of Kilmore said when, in the winter of 1870, he appealed for money with which to build the diocesan college, they had 'no spoils of the past on which to rely'.[13]

It could then be said that for much of the last half of the nineteenth century the Catholic Church was walking on an educational tightrope. Retention of control in the schools necessitated a variety of political dealings with the British government. An awareness of the growing power of nationalism was to make it equally necessary to establish and maintain links with the new class then emerging and which was later to provide the leaders of the Gaelic League, of the

Gaelic Athletic Association and of 1916.

The Catholic Church took the view that as the middle class grew in numbers and influence so, too, would the secondary schools. The national schools had given the people a belief in the benefits of education which the secondary schools were later to capitalise on, and so it was that even as early as 1870, when there were no more than 5000 pupils in secondary schools, Catholic teaching orders continued their policy of expansion.

To explain the low proportion of Protestants attending secondary schools is more difficult. Protestants, perhaps because of a belief that their inherited wealth and social position rendered a lengthy education unnecessary, seemed less eager to send their children to secondary schools. It was also true that a school of appropriate religious persuasion was not always available to them unless they had the means to afford a boarding-school education. Some of those who had the means preferred to send them to England, and Hime, writing some years later, quoted the figure of 1500 or 1600 Irish boys who were then going yearly to school in England.[14] Reasons can fairly readily be adduced for such scholastic traffic but how account for the flight of the headmaster, staff and boys of Portarlington School, who, in 1882, moved to Kingsley College in North Devon!

A report compiled by a Committee of Irish Catholics gives an estimate of the number of Catholic boys attending 'superior' schools in 1870. On their reckoning there were no more than 5000, divided almost equally between boarders and day pupils. From figures given in the report it is reasonable to assume that some 20 per cent of the pupils may have been in regular attendance by the age of twelve, and the figures show that many stayed on at school after reaching the age of eighteen. This assumption must, however, be balanced against the known fact that few parents could afford such a lengthy period of schooling, and some years later we find the President of St Jarlath's College stating that some pupils did not come to intermediate education until the age of sixteen or seventeen, particularly in the case of diocesan colleges.[15] Nor was the attendance of day pupils likely to have been at all regular because of the need for family labour, particularly at harvest and seed time. Many more would undoubtedly have gone on to superior schools had the education given in the national schools not have been considered adequate, but by 1871 the national schools had begun to educate the great mass of the people.

Education beyond that given in the national schools was in an undeveloped state and one writer feared that 'Unless prompt steps were taken by the State to encourage Secondary instruction, the

youth of Ireland could lapse into a condition of deplorable ignorance.'[16] Yet even in quite small towns there were select academies,
commercial colleges and classical schools which provided a rather
specialised type of education for small clusters of pupils. The
academies and commercial colleges survived and some are still with
us, but the classical schools, often taught by a priest or ex-Maynooth
man, declined in importance with the decline of the classics
themselves. Protestant clergymen, in addition to giving tuition,
occasionally received pupils in their homes where they were educated
with the family; one rector, advertising in *The Irish Times* of 9
August 1879, was prepared to accept ten of these 'parlour boarders'
in his house.

That instruction was to be had in some form by anyone with even
slender means is clear. That the efficiency of such instruction was
very much dependent on a wide variety of circumstances is equally
clear, and it was this educational anarchy that the President of
Queen's College, Cork, doubtless had in mind when he referred to the
type of school from which his own and other universities drew their
students:

> The teaching staff in one of these institutions often consists of a
> master and a couple of ill-paid assistants. Indeed, I remember one
> instance in which a claim was made on the part of an 'Academy'
> with one master to be admitted, under the Supplemental Charter of
> the extinct Queen's University, to the rank of an affiliated
> University College. These Colleges, some of which might grow
> into excellent Grammar Schools, undertake to teach the alphabet
> and all the 'Liberal arts'. It is not given to any man, however great
> his abilities may be, to do this.[17]

If the standard in many of the schools was low, so, too, was the
status of the teacher if we are to judge it by reference to such criteria
as salary, pension, security of tenure, etc. This was all the more
strange because of the traditional respect in Ireland for the man of
learning, as evidenced in the social standing of the hedge school
master and, later, the national school teacher. The truth of this statement does not alter the fact that Ireland was then served by a very
informal system of education in which there were almost no trained
practitioners at secondary level. Those who sought positions as
ushers and assistants, particularly in boarding-schools, were without
qualifications of any kind and were treated accordingly. Many of the
staff in Catholic schools were ex-Maynooth men who, *faute de
mieux*, were glad to accept positions as teachers. They found the

schools controlled by religious and had to be content with a very subordinate role. For them, teaching was a second choice, and they
embraced it in a spirit of grateful acceptance. Of professional rights
they thought not at all and they neither made nor, indeed, sought to
make any impact on educational policy. Society's estimate of their
status may have been harsh but it was accurate.

No official salary scales are, of course, available for those years,
but we have figures for one of the foremost colleges in Ireland at the
time, St Stanislaus College, Tullabeg, which were almost certainly
above rather than below the average for the country. There were a
number of laymen on the staff of the college in 1877 who were paid
as follows:

> Mr. D. Turner, teaching the piano at £40 a year; Mr. Kasper
> Meier, teacher of piano, violin and the school band, at £60 a year;
> Mr. Cottuli, paid £6 for dancing lessons once a month; Mr. James
> Flanagan, who taught drawing, kept school accounts, and took
> Elements for arithmetic; and Mr. John Flanagan, who taught
> Elements and aided in teaching philosophy. Both of these were
> paid £50 each *per annum*. Finally, there were two men with
> university degrees: Mr. John Collins, B.A., teaching mathematics
> to first B.A. at a salary of £80 a year; and Mr. Dan Croly, B.A.,
> who taught English language to first B.A. and Matriculation
> students and mathematics to non-matriculation pupils. Croly was
> studying privately and received no salary.[18]

Such salaries may best be judged by comparison with those paid to
teachers in national schools in the same year (1877) when *Thom's
Directory* gives the average salary for men as £66 and for women
£59.

If the education provided for boys was haphazard, that of their
sisters was even more so. First of all, girls were excluded from a share
in all endowments of schools and colleges which the generosity of a
former age had supplied. Dr Traill, Provost of Trinity, could say
during his examination of a witness before the Educational Endowments Commission that, 'in 1872, when I read a paper on this subject
[i.e. the education of girls and women] before the Statistical Society
in Dublin, there was absolutely no endowment for the secondary
education of woman at all'. It was a widely held belief that they
needed little or no education and that the little they did need could be
provided at home. Yet, even on the assumption that no more than ten
girls in every thousand needed a secondary education, there were
then in Ireland '54,000 (Census 1871) girls requiring a higher than

elementary education'.[19] Few girls' schools thought of presenting for such examinations as then existed, even after 1878 when the Joint Board of Oxford and Cambridge admitted girls to their examinations. The first to do so were Alexandra College, the Dominican Convent, Eccles Street, Dublin, and the Ursuline Convent, Waterford.

It would appear that it was only when governesses became increasingly hard to find that separate schools for girls came to be established. They seem to have become quickly popular if we are to judge by the number founded in the last quarter of the nineteenth century but, as few girls in those days embarked on a professional career, the academic content of their studies was not always high. An advertisement for the Convent of Mary Immaculate, Loretto, Omagh, which appeared in *The Irish Catholic Directory* for 1878, shows that the emphasis remained very much on the social graces. It gave as the aim of the school, 'To form young ladies to virtue, ornament their minds with useful knowledge, accustom them to habits of order and economy, and to cultivate in them those qualities which render virtue both amiable and attractive, not only in the family circle but also to society.'

The boarding-schools of the period give us a useful insight into the daily life of the pupils in Ireland a century ago. Most schools allowed but two vacations in the year, one in summer and one at Christmas, and even then, in at least one college, 'the privilege of visiting home [at Christmas] is only granted as a reward for merit.'[20] The prospectus of St Peter's College, Wexford, pointing to the hazards of Christmas travel, stated that but one recess is allowed in the year, 'during which no additional charge is made for those pupils who may find it inconvenient to return to their friends'.[21] And, if we are to believe a writer in *The Clongownian,* even 'home-going for Christmas was unknown until about 1870'.[22]

Life in many of the boarding-schools was bleak to the point of harshness. Pupils generally rose at six o'clock in summer and at seven in winter and, to compound the misery of early rising, there was in most Catholic schools a period of study before breakfast. Nor was the food marked by any great variety if we are to judge from a description of life in Clongowes Wood College in the last half of the nineteenth century when 'the majority of boys still had bread and milk for breakfast and supper'.[23] There is some reason to believe that the boys boarding in the school of the Incorporated Society at Santry were better fed than those elsewhere, as an allowance for diet of eleven pence a day was decided on by the Committee in 1873 to ensure that meat or fish would be served at the main meal each day. The classrooms were usually heated by open fires and 'slates and slate-pencils were in common use until about 1900'.[24]

Little or no provision was made for games but, doubtless, the boarders brought with them a knowledge of their local sports and pastimes, many of them now forgotten. One such account speaks of

> the usual boys' games, such as prisoner's base, rounders, fives, for which we had a large alley; swimming, sliding and skating, in their seasons, cricket and football were not much indulged in, probably the school was too small to make two good sides to play these games properly.[25]

Boarding-schools were really small villages isolated from one another and populated largely by young people who played their own games in accordance with their own rules. For instance, at St Stanislaus College, Tullabeg, football was played on a gravel surface by eighteen players a side. The season began on 20 September each year and ended on St Patrick's Day when football was replaced by cricket, rounders and stilts. Not until the Intermediate Education Board was set up and school life regulated to follow a more definite pattern were team games organised as a leisure activity in schools. Probably the first mention of games in a school prospectus is to be found in that of Mungret College for 1897, which announced that 'in addition to the playground and cricket field, there is an extensive ambulacrum for exercise and games in wet weather'. It is disappointing to be told of a school 'recreation ground' and learn nothing of what games were played there. The typical recreation ground may, indeed, have been less of a playground and more of an exercise-yard such as that in St Patrick's Collegiate Seminary, Tullow, which was described as being 'completely walled round, so that no student can have any communication from without unless when allowed by the Superior, and accompanied by one of the community, a parent, or guardian'.[26]

The events on the programme of sports at the French College, Blackrock, in the summer of 1879 give some idea of the range of sporting activities at the time. 'Throwing the Cricket Ball' and 'Dropping Football' were tests of distance and direction, while 'Walking Matches', especially that for seniors over a course one-and-a-half miles in length, were stern tests of stamina. There were tug-of-war contests and a great number of weight-throwing competitions, two events in which Irish athletes had always been outstanding. The prizes may not have infringed the strict code of amateurism but they were, by present-day standards, unusual. They included a steam engine, a butter cooler, a thermometer, a sardine box and, for the sack race, the prize was marmalade!

Built into the fees charged in secondary schools today is the cost of physical education and games. But, at a time when most of the schools advertising in *The Irish Catholic Directory* of 1870 were quoting fees of twenty-five to thirty guineas for board and tuition, there was little likelihood of money being available for developing sport in schools. Fees in Protestant schools were at all times higher and the 1871 prospectus for St Columba's College, Rathfarnham, gives the figure of 60 guineas. This was certainly higher than the average and, some seven years later, Lord Randolph Churchill gave the range of fees in the Royal Schools and in those of Erasmus Smith as '£65 to £40 per annum'.[27]

One annual event common to Protestant and Catholic schools was Prize Day or Academy Day, with which the summer term ended. On that day the pupils gave proof of their ability in the subjects taught in the school before an audience consisting mostly of parents and university professors, a debate was held, specimens of work exhibited, and speeches delivered in Latin and Greek. In many schools it seemed to have been very much a classical occasion when the pupils were questioned on such authors as Cicero, Horace and Tacitus by 'Maynooth professors, or university professors, or even the Archbishop'.[28] It was for many schools as it is to this day, very much an exercise in public relations. The Jesuits seemed more conscious than other religious orders of the importance of developing closer relations not only with the public but with influential figures of government. During the headmastership of Father Delany of Tullabeg,

> many notabilities were invited to visit the school. Lord Portarlington's arrival was an occasion celebrated by a special half-day. On 17 October 1878, just after the introduction of the Intermediate system, Lord Randolph Churchill and Lady Londonderry came on a visit. They were received with great *éclat*. The following year, after a number of pressing invitations from the rector, the Lord Lieutenant himself and the Duchess of Marlborough visited the college.[29]

Stephen de Vere may have been anxious to maintain the tradition of Prize Day while, at the same time, recognising the need for some more impartial test when, in his evidence before the Powis Commission, he suggested the holding of meetings or concursus 'in different central spots'. He would have scholars from different intermediate schools attend and subject themselves to examination with, as a reward, premiums for those who showed more efficiency.[30] Behind what he was outlining, which was no more than a national Prize Day, can be discerned the outline of the nation-wide system of examinations which within ten years was to enmesh 'the scholars from different intermediate schools'.

In the absence of any generally accepted system of examination, schools were free to teach what they liked and the range of subjects offered was, to say the least, extensive. In the year 1871 the headmaster of Dundalk Educational Institute, with the aid of four assistant masters, was prepared to give instructions in 'Greek, Latin, French, German, Geometry, Algebra, Mensuration, Trigonometry, Mechanics, Electricity, Chemistry, Physical Geography, Metallurgy, Navigation, Geology, Arithmetic, Drawing, Writing, Reading, Spelling, Grammar'.[31]

Classics were taught in almost all schools, though to this general rule the schools of the Incorporate Society formed a notable exception. When giving evidence before the Powis Commission, the representative of the Incorporated Society said in answer to a question on this point:

We do not undertake the classical education at all, for our Society was incorporated for promoting English Protestant schools in Ireland. The object is to educate them for commercial situations, and classics have been superadded where the boys expressed a desire for them.[32]

The influence of the Catholic Church ensured that they were widely taught in boys' schools controlled by religious, and one estimate was that, 'of the 5,178 boys in Irish Catholic Intermediate Schools, 3,188 or 61.5 per cent., were stated to be learning classics'. These figures may seem high when it is borne in mind that Latin and Greek were not taught in many of the schools of the Christian Brothers. In fact a writer in the *Synge Street Centenary Record* goes as far as to say, 'Brothers were forbidden by rule to teach Latin.'[33] This is almost certainly too extreme a statement. The Rule of the Irish Christian Brothers was based to some extent on the Rules of the De La Salle Congregation, which rules forbade the Brothers to *learn* Latin. Hence there was little question of their teaching Latin. It will, I think, be found that when Greek and Latin came to be highly marked under the Intermediate Board and when proficiency in them led towards scholarships as well as to the highest posts in the civil service, the Christian Brothers taught them.

It is not always easy to trace the names of the textbooks in use in schools one hundred years ago. However, in the official Programme of Rules for the first examination under the Intermediate Education Board in 1879, a catalogue of books is given 'suitable for Pupils Preparing for the Examinations' and it is highly probable that many of these books were to be found in the satchels of the school-goers at the time. What does strike one when glancing through the list is the high cost of the books given under 'Irish Literature etc'. O'Donovan's *Large Irish Grammar* is quoted at 16s., and *The Student's History of Ireland* by Cusack cost 6s. In the classics, Arnold's *Latin Prose* and *Greek Prose* were in general use, as well as Bradley's *Latin Prose* and Smith's *History of Greece*. Texts by Thompson, Casey and Bryce were available in mathematics and both Williamson's *Chemistry for Students* and Galloway's *First Steps in Chemistry* appear in book-lists of the seventies. The Christian Brothers provided many of their own texts and 'A Series of Reading Lessons' ran through many editions and was, with Sullivan's *Geography of Ireland,* in use in my own schooldays. At the Brothers' school in Richmond Street 'in the early eighties of the last century' a writer speaks of using their 'Catechism of Irish History' as well as their 'Historical Class Book of European History'.[34]

Perhaps because of the wide range of subjects offered, a few schools found it necessary to separate into two distinct departments. The Methodist College, Belfast, prepared pupils for clerkships in the city as well as for the university; a former teacher in the school describes how the division was made:

> On the one side was the Commercial Department intended for those who did not plan to go to University. The subjects studied here were English, Science, a modern language or languages, Arithmetic, Book-keeping, Handwriting, Commercial Correspondence and the Principles and History of Commerce. The boys who opted for the other section would study the usual curriculum of the Grammar School — English Literature and Composition, Classics, Modern Languages, Mathematics and Science.[35]

The Methodist College system was by no means typical, but it did indicate an alternative curriculum to that of the more professional or university-orientated schools.

In England, examinations of all kinds were to increase very rapidly in the second half of the nineteenth century and 'by 1875 boys leaving secondary school could choose between seventeen different examinations'.[36] Ireland could never match that figure but Irish boys were eligible for all the clerkship examinations and found employment in the Post Office, the Board of Works, Local Government Board, Agricultural Department, and the Education Office.

Whether their success was to be attributed to the schools or to their natural intelligence, the fact is that Irish pupils were immediately successful in the public examinations both for the Home and Indian Civil Service. It may be that they availed more eagerly of the opportunities offered to escape from the poverty of home conditions in parts of rural Ireland than did boys of their age elsewhere. Whatever the reason, there is evidence to show that they gained a disproportionately large number of places for clerkships in the government service. One report, published in 1872, states that

> on the 22nd of February last Irishmen obtained 46 places out of 60 in the Excise; on the 28th of February 8 clerkships out of 20; on the 23rd of June 42 places out of 60 in the Excise; on the 22nd of August 6 clerkships out of 20. In all, during the year 1871, Irishmen obtained 102 government clerkships out of 180 by open examination between England, Ireland and Scotland, although Ireland did not contribute one-fourth of the candidates.[37]

Confirmatory evidence came from another source a year later when, commenting on the opening of public offices to competitive examination, R. D. Lyons writes,

> I am informed that of 133 second-class clerkships, the Irish candidates have taken 35, i.e. 26 per cent, while the population is but 16 per cent of the population of the Empire. Again, of 341 Excise places, Irish candidates took 205, English 108, and Scotch 28, or 60, 32 and 8 per cent respectively.[38]

At the very time when the products of Irish schools were achieving distinction in examinations, the President of Queen's College, Cork, was showing his marked disapproval of the teaching in secondary schools. He corresponded frequently with Lord Emly and in one letter, undated, but which was almost certainly written in the middle seventies, he criticised Protestant and Catholic schools alike. There had been complaints of students who were unable to follow courses at university level yet he must have been aware that the Queen's Colleges were inclined to admit all students who matriculated, especially Catholic students, if only to prove to the government that the university had come to be accepted by all denominations.

He laid the blame for the low educational standards on the poverty of the schools, both Protestant and Catholic:

> They have [he wrote] practically no endowments, and consequently do not attract men of ability to them. And both alike are obliged to use in the lower classes teachers who would in many cases not be entrusted with a good National School. Our Catholic schools have special defects of their own. They are rarely got up with education as their primary object. They are intended to form nuns and priests for missions or as Diocesan Schools at home, the secular education of the boys is a very secondary consideration. The priests either employ very inferior and ill paid teachers to do the work, and even when they do the work themselves they do it very badly, because they have not qualified themselves for the work, and because, and this is a very important reason, *it is not their chief business*.

The underlining in the President's letter takes on an extra significance when it is remembered that it was at that very time that religious were everywhere in Ireland opening schools as if it were, indeed, 'their chief business'. He goes on to reflect on the sad lot of the teacher:

> No words can give you an idea of the degraded position a lay teacher holds in an Irish Catholic school. A London West-end footman is so far above him in relative social standing that he wouldn't for a moment brook the treatment I have known one to receive.[39]

Dr Walter McDonald expressed very similar views when recalling his own school days at St Kieran's College, Kilkenny, where, he said, the teaching was poor and 'the teaching staff defective'. There was no endowment, the pension was low and as a result 'the president was forced to content himself with an insufficient staff — too few in number, and not sufficiently prepared to teach'.[40]

CHAPTER 2

RISING DEMAND FOR STATE AID FOR
SECONDARY EDUCATION

As Ireland entered the last quarter of the nineteenth century the government was being forced to realise the need for some form of State assistance to help those secondary schools already in existence and to encourage the setting-up of new ones, 'but owing to the difficulties that had arisen in connection with the primary system and with university education, neither of the English political parties wished to undertake the work'.[1] The story of the educational developments which follows may not be as dramatic as that of the political movements of the same period, but, in regard to the principles at issue and the effects upon the country, it is almost as important.

The leading actors are the Irish Catholic bishops on the one hand and, on the other, the English politicians and civil servants both in Whitehall and Dublin Castle, bent on their perennial goodwill missions of short-term and, often, short-sighted reform. Because of certain factors, internal and external, the bishops found themselves on a rising arc of influence; the contemporaneous fear of Fenianism inclined the government to support any force of conservatism and, at the same time, the Liberal Party in England seemed not unwilling to satisfy some if not all of the educational needs of the Irish people. So, on the whole, Irish remedial legislation in educational matters was to run on lines favoured by their lordships, and these lines were unequivocally denominational.

The first draft plan, which might seriously be considered as foreshadowing the legislation of 1878, was outlined by Edward Howley, former teacher at the French College, Blackrock, who was called to the Bar in 1874. Towards the end of 1870 he published in the *Evening Post* a series of letters, which, in November 1871, he embodied in a book or pamphlet entitled *The Universities and the Secondary Schools of Ireland with proposals for their improvement*. In it he traced the system of Capitation Grants in Trinidad 'where the government of the colony appropriates a sum of money to each classical school, under any religious management, in exact proportion to the number and proficiency of the students who have passed a satisfactory examination'. The idea was not entirely original as a scheme very similar in form had been proposed in 1863 by George F. Shaw in a lecture on 'How to improve School Education in Ireland',[2] but it contained most of the essentials of the scheme drawn up by Patrick Keenan, the Resident Commissioner of National Education, who had been sent to Trinidad to report on the system of education there and make recommendations.

Keenan himself recalls the shaping of the plan in a letter in which he says,

> I can never forget the meetings I had with him and you [the 'him' refers to Father Jules Leman, founder and then President of Blackrock College; the 'you' refers to Father Reffe, Dean of the College, to whom the letter was addressed by Keenan] while I was preparing the Intermediate scheme, a scheme first suggested to me by the position of your College in Trinidad, about which I had to make a report in 1869.[3]

That College, run by the same order of religious as the French College, Blackrock, was, within five years of the completion of Keenan's report, earning 'as a capitation grant the maximum of £1000 a year' and, naturally, hopes were held that a similar system of payments would be introduced to the benefit of pupils and teachers in Ireland.

The ideas of Keenan were taken up by Howley and presented, as adapted by him, to the needs of Ireland. The idea of capitation grants, the proposal to award small exhibitions and to make the payment of grants to schools on the basis of the number of academic attainments of the pupils, were all put forward in his pamphlet and, later, in association with the staff and students of the French College, in the form of a Memorial to the Chief Secretary. They recommended the holding of an annual examination for boys classified according to age, beginning at twelve years, so that education might be gradually stimulated and not suddenly forced to take a single competitive leap at the end of a school career. The standard in this qualifying examination should be attainable by a large percentage of pupils, so that slow or stupid boys might not be sacrificed by the teachers for the credit usually gained by pushing forward a few quick and clever boys. And, with an admission that religion was never too far from the surface in any discussion of education in Ireland, they would have the examiners give their decisions before knowing to what school the candidates belonged.

Howley's pamphlet was followed by another, written 'in order to confirm the conclusions of the first pamphlet', and this appeared in November 1871. He sent copies of each to Cardinal Newman who acknowledged them in letters which could serve as models of restrained approbation. In the course of a letter written after he had received the first pamphlet, Cardinal Newman wrote:

> It is not in my line, or in my power to originate, or to judge of proposals of a practical character. I have never gone further than investigate principles; but as far as I understand, or could dare to intrude into ecclesiastical or political measures, I should entirely concur, and did, when I was in Dublin, concur in such general views of legislative action, as you recommend.

His letter acknowledging receipt of the second pamphlet skirts any reference to its contents and he simply thanks the author 'as well for the principle on which it is based, as for the information which it supplies in detail'.[4]

Much more significant than anything that Howley had written was the Pastoral letter of Cardinal Cullen written in the autumn of 1871, which put the Catholic case in forthright terms:

> As to Intermediate Education, we demand that the large public endowments now monopolised by schools in which you and we have no confidence and many of which are directly hostile to the Catholic religion, should be taken up by a Commission in which the Catholics of Ireland would have full confidence; that the Commission thus appointed should be merely for financial purposes and should hold the endowments in question, for the benefit of the whole nation, of all the Intermediate Schools in Ireland without religious distinction and for the general advancement of middle-class education; that the national fund thus held should be devoted to the encouragement of Intermediate Education by means of Exhibitions open to the competition of all youths under a certain age, and to payment by results to every institution established for middle-class education. . . .

The suggestion that endowments, many of them more than two centuries old, should be diverted and used for all the children of the nation was a daring one which the Cardinal tempered by a mildly-phrased wish that the examinations be 'conducted in such a manner as to preclude the possibility of partiality or of interference with the religious principles of any competitor or of any school'.

Less than a month later the Cardinal decided to convene a meeting of the Catholics of his diocese in the Pro-Cathedral on 17 January 1872. The meeting decided to forward an address embodying the resolutions, all on education, passed at the meeting to the Prime

Minister, 'in the name of the Catholics of Dublin'. That which dealt with intermediate education ran as follows:

> We further ask that the funds, which, having been originally derived from public sources, are devoted to promote Protestant education in the Royal and other endowed schools in Ireland, shall be made available for the intermediate education of the whole nation, by admitting students in Catholic schools and colleges to their fair share in those endowments.

Following the conference Cardinal Cullen put the Catholic case to Gladstone in a letter, in the course of which he said:

> It cannot be denied that the Catholics of Ireland have suffered in the past and are still suffering serious grievances in reference to education. They now expect that their wrongs will be redressed and that through your powerful influence some compensation will be made for past injustice, by establishing a system of public instruction of which Catholics rich and poor may avail themselves for their children without exposing their faith and morals to danger.[5]

Unfortunately for the expectations of those Catholics who had hoped to see a bill dealing with intermediate education introduced during the session, Gladstone decided to bring in a measure intended to settle the Irish university question. The measure he proposed would make Trinity but one of a number of colleges sharing in the government and privileges of the University of Dublin; the Catholic University, Magee College and the Queen's Colleges of Belfast and Cork being the others. When the bill came before the House, Gladstone did make reference to what he called 'a subject of great importance collateral to that immediately in hand, to which I will only refer for the sake of putting it aside; it is that which relates to the intermediate or proprietary schools in Ireland'.[6] He went on to say that 'legislation with regard to its schools must arise as a necessary of the legislation which Parliament may think fit to adopt with regard to University Education'.[7] Parliament did not, however, adopt any legislation to deal with universities because, as Graham Balfour said, 'The Protestants did not like the measure, because it deprived them of power, the Catholics did not like it because it failed to provide them with endowments and on the second reading it was rejected by three votes.'[8]

Following the dissolution of Parliament the Conservatives secured a majority at the election which followed and on 17 February 1874

Gladstone resigned. In the same month the new Chief Secretary, Sir Michael Hicks-Beach, arrived in Ireland. He was a friend of Dr Woodlock who had succeeded Newman as Rector of the Catholic University and so we can assume knew something of the Irish educational scene to the extent that he was almost certainly made aware that nothing less than denominational education would satisfy the Irish hierarchy. While this is but a conjecture, there is positive evidence that he was forewarned of the very real danger of agreeing to denominational education. It appears that he began working on a plan for Irish education in the winter of 1874 and that a copy was sent to Disraeli.[9] There is no trace of the plan but we have Disraeli's letter of acknowledgement and his observations on the uncompromising attitude of Victorian England to sectarianism in education. He begins with a reference to 'the temper of the time', when 'the national spirit is full of alarm about Popery and Sacerdotalism, and jealous of any move they may deem in their direction',[10] and reminds the Chief Secretary that 'An attempt to deal with National Education in Ireland, even in quieter times, had broken up two governments.' Disraeli points to the contrast between England, where the Church educated the people 'and denominational education was a necessity', and Ireland where 'it is Parliament that has educated the people, and Parliament has declared against denominational education'. This does not mean that it does not exist but he goes on to say that 'many, who are aware of it, shut their eyes to the result', and he ends with a warning: 'Any measure, which advances or sanctions Denominational Education in Ireland, will array the whole of England against it, except a portion of the Clergy and a few country gentlemen.'

It was against this background that two men, the Chief Secretary and the Resident Commissioner of Education in Ireland, began their work.

Keenan had been, in turn, teacher, inspector, headmaster and professor in the Training College before being appointed Resident Commissioner of Education in 1871. Having, as we have seen, reorganised the system in Trinidad in 1869, he had returned to Ireland in 1871. Of his ideas on educational matters we know a great deal, thanks to his many letters to his friend, William Monsell, the Limerick M.P., who, in 1874, was raised to the peerage as Baron Emly. These letters are, however, largely the expression of his personal feelings on education and they do little to reveal the pressures to which he must have been subjected when he undertook the work of preparing a plan for the development of secondary education in Ireland. To steer a course between strongly-held Catholic convictions and the obduracy of English non-conformist opinion was no easy one and a warning shot, in the form of an editorial in *The Times,* must have told him, if he needed telling, that any endowment of Catholic schools would be resisted. Referring to Catholics and their demands, it said,

> ... to give them separate establishments for themselves, supported by the State, would be to create a distinction in their favour inconsistent with the tenor of our recent policy, not only in Ireland, but in England and Scotland, and justified by no existing precedent.[11]

Professional organisations of teachers might have been expected to make proposals as to how to overcome this obstacle but there was only one such body in existence at the time. This was the Schoolmasters' Association consisting of headmasters of Protestant schools and the members decided at their annual meeting on 29 January 1875 to send a deputation to the Chief Secretary. The deputation was received in January 1876 and the Minute Book of the Association contains a pencilled note saying that 'a complete scheme proposing financial aid for intermediate education was forwarded in writing to the Chief Secretary who acknowledged its receipt'. There is no copy of this scheme in the Minute Book but, in a *Memorial ... to the Commissioners of Intermediate Education,* the Honorary Secretary of the Schoolmasters' Association refers to the fact that 'from it [the Schoolmasters' Association] proceeded, in January, 1876, the first suggestion of the measure that has now become law'.

Keenan was scarcely unaffected by the opinions voiced at the time, but his chief task was to collect information, consult responsible authorities and press on with the shaping of a system. His letters occasionally reveal how difficult it was to get information:

> Reliable information on the *quality* of the Irish seminarial education is next to impossible to obtain. It is admitted on all hands to be bad: to be given mainly by young Ecclesiastics, fresh from College, utterly destitute of all didactic qualifications. But you can get no *authority* to vouch this, with permission to quote him.[12]

How the schools could be otherwise than bad would be, he says, a miracle because, 'except in a few cases the teachers are priests, waiting and longing for a *mission* and abhorring their enforced occupation'.[13] It was their 'enforced occupation' which, in Keenan's eyes, made 'the pursuit of teaching to a lay Catholic scholar of distinction . . . impracticable'. But we can see something of the working of his mind when he adds that Catholics will not 'dream of becoming teachers, until the Intermediate Schools are in some way recognised by the State and open to lay as well as clerical professors'.[14]

However, before the end of 1876 he was in a position to write a letter, marked 'Awfully Private and Confidential', in which he told Lord Emly that he had been

> terribly poorly of late and have night and day been occupied like a hack at my estimates for '77-78. I am, however, better today and have been able to go out to Sir M.H.B. *Great* news: but to any human being you must not breathe it. To you and to Lord O'H. only shall I commit the secret. Sir Michael submitted my *Intermediate Memo* to the Cabinet. You cannot conceive how well the project was received. So well — that this very night I *begin* the preparation of the measure. . . .

How carefully he had to tread is revealed in a footnote to that letter in which he adds, 'But if it got wind that it is *I* who am preparing the measure, and that the funds are to come from the Church - there might be a collapse of the whole measure.'[15]

The reference to 'the Church' was to the decision to finance intermediate education with the interest of a sum of £1,000,000 from the disestablished Church of Ireland. Keenan obviously feared criticism from Protestants of what might be considered misappropriation of Church funds. This and the composition of the body to administer the funds presented a problem. It was utterly unlikely that any single individual could be found acceptable to the various interested parties and he complains to Lord Emly of the 'small, unpaid board' to which he must, reluctantly, turn. But, he adds, 'conscious of the utter inefficiency of any such Board, I shall bring to its aid a small Council of the Examiners'.[16] Three days later, with the matter very much on his mind and anxious to be told of any alternative, he returns to the question when he writes to tell him: 'These unpaid Boards are full of dangerous elements. . . . However, for my scheme, there is nothing else for it. We must have an unpaid Board.'[17]

While Keenan was voicing his fears on the efficiency of a Board even when fortified by 'a small Council of Examiners', Bishop Conroy of Ardagh, who was the mouthpiece of the Irish hierarchy, had already expressed fears as to the ability of Catholic schools to meet the examination requirements of the proposed Board. He wrote to the Earl of Granard, who was known to enjoy 'the full confidence of Cardinal Cullen', and in his letter said:

> Your Lordship knows that the resources of the Catholic Body are not sufficient to maintain with any prospect of success the struggle which such an Examining Body would inaugurate between the students of well-endowed State establishments, and those of the unaided Catholic schools. To be sure, in that event, the Catholic University would have a right to claim degrees for her children as well as the present University but to play Cinderella without the useful slipper, and to play it for ever, is not an agreeable or useful destiny no matter how condescending the Elder Sisters may become.[18]

Later on in the same letter he referred to 'the competitive examinations for the Civil Service' which, he said, 'have done great harm to Education in Ireland by lowering its standard and debasing its method. What would it be if every High School and College in the country became a grinding Establishment?'[19]

The importance with which the hierarchy viewed the Examining Body and its composition was at once a measure of their fear that such a body might act prejudicially against the interests of Catholic education and also of their lack of confidence in the instruction given in Catholic schools. Bishop Conroy returns to the theme in the course of a further letter to Lord Granard in which he warned: 'it would be fatal to the success of the scheme to appoint an examining body the members of which should be exclusively Protestants or Secularists, or Catholics who have identified themselves with Godless Educational Establishments'.[20] Nor were they indifferent to the threat which inspection could pose to schools lacking in the amenities enjoyed by their better-endowed rivals. Writing to the Chief Secretary towards the end of 1876, Bishop Conroy puts the objections to it courteously but firmly:

> I trust that your plan for the improvement of Intermediate Education will not include a demand of the right to inspect Catholic Schools *otherwise than by testing their results in the examinations*. We should be jealous of such inspection; and to claim the right of making it, would signally interfere with the success of the proposed scheme.[21]

If the opposition of the bishops to inspection was based largely on material grounds, their resistance to the suggestion that national schools and model schools be allowed participate in the intermediate system was rooted in profound religious convictions. Nothing could be more clear than Conroy's rejection of the suggestion when he affirmed that were they to accept it

> then we should be in the position of men who tolerate and even recommend the Mixed System, by allowing our schools to be placed on the same list with the schools of the Model System, which we must ever condemn and with which we will never make terms. This would be the undoing of all our work for the last 40 years. In fact I see no possible *modus vivendi* with the Mixed System.[22]

The point was carried and the final scheme excluded from participation all schools under the National Board. They had, however, been included in an earlier document which may have been the first outline of the scheme, and to which Keenan refers when describing the fears of a bishop to whom it was shown:

> . . . this Bishop must have seen the Memorandum (historical) which I wrote for Sir M. H. B. *three* years ago and has taken it for granted that a few notes in which certainly the Model schools do figure, at the end of the Memo, are the scheme of the moment.[23]

Yet 'the measure', which Keenan had begun to work on some months earlier, was to wait for well over a year before it would be made public. His impatience with the politicians whom he blamed for the delay shows itself in a letter written early in 1877: 'How I regret the postponement of Intermediate Education. Parnell and Biggar!! I think of them only as I think of a sandbank at the bar of a river, impeding the progress of everything useful.'[24] It is hard to see how Parnell and Biggar could be accused of barring the way either to the drafting of a bill to deal with intermediate education in Ireland or to its introduction in the House, since they at no time showed any interest in education. Keenan kept working away; in fact he tells us that he was 'incessantly at work on the Intermediate and other questions', but he must have known that, with the Catholic Church satisfied, he could congratulate himself on what had been done. Conroy says as much in a letter which he addressed to Hicks-Beach in February, 1877. In it he says:

> . . . I have endeavoured all through to put before you what I judged to be *the gravest* of the difficulties likely to be urged on our side against the measure . . . but the general feeling is that your plan is excellent in its outline and in most of its details. I have been

requested by all those whom I consulted on this matter to convey to you that they are most sensible of the courtesy you have shown and of the confidence you have reposed in them, as well as of the fair and impartial spirit in which you have addressed yourself to so vexed a question. I need hardly say that I have deep pleasure in discharging this most agreeable commission.[25]

The years of waiting were over, the 'Memorandum on Intermediate and University Education in Ireland' was ready for submission to the Cabinet. The copy in the political papers of Sir Michael Hicks-Beach, now in the Records Office in Gloucester, is dated 24 December 1877 and is chiefly of interest for certain matter contained in it but omitted from the bill as later presented to Parliament. It is a lengthy document which begins with a glance at the Royal Commission of 1858 with its recommendation that a Board, including one paid Commissioner, and representing the principal religious denominations in Ireland, be appointed and entrusted with 'very great powers of inspection and control over "non-exclusive" schools (i.e. those not founded for the exclusive benefit of one denomination)'. It gives as the reason why this recommendation was not followed that

the Board which I propose would be more efficient and more popular than the copy of the National Board of Education which the Royal Commission suggested; and if it were once established, any duties or powers might subsequently be vested in it, instead of in the present Commissioners of Endowed Schools.

There follows a description of the Board as it was to be constituted under the Act of 1878.

What the Memorandum included but which was not to find inclusion in the bill as presented to Parliament was a proposal for the building of schools:

The building of new Intermediate Schools, to be encouraged by the establishment of grants for building or school requisites to be made by the Board, on similar conditions to those made by the Commissioners of National Education to Schools vested in Trustees for the purpose of elementary education, or in the case of non-vested Schools by loans for the same purpose, on the plan sanctioned by the National Teachers Residences Act of 1875.

It must have been tempting to give such material encouragement, as building grants would represent, to the intermediate schools. It would almost certainly extend their spread to areas especially in the west, where a thinly scattered population could not be expected to support a sufficient number of such schools. It would have been looked upon as an earnest of goodwill by Catholics who could reasonably claim that the government should not rely on private endeavour to supply a public need. But over and against such arguments was the encrusted weight of opinion which, one hundred years ago, was opposed to endowing denominational schools.

In his first letter to Lord Emly in what was to be for him an eventful year, Keenan, never the most optimistic of men, did not conceal his satisfaction that all his efforts to draw up an acceptable scheme were proving successful. He tells Lord Emly that he feels *'quite satisfied'* (his italics) and goes on to ask him if he had read Lord Randolph Churchill's pamphlet: 'A more impracticable scheme could not be devised. He was with me yesterday for some hours. Strange to say he had not the *remotest idea* of the government plans.'[26] This was a reference to a proposal which first appeared in the form of a letter published in the *Freeman's Journal* of 31 December 1877. Briefly, Churchill's proposal was that new schools should be established and he, too, pointed to the same source of money for financing a system of intermediate education as did Keenan when he referred to 'the surplus property of the Disestablished Irish Church'. And, even if he must have felt justifiably disappointed at the manner in which his carefully prepared document was put aside, it was his motion for a Select Committee of the House of Commons to inquire into the conditions and management of the endowed schools in Ireland that led to the legislation of 1885 and the important results that followed from it.

A letter from Hicks-Beach which simply bears the date 'January 1878' may well have been written to accompany the copy of the bill sent to Cardinal Cullen and which the latter acknowledges as having already received when writing to Hicks-Beach in February of that year.[27] It contains what might be considered as marginal notes on the draft scheme which was then, as we know, in its completed form. In it the Chief Secretary makes the rather ingenuous suggestion that 'arrangements might easily be made between students and their teachers, by which the whole, or part of, the grants thus earned by the students might be passed on from them to the teachers'.[28] What is of far more interest in the light of the difficulties the matter raised when the bill was before the House and, later, when the Intermediate Board found itself in financial straits, is his definition of 'students' as including girls: 'The term "students" is intended to include girls as well as boys: but it might be advisable to reduce the value of pay ments to the former, and of their prizes and exhibitions, below that named for boys.'

To read the Memorandum of 1877, to consider the arguments put forward for giving building grants and then to study the terms of the bill sent to the Parliament six months later, is to be made aware of the power of the Catholic Church which found itself forced to reject all such aid through fear of the extension of State power that would almost inevitably accompany such grants. Yet there must have been pressure on Hicks-Beach to embody the suggestion of building grants in the bill and, even after it had come before Parliament, we find the Moderator of the Presbyterian Assembly, Dr Porter, recommending that a clause be added

> to give loans (not grants) to encourage local efforts in building schools. The Presbyterians especially require this. The Church of Ireland has many endowed schools: the Roman Catholics have convent schools: we have none, and are thus placed at a great disadvantage.[29]

Whether in the form of grant or loan, the State could not give money unconditionally and the Churches were not ready for conditional assistance.

Cardinal Cullen in his comments on the Memorandum seems rather non-committal, but it must be remembered that he had never been less than thoroughly informed of its probable contents and that he had, through Dr Conroy, made known his objections and recommendations. His comments are contained in a letter which begins by acknowledging that 'there are many useful things in it for which we are thankful, but that at the same time it cannot be considered as fully satisfactory or lead to a final settlement of the question at issue'.[30] He particularly regrets that 'nothing is proposed as to the property of the endowed schools in Ireland, so that they retain their Protestant character and their rich endowments generally derived from the confiscation of Catholic property in penal times'. This historical aside was probably made to give point to his next remark that 'no grant or subsidy is given to Catholic intermediate schools'. Equally serious was the lack of provision for 'any emolument or remuneration to teachers or professors in the proposed intermediate schools', which, he said, would press 'very heavily upon Catholics who cannot afford to give proper salaries to the teachers they employ'.

If Hicks-Beach had seemed uncertain as to the advisability of allowing girls to benefit fully from the financial provisions of his measure, the Cardinal was plainly reluctant to have them benefit at all. He refers to the intention of extending the provisions of the bill to intermediate schools for girls as well as for boys, and goes on to say,

> This might do very well for infant or primary schools where children of both sexes learn the more fundamental rudiments of knowledge, but it should not be extended to higher schools in which the training and teaching separate into diverging channels for the different sexes. In the intermediate schools the boys begin to train themselves for the army or navy, for the bar or magisterial bench, for the medical or surgical professions, or for other occupations to which men alone can aspire; females go in a different direction and require other sorts of training and teaching; and it seems strange that regulations for the two classes should be united in the one bill.

He also sought safeguards for Catholic interests by asking that the powers of the new Board be 'accurately determined' because, as he said, 'the powers of the Board were always directed against Catholic interests'. This may have been a reference to the Commissioners of National Education who administered primary education. Nor did he see any advantage in opening the existing endowed schools to Catholics in a country where 'sad experience convinces us of the dangers of the mixed or non sectarian system, and we must protest against any extension of it not only in day schools but especially in boarding schools'. An examination of the Cardinal's criticisms will show that no word of his could be interpreted as *opposing* the proposed measure, and he ended by saying 'if the bill be amended or explained so that it may not clash with catholic interests and doctrines, I think that the catholics in general will be thankful for it'.

Among other things, the letter makes clear that Cullen had accepted the 'Conscience Clause'* to which he makes no reference, but which had at one time so threatened the bill that 'an appeal to Rome was seriously contemplated by the cabinet'.[31] In the light of Protestant opposition, and in the face of what we know to have been the extremely firm attitude of the government on this question, the Catholic Church was probably wise to concede ground.[32] Dr Porter, head of the Presbyterian College, Belfast, had voiced the opinion of Protestants in general when he wrote: 'The Conscience Clause is that to which Protestants in this country will most jealously look. In fact if

---

*The Conscience Clause permitted parents of children in schools affiliated to the Intermediate Education Board to withdraw them during religious instruction.

it be unsatisfactory, the advocates of United Education will resolutely oppose the Bill.'[33] The government seemed equally inflexible and, in the course of an interview, Hicks-Beach told Dr Conroy that, in his opinion,

> a 'conscience clause' violated no principle, that it was already accepted by English and Irish Catholics, that without it no government *could prepare* any educational measure [and that] should the Intermediate scheme fall through, when it assails no Catholic principle, the question of Intermediate Education will be relegated to the Greek kalends.[34]

For any political measure to find general acceptance, there must be some element of compromise though not necessarily at the expense of principle and such an element may be discernible in a letter of Dr Conroy's which closed the discussion on the Conscience Clause. He wrote as follows:

> I have communicated to the Cardinal at Dublin the reasons why you find it necessary to insist on a Conscience Clause in the case of all affiliated schools. I am glad to tell you that His Eminence will offer no objections to the arrangements. He believes that the simple *omission* of the National and Model Schools will do much to recommend the scheme to those who distrust the National System.[35]

CHAPTER 3

THE BILL OF 1878 PRESENTED TO PARLIAMENT

'The introduction of the Intermediate System in 1878 marks the beginning of that new era in secondary education in Irish schools. The inherited notion that secondary education was the exclusive privilege of children of a higher social position prevailed in this country as well as in England, then and for many years after the introduction of the Intermediate Act. The framers of the Act devised the term "Intermediate" to meet the difficulty created by this confusion of thought and terms. It means secondary education or higher education than elementary and not higher in the sense of befitting a higher social class.'[1]

It is clear from Keenan's correspondence, as well as that of Hicks-Beach, that the bill was ready early in 1878. It was drafted by the Rt Hon. Edward Gibson, the Attorney General, and Mr Gerald Fitzgibbon, the Solicitor General, but 'It is more than likely that they had consulted Father Delany, the Rector of Tullabeg College, and accepted at least some of his recommendations.'[2] If further proof is needed, it is contained in the Queen's speech at the opening of the Parliamentary session of 1878, in the course of which she said: 'Your attention will be invited to the subject of Intermediate education in Ireland. . . .' Yet the bill was not to come before Parliament until 21 June, that is within two months of the end of the session. If the government held back the bill, it could only have been to restrict debate and, by doing so, lessen the danger of arousing controversy over its contents outside Parliament. Hostile to Home Rule and land reform, the Conservatives had every reason to desire a safe passage for the education bill, and the setting-up of the Commission to deal with endowments must be seen as part of the plan to divert attention from the controversial aspects of education which could have endangered the entire measure.

Even with the bill in the hands of the Parliamentary draftsmen, there was still the danger that it could be put on one side because of political pressures and, to the Irish members, the answers of the Chief Secretary to their queries in Parliament must have seemed evasive. On 22 February 1878, in answer to Mr O'Shaughnessy, Lowther said that he hoped to introduce the bill on Intermediate Education 'when some progress has been made on the Grand Jury Bill'. A month later, on 22 May, he gave an almost identical reply and, even as late as 9 May, he could give no firm date for its introduction. So we can share Keenan's dismay when, early in the spring of 1878, he heard of the impending departure of Hicks-Beach and hurried to confide his fears to Lord Emly:

> How my heart quaked when I found that Beach was to go. *He* himself did not expect the move. If Lord Sandon is the new Chief we are all right. I know him and he is very sympathetic with me. But if Lord G. Hamilton or Plunkett comes, we are in great danger. Lowther I know nothing of, but I should prefer him to any Irishman.[3]

In the event it was Lowther who was appointed, but this did not quite dispel Keenan's fears and he showed his impatience when remarking on the former's first appearance in his new role. 'This new Chief Secretary has made no sign at all of preparation. His answer to Martin on Friday evening was anything but promising.'[4] And, as a further cause of aggravation, he remarks in a later letter: 'The Freeman had a mischievous article urging — in the interest, I suppose, of Dr Woodlock — priority for a University Bill.'[5]

While Keenan had to wait, as we have seen, impatiently, the pressure on the government was maintained and what the newspapers of the time described as 'A Great Aggregate Meeting of the Catholics of Ireland' was held at the Rotunda in Dublin on 26 April 1878, when among the resolutions passed was one requesting that the bill on Intermediate Education promised in the Queen's speech be introduced. It was to be the last of such motions as little more than a month later it was announced in Parliament that the bill was ready and only awaited a suitable moment to be introduced. On 4 June 1878 Churchill, still apparently unaware of the government's plans, moved his own motion:

> That a Select Committee be appointed to inquire into the condition, revenues, and management of the Endowed Schools of Ireland, with instructions to report how far these endowments are at present promoting or are applicable to the promotion of Intermediate Education in that country without distinction of class or religion.[6]

In introducing his motion which, incidentally, 'did not improve his reputation in the Conservative Party',[7] he apologised to the Irish members for taking up 'what might be considered their peculiar property'. He gave as his reason the fact that the question of Irish education was really one of the most important imperial questions of the day and that if the endowed schools were efficiently managed they would have a most beneficial effect upon the middle classes in Ireland. He added significantly that 'though these endowments were in such a state of inefficiency as to demand the attention of the legisla-ture, no Irish member had devoted any attention to the subject'. The Chief Secretary asked that the motion be withdrawn and that the House should agree to the setting up of a small Commission to inquire into the management of endowed schools. He further promised that 'It was the intention of the Government at an early period to introduce in the other House of Parliament a measure dealing with that important subject.'[8] By announcing the setting-up of the Endowed Schools Commission *before* the introduction of the Act of Intermediate Education, the government forestalled any possible criticism of the terms of the Act, which contained no reference to the need for reforming many of these schools.

The Lord Chancellor introduced the Intermediate Education (Ireland) bill on 21 June 1878 in the House of Lords. This was not unusual when there was a great congestion of business in the Lower House, the Lords having, in fact, the same rights as the Commons to originate every sort of measure which was not a money bill. Again, when so many weeks of the session had gone by, time was, as the Lord Chancellor said, precious, 'and in the state of Parliamentary Business it is desirable if a measure on the subject is to be intro-duced, it should be introduced now in your Lordships' House'. He referred in his speech to the Returns of the Census Commissioners of 1871 and, in particular, to one item which stated that in June 1871, out of a population of 5,500,000 there were but 10,814 boys learning Latin, or Greek, or any modern language, or mathematics.

> My Lords [he said], if I describe what is the state of Intermediate Education in Ireland at present, I can only use an extremely short expression — its state is decidedly bad. Intermediate Education in that country is defective in quality, and it is inadequate in quantity.[9]

The debate that followed stretched over eight weeks and was remarkable for the goodwill shown by members of the two great English parties to the bill and by the lack of criticism from Irish members who contented themselves with proposing amendments all concerned with the contents and administration of the bill. Their leader, Isaac Butt, seemed reluctant even to introduce amendments but urged that 'the Bill, the whole Bill, and nothing but the Bill' be passed. As if to underline the importance of his words in the House, he wrote a letter, dated 'Dublin, June 25, 1878', to the Home Rule Parliamentary Party, in the course of which he said, 'we must endeavour to facilitate the progress of public business and avoid every course of conduct which would fairly expose us to the charge of impeding it'. He did not conceal his eagerness to have the measure passed, adding that he would regard with great apprehension 'the postponement of the measure to another session'.[10] Clearly, Butt was appealing to the obstructionists in the Party to desist from any action which might prevent Parliament from passing the bill. There was, of course, little doubt but that it would go through. First of all, it made no demands on the British Treasury as it was deriving its funds from the money raised by the Disestablishment of the Irish Church. Secondly, neither Conservatives nor Liberals wished to forfeit the support of the Irish Party by opposing a bill which 'was approved by the representatives of the Roman Catholics and by Cardinal Cullen, and which at the same time received the support of the hon. and learned member for the University of Dublin'.[11]

The press in general gave a hesitant welcome to the bill. The leader-writer of the *Freeman's Journal,* in a reference to the many wrongs under which Ireland laboured, said that none surpassed in importance what he called 'the great educational grievance'. The London correspondent of the same paper saw no reason for the inclusion of a Conscience Clause, arguing that pupils in Ireland went either to Catholic or Protestant schools but never mixed.[12] *The Times,* in Cassandra-like mood, referred to the fate of previous bills, abandoned because of what it called 'the impracticable claims of the Roman Catholic hierarchy'.[13] *The Nation* was equally pessimistic though for a very different reason. The leader-writer in that paper felt that 'the Government may not really be in earnest about it' and he commented upon some, admittedly unusual, features of the bill:

> It has been introduced, not in the House of Commons, but the House of Lords, by Lord Cairns, at the fag-end of a profitless session; and it certainly appears to us that even if every facility be given by every party in the House for the passage of the bill — a supposition which involves an unwarranted assumption — the chances of its getting through every stage and becoming law before the prorogation of Parliament are peculiarly weak, in view of the amount of Government business that must yet be disposed of.[14]

Keenan must have waited like a producer in the wings for the reaction of the public and, though he does not appear to have been a man of excessively optimistic temperament, his letters at the time show him to have been confident and reveal that his only fear was that the bill might be held up in its passage through the House. In a letter to Lord Emly a few days after the bill had been introduced, he says, 'I asked Dr. Dorrian [the Catholic Bishop of Down and Connor] particularly to muzzle the Home Rulers, especially Biggar who is a Belfast man. His Lordship's reply was characteristic - "What" he said "have they to say to this matter? What have the laity to say to it? Of course they must not interfere.' Where was, however, very little overt disagreement with the contents of the bill if we are to judge by the remarks that follow in the same letter: 'The Methodists are in conference here. They are enthusiastic about the bill. Trinity College is loud in its praise. The president of the Belfast Queen's College was here today rejoicing *immensely* also.' It may have been his own weariness that caused him to add: 'The great thing will be to pass it this *session*. Direct your tactics mainly to this.'[15]

The bill had its Second Reading in the Lords on 28 June when, for the most part, the speakers showed more familiarity with isolated aspects of education than with the contents of the bill under discussion. Lord Emly, as was only to be expected, enthused over the bill which, he said, proposed 'not only the only possible system, but the best possible one'. Lord O'Hagan, though no less enthusiastic, chose to concentrate on 'the principle that it [the bill] adopted', a reference to the recognition given to Catholic schools and the acceptance of the principle that these schools might earn money from the State. His words appeared to be those of a churchman, voicing gratitude for the benevolence of a State which had discovered that money went far towards appeasing sectional differences. He praised the bill because,

> It respected the rights of conscience; it did not interfere with religious susceptibilities; it encouraged individual effort and rewarded it; it absolutely and impartially dispenses the bounty of the State; it aided and improved and consolidated the efforts of scholastic institutions; and it did all this without vexatious interference with the internal management of these institutions.[16]

His speech must have seemed excessively chauvinistic to English ears as he went on to show, by reference to examination results, the superior intelligence of Irish boys:

In 1878, England had $72\frac{1}{2}$ per cent of the population of the United

Kingdom; Ireland 17 per cent; Scotland $10\frac{1}{2}$ per cent. Since 1871, there had been 1918 places in the Customs bestowed in public competition. For these places there had been 11,371 candidates, of whom 11 per cent were Scotch, 46 per cent English, and 43 per cent Irish. Of the places, Scotland gained 6 per cent, England 38 per cent, and Ireland 56 per cent. Of every 100 Scotch candidates 9 passed, of every 100 English 14, and of every 100 Irish, 22.

It may have been these statistics which caused Viscount Midleton to point to the material advantages accruing to the empire from assisting the class of pupils 'from which they might expect to get good public servants'. Undue concentration on academic achievement was not to the liking of Lord Oranmore and Browne, who recommended that attention be given to the more practical side of education and, in doing so, anticipated many of the criticisms levelled against the intermediate system in later years. To him,

> Intellectual education was an excellent thing; but he did not know that if it were carried too far, without being applied to those pursuits in which a man's life was to be spent, it might not become an injury. We might educate children and bring them up as if they were to get their living by education alone; whereas, do what we would, the majority of men must live by the sweat of their brow.[17]

He believed that, if it were possible, it would be advantageous to extend the subjects of examinations even to agriculture and different trades, adding that in Prussia, 'every man was obliged to learn a trade, whatever else he might learn, from the Prince Imperial downwards'.

Few speakers trod on ground that might have been considered dangerous because of religious susceptibilities — such as inspection. Lord Dunsany did so, unaware, perhaps, of the strength of feeling on the question and out of a genuine desire to have schools of an acceptable standard affiliated to the Board. The attitude of the Catholic Church seemed to be that, in general, inspection was favoured if it was confined to the buildings, equipment, methods of teaching, texts used, etc., and was not extended to the internal management of the school. He boldly declared himself in favour of inspection and asked what was meant by saying that the Assistant Commissioners should act, when required, as inspectors.

> From the use of the words 'when required' [he said] it would appear as if inspection was something contingent. Did the words 'when required' mean that there was only to be inspection when

glaring irregularities were discovered. In his opinion, there ought to be more provision than that for the inspection of these subsidized schools.[18]

While the measure was being piloted through the House, Keenan appears to have been particularly sensitive to the attitude of individual members towards the Conscience Clause. Writing on 30 June he even suggests that it might have to be omitted:

Logically, it is out of place. But its appearance in the measure wins the secularists of England and the Protestants generally over here. I am writing Lord O'Hagan advising its retention. Father Delany, S.J., is in favour of retaining it. As it stands it can be no inconvenience — but at the same time it would be wise to have it understood that the clause imports no iconoclastic projects. As it stands it is safe. No Bishop expressed any opposition to it.

In a footnote to the letter he adds, 'Dr. Croke, I heard, was the only Bishop at Maynooth who failed to applaud the Bill. He characterised it as designed to produce fodder for the Queen's Colleges.'[19] While Isaac Butt, the leader of the Irish Party, had ceased to be a decisive influence in Irish affairs by the summer of 1878, he did add his voice to those favouring the inclusion of the Conscience Clause, reminding Hicks-Beach that 'nearly 70 of the Irish members have been returned on a pledge to support denominational education'.[20] Parnell, the man who was later to become leader of the Irish Party, remained a looker-on and the few comments on the education issue traceable to him show little real concern. Frank Hugh O'Donnell, M.P., quotes his lapidary reply when asked what he thought of the bill: ' "Well", he said meditatively, "there does not appear to be much clericalism in it. It seems to steer clear of that. Looks open to everybody equally." '[21]

When on the 9 July the bill was read for the first time in the Commons and when Charles Lewis, the member for Londonderry, moved that it be read a second time that day three months, a cold draught must have been felt as when a door is unexpectedly opened on a warm and, for the most part, friendly assembly. He first criticised the haste with which the measure was being hurried through the House, remarking that 'there was something remarkable, and indeed extraordinary, in the conduct of the Government with regard to this Bill'.[22] To him their conduct was inexplicable:

It was a measure that had been heralded by discussions and investigations; it was simple in its construction, and not complicated in its details; it must have been framed some time ago; it was a measure in which the various religious parties in Ireland were deeply interested; and, notwithstanding all that, the Government keep the Bill in the drawer until five months of the Session had elapsed.

He then went on to make a statement, the significance of which we can appreciate even after a lapse of one hundred years:

The result of the Bill must be to endow schools which were now exclusively sectarian, which were likely to continue sectarian, and which were not only likely to continue sectarian, but to be made more intensely sectarian by the operation of its provisions.

To him the real want, so far as intermediate education in Ireland was concerned, was more schools for the middle classes. But there was nothing in the bill on 'loans for building new schools', nothing to check the race then begun between different congregations to open new schools and to extend their missionary aims in the absence of any consistent educational philosophy. He saw in the objection to inspection the power of religious influence and the real reason for rejecting inspection was, he said, that it was a 'denominational Bill . . . a Bill for the purpose of endowing denominational education in Ireland'.[23] Indifferent to the pain he must have caused those who had hoped that no mention would be made of the source of the money with which it was proposed to finance the system, he quoted from the 68th Clause of the Disestablishment Act of 1869, which provided 'that the surplus derivable from the disendowment of the Irish Church should be mainly applied to the relief of unavoidable calamity and suffering'.[24]

Gladstone sought to allay the fears of the member for Londonderry. He was satisfied that the bill should have the support of his party because it promised assistance to the youth of Ireland while 'asking no questions as to the place in which they were educated, as to the persons by whom they were educated, or as to the religious principles in connection with which that secular education was obtained'. The Second Reading of the bill concluded on 22 July.

During the debate on the Second Reading the O'Conor Don, member for Roscommon, raised the question of including Irish among the subjects for examination and on 25 July he moved an amendment to the bill. It simply requested that 'The Irish language, literature, and archaeology' should be included in the list of subjects. He was strongly supported by Mr O'Conor-Power, member for

Mayo. The discussion that followed was conducted with the utmost goodwill and, as a result, 'Celtic language and literature' appeared among the subjects prescribed in the Schedule of Rules. The history of Ireland, which might otherwise have been ignored, was joined, also as a result of a motion by O'Conor Don, with that of Great Britain as an examination subject.

The men who designed the Act of 1878 worked on the assumption that any measure of superior education would, initially at any rate, concern itself with boys only and, at an early stage in the Parliamentary debate, the Lord Chancellor made the clear statement that 'the Bill, as at present framed, did not contemplate the application of the scheme to female students'. But when the bill was committed to a Committee of the whole House Earl Granville asked if it was intended to admit female students to the advantages of the bill and the Lord Chancellor replied in terms which, while similar to those employed by him in his earlier statement, gave hope to those dissatisfied with the bill before them. He reiterated that, while the bill was intended to promote boys' education, if

> in the opinion of Parliament, the measure should be extended so as to include girls, Her Majesty's Government would desire to consider whether it would not be necessary to make some modification of the rules and to consider also, whether the financial arrangements of the Bill being framed on the principle of providing only for boys, would not require material alteration.

Earl Granville followed up his question with a Petition, which he presented, from The Ladies' General Educational Institute asking that females should be admitted to the benefits of the bill. He strengthened their case by saying that he was advised on high authority that the bill before the House did *not* exclude girls from its benefits. With this view the Lord Chancellor concurred, adding that 'there was nothing in the Bill to prevent the Board under it admitting women to the advantages provided'. This was an advance on his earlier position and when, on 9 July, the bill came before the Commons, Mr Gladstone favoured the admission of women 'in the fullest measure to share in the advantages of the Bill'. However, a proposal by Mr Corry that the Board be given 'a certain sum to be extended on promoting female Education in Ireland' found no support. The scant attention paid to this proposal scarcely reflected the considered opinion of the House and must be ascribed, as the Report of the Educational Endowments was later to imply, to 'the lateness of the session'. When on 25 July the bill came to be considered in Committee, the Chief Secretary said that the government was now willing to have the provisions of the bill applied to girls, and, therefore, he moved an Amendment to insert, 'For applying, as far as conveniently may be, the benefits of this Act to the education of girls'. In what was an effort to avert the financial difficulties which, as we shall see, were to beset the Intermediate Board at every period of its life, Sir Joseph McKenna asked the House to bear in mind that 'the fund to be disposed of under the Bill was not very large, and, indeed, was not sufficient to provide for the requirements of the male youth of Ireland; and, therefore, it would not be expedient that it should be divided equally between girls and boys'. His warning went unheeded and the Amendment was passed.

The bill came before the House on 12 August for the final Reading. It was not a particularly propitious day for the further discussion of a bill that had already been extensively debated. The opening of the grouse-shooting season in Scotland had thinned the ranks of Parliament and as the member for Londonderry, unflagging in what he conceived to be his duty to oppose the bill, remarked, 'if it were not for the serried ranks of Irish members opposite, who had so loyally answered the call of their distinguished leader, there would hardly be a quorum'.

The Chief Secretary began by announcing the names of the Commissioners who had agreed to act on the Board of Intermediate Education. Unsuccessful efforts had earlier been made to ensure that the Board would be representative of educational and academic interests and one amendment sought to establish a Board consisting 'of laymen and graduates of any University of Great Britain', with a view to excluding clerics and to ensure 'some sort of prima facie academical position and potentiality in the Board'. The mover of the amendment, Mr Jenkins, member for Dundee, explained that he feared 'a combination of clerical elements which might be injurious to the promotion of intermediate secular education'. Sir Michael Hicks-Beach intervened to say that 'the wish of the Government was to secure for the Board gentlemen of position, of learning, of experience in educational work; and if it were necessary to include clergymen or persons not having a university degree'. It was perhaps inevitable that there was some lobbying for nominations to the Board and Father Woodlock, Rector of the Catholic University, had on two occasions written to Hicks-Beach mentioning certain prominent figures acceptable, presumably, to Catholic interests.[25] In the event, the Commissioners chosen represented the Protestant Church, the Catholic Church and the Presbyterian Church, thus perpetuating 'the notion that they could not appoint a Catholic to an office of this kind, without having a Protestant to watch him, and *vice versa*'.

The first Commissioners were:

> Chairman: Right Hon. J. T. Ball, Lord Chancellor of Ireland.
> Vice-Chairman: Right Hon. Lord O'Hagan, Commissioner of National Education.
> Right Hon. the Earl of Belmore.
> Right Hon. C. Palles, Commissioner of National Education.
> Rev. Dr George Salmon.
> The O'Conor Don.
> James P. Corry, M.P.

The two Assistant Commissioners were the Rev. Dr Molloy, afterwards Rector of the Catholic University, and the Rev. Dr Porter, who later became President of the Queen's College, Belfast.

On 16 August 1878 the Royal Assent was given to *An Act to Promote Intermediate Education in Ireland* and Her Majesty in her speech, delivered by the Lord Chancellor, expressed a hope for 'the best results from the wise arrangements which you have made for the encouragement of intermediate education in Ireland'.

The Act was passed and if joy was not unconfined among the interested parties, there was general agreement that there was at least one problem less for those whose responsibility it was to contain Ireland's dissatisfaction with English rule. Time was to show that the Act had many deficiencies. The Act as passed contained no provisions as to salary, training and conditions of employment of teachers. It placed no funds at the disposal of the Commissioners for the building or equipment of schools. It failed to stipulate how the results fees were to be used and, in consequence, school managers could do what they pleased with the money. The imprecision of the clause which stated that the two Assistant Commissioners could function as inspectors resulted in there being no inspection. And, as if to compound its shortcomings, the Act recognised the right of girls to inclusion under its terms, even though no additional financial provision was made for them.

CHAPTER 4

THE WORKING OF THE ACT OF
INTERMEDIATE EDUCATION

The first meeting of the Commissioners of Intermediate Education was held on 1 November 1878, at three p.m. in the Privy Council Chamber of Dublin Castle. While the Commissioners were beginning the task of framing a programme of studies in each subject, devising a means of examining candidates from the intermediate schools throughout the country and deciding the terms of appointment and duties of examiners and superintendents, the headmasters were also at work.

There were at the time two bodies in the country representing the headmasters — one Protestant and the other Catholic. According to the biographer of William Walsh, the then Archbishop of Dublin, 'the Catholic headmasters had declined an invitation to join forces with their Protestant colleagues'.[1] However that may be, as early as October 1879 a joint meeting of the Schoolmasters' Association and the standing committee of the Catholic Headmasters' Association was held. The two standing committees sought and secured a meeting with the two Assistant Commissioners and, as a result, the programme of examinations for 1879 was drawn up 'in consultation with representatives of intermediate schools'. A booklet containing the Schedule of Rules and the Programme of Examinations was published on 16 December 1878.

Some knowledge of the Rules governing the payment of results fees, which, it must be remembered, was a first charge on the income of the Board, is necessary for an understanding of the later tribulations of the Board. The relevant section ran as follows:

Results fees shall be paid to the managers of schools for students who, having attended their schools from the 15th October of the year previous to that of examination, and having made at least one hundred attendances from that date to the last day of the month preceding the examination, may obtain passes according to the scale below. For the purpose of this rule a school shall mean any educational institution (not being a national school) which affords classical or scientific education to pupils not exceeding eighteen years of age, of whom not less than ten shall have made one hundred attendances at the least in the period between the fifteenth of October and the last day of the month preceding the examination in respect to which the results fees are claimed.

	One division	Two divisions	Three divisions	Four divisions	Five divisions	Six divisions
	not exceeding	not exceeding	not exceeding	not exceeding	not exceeding	not exceeding
1st Year	nil	£3	£4	£5	—	—
2nd Year	—	£4	£5	£6	£7	—
3rd Year	—	£5	£6	£7	£8	£10

While the Programme also contained the names and authors of textbooks, it was made clear that such books were neither prescribed nor recommended. They were there to indicate 'the *amount of matter* in which the examination will be held'. One marked difference between the early question papers and those of later years was that but one paper was given to each candidate so that he could decide in the examination hall whether to take the 'Higher' or 'Lower' course. Rule V stated as much in a rather prolix manner:

> In each Examination Paper there will be a large proportion of comparatively easy questions to test the knowledge that may fairly be expected from the average class of students. These will be known as 'Pass Questions', and they will not require a knowledge of the subjects marked 'optional' in the Programme. But questions of a more difficult nature will also be given to test the higher proficiency of more advanced students. These will be known as 'Extra Questions', and will be marked with an asterisk in the Examination Paper. They will require a knowledge of the subjects marked 'optional' in the Programme, as well as a more minute and thorough knowledge of the subjects not so marked. Every candidate will be at liberty to attempt the 'Extra Questions' or not, as he may think fit.

There was more to Rule V, but this is the substance of what mattered to the candidate.

The Rules governing prizes and exhibitions were undoubtedly drawn up with a view to preventing too narrow a specialisation, but they contained nothing to enable the examiners to withhold these awards when a sufficiently high standard was not reached. Exhibitions worth £20 a year and tenable for three years were awarded to students obtaining the highest places at the examination for the first year and who passed in at least three divisions. Exhibitions worth £30 a year and tenable for two years were awarded to students obtaining the highest places at the examination for the second year and who passed in three divisions at least. An exhibition holder would, however, lose the award 'unless in each subsequent year he presents himself for examination and passes in three divisions at least, and obtains a certificate of merit in one of such divisions'. In addition to the exhibitions, it was decided that 'silver medals and prizes in books will be awarded to students of merit, who pass in three divisions in any year, and obtain certificates of merit in two of them, but fail to obtain exhibitions'.

There is little doubt that the amendment which enabled the provisions of the Act to be extended to girls was a serious embarrassment to the Commissioners. In an attempt to remedy the situation, they decided to reserve a special part of their funds for exhibitions and prizes for girls only. This modification of the Act was added, as if as an afterthought, at the end of the Rules relating to the examinations. It made absolute the division of the sexes, a division which was to be respected during the lifetime of the Commission. It read as follows:

> There shall not be any competition between girls and boys for prizes or exhibitions. The number of prizes and exhibitions to be awarded in each year to girls shall be determined by assigning one prize or exhibition, according to the respective years, for every ten girls in the aggregate who shall have passed in three Divisions for each such year; and in the same way the number of prizes and exhibitions to be awarded to boys shall be determined by assigning one prize or exhibition, according to the respective years, for every ten boys in the aggregate who shall have passed in three Divisions for such year.

At the second meeting of the Commissioners, that of 7 December 1878, the scale of marks for the different subjects was decided on. The disproportionately large number of marks given to Latin, Greek and English, each of which carried 1,000 marks, greatly encouraged the study of these subjects. Languages, generally, were well favoured, with 700 marks for French, 500 marks for German, 500 marks for Italian and 600 marks for Celtic. Mathematical subjects carried on average 500 marks, in the Middle and Junior Grade, algebra, Euclid, and arithmetic each carried 500 marks and only in the Senior Grade did a mathematical subject (plane trigonometry) earn more - 600 marks — but this was balanced by the 400 marks allotted to elementary (*sic*) mathematics. None of the science subjects reached the 500 mark level and such sections as botany (200 marks) and zoology (200 marks) seemed doomed to disappear from the curriculum of schools intent on earning result fees. Drawing and music, comparatively speaking, did better as each was given 500 marks.

Having issued the Rules and Regulations and having held the first of many meetings with headmasters of schools, the Commissioners were then faced with the task of finding suitable premises for the examinations. The Act of 1878 had laid down that the examinations should be held 'if possible, in the Town Hall or other public Building' but, in the Ireland of the last century, there were few town halls and fewer other suitable public buildings. 'The difficulty was met by the public spirit, the generosity, and the good feeling shown alike by public bodies and by individuals in all localities': thus the Report of the Commissioners for 1879 in which they praised the efforts of all those connected with the schools, adding that 'nothing could be more satisfactory than the harmony which prevailed, and the good feeling with which the headmasters of the schools of different religions co-operated in arranging the local details'. Sometimes they were forced to accommodate the candidates in rather unusual places. In Cork, the examinations were held in the Assembly Rooms and in the Round Room of the Theatre, while in Galway, one of the centres for the examinations in 1880 was Irvine's Auction Rooms. In all, there were 56 centres for the 3054 candidates, of which 43 were for boys and the remainder for girls.

In that first year of the intermediate examinations, the word 'examiner' seems to have been used to describe those who did the work of supervising the examinations as well as those who actually *examined* the candidates' papers. Whether as examiners or supervisors, they seem not to have been ungenerously paid, as an extract from the Minute Book of the Commissioners shows. At their April 1879 meeting, the Commissioners resolved 'that the sum of £20 be paid to each male local examiner in addition to his locomotive expenses, for his services in connection with the Examination', and 'that the remuneration of lady examiners shall be at the rate of £2.2.0. for each day on which they shall be actually engaged in examining'. A minimum of £50 was paid to examiners in Greek, Latin, English and mathematics up to a maximum of £100. A minimum of £30 was paid to examiners in modern languages, physics, drawing and music up to a maximum of £60. A minimum of £20 was paid to examiners in arithmetic up to a maximum of £100. To earn the maximum, most examiners were required to correct 500 papers.

The first examinations held under the Intermediate Board inspired a leader-writer in *The Irish Times* to fill a column and a half of which the following extract will give the literary flavour:

On Thursday there closed one of the most gratifying and most general contentions that has taken place in the modern history of Ireland. An intellectual tilt and tournament, which lasted for nine days, in forty of the leading cities and towns of Ireland, has just terminated, in which about 5,000 of both sexes, 15 or 16 to 18 years of age, took part. Every locality and social caste in the country entered the lists. From the colleges of the three Universities, but in small numbers, from the Royal, the Diocesan, the Erasmus Smith, the Incorporated and other endowed schools; from 5 colleges under the Jesuit fathers; from the Magee Presbyterian College, Londonderry; the Episcopalian College, St. Columba, Rathfarnham; from all the Catholic Diocesan and Grammar schools; from the numerous Collegiate schools under Dominican, Vincentian, Augustinian, Marist, Franciscan, and other Regulars; from the Christian Brothers, the Church Education, the Model and the ordinary national schools; from private tutors, from the numerous convent schools for Catholic young ladies, from the Alexandra College, and other establishments in Dublin, contingents were sent to swell the muster of candidates for intellectual distinctions. No such hosting ever before assembled in Ireland.[2]

Of those examined, the number who came up to the standard fixed by the Schedule of Rules as the lowest for paying result fees, i.e. candidates who passed in at least two divisions, was 2327, of whom 482 were girls. The figure of 2327 represented almost 60 per cent of those who presented themselves for examination. The exhibitions for the year totalled 131 and they were divided as in table 1.

Table 1

	Junior Grade	Middle Grade	Senior Grade	TOTAL
Boys	74	20	15	109
Girls	18	3	1	22

On the publication of the results, managers were entitled to claim results fees, but such claims had to be accompanied by a declaration which was, in effect, the Conscience Clause in shortened form. It read:

> I declare that no pupil who has attended the school from October 15 last has been permitted to remain in attendance during the time of any religious instruction which the parents or guardian of such students have not sanctioned, and that the time for giving such religious instruction has been so fixed that no pupil who did not remain in attendance was excluded directly or indirectly from the advantage of the Secular Education given in the school.

The year of 1879 was, as we have been made aware if only by the leader-writer in *The Irish Times,* a year of great importance to all the intermediate schools. However, we know little of the quality of the answering in individual subjects as the Examiners' Reports for 1879 were not made public, as was the case in subsequent years. What was made public were the names and private addresses of the successful candidates, but the colleges and schools that sent up pupils for examination remained unknown, 'hence many letters appeared in the Press advocating a change of policy in this respect. The following year, 1880, the Board gave the names of the institutions that sent forward the successful candidates.'[3]

If all schools were somewhat apprehensive of the outcome of the first intermediate examinations, Catholic schools were especially so, and one writer recalled being told 'by some of those who were teaching in Catholic schools at the time, that they sent their pupils to the first year's examinations with fear and trembling'.[4] They had no long tradition of scholarship behind them, nor had they the resources to pay qualified graduates, and many years later Archbishop Walsh was to recall the words of a Maynooth professor who had predicted that 'for the first ten years, 90% of the honours, and 95% of the prizes and exhibitions, will go to Protestant schools'.[5] The results must have been highly satisfying to them and the *Cork Daily Herald* even went so far as to state: 'The great success of students from Roman Catholic Colleges is said to have caused a great deal of surprise to the Commissioners.'[6] The newspapers had their own way of assessing the

Table 2

School	Junior		Middle		Senior		TOTAL
	Ex.	Prizes	Ex.	Prizes	Ex.	Prizes	
The French College, Blackrock	8	23	1	9	2	5	48
St Stanislaus' College, Tullamore	3	17	1	9	1	9	40
Royal School, Armagh	2	10	1	3	3	9	28
Royal Academical Institution, Belfast	9	10	1	5	0	1	26
St Vincent's College, Castleknock	4	9	0	1	0	9	23
Academical Institution, Coleraine	2	13	0	1	3	4	23

results and, in table 2 based on the total exhibitions and prizes gained by each, we find that in 1879 three Catholic and three Protestant schools shared the first six places.

And, lest history fails to record their claim to distinction, here are the names of those who headed the list of the first-ever exhibitioners under the intermediate system. First in order of merit among the boys in the Junior Grade was Charles F. Doyle of Limerick, in the Middle Grade, Peter Paul Greer of Galway and, in the Senior Grade, William Andrew Russell of Londonderry. First in order of merit among the girls in the Junior Grade was Alice M. Baxter of Belfast, in the Middle Grade, Kathleen Morrow of Dalkey and, in Senior Grade, Lucy Moore of Belfast. (The names of successful candidates were not the only ones preserved for posterity; lists of unsuccessful candidates were also published, but this practice was discontinued after 1884.)

The publication of the results of the examinations of 1879 marked the end of a year's scholastic work and, almost immediately, a new cycle began. Henceforth, in November of each year, headmasters were obliged to send a list to the Board of all the pupils in their schools. In the February following, an application had to be forwarded, signed by each pupil who intended to present for examination. Finally, in the month of May, headmasters had to supply a statement saying that the studies of such pupils were pursued in Ireland.

After the year 1888 each examiner furnished a comprehensive summary of the work of the candidates whose papers he examined. These summaries appeared in the annual reports of the Board but it is difficult to know what educational purpose was served by their publication. That they were studied by teachers anxious to prepare their pupils for examinations is not in doubt, but at no time did the examiners comment on the suitability or otherwise of the curriculum on which the examination papers were based. Pass lists were published and printed in October of each year, giving the name and address or school of every boy and girl who passed the examination, with the marks obtained in each subject. These, in turn, came to be extensively used in the advertisements proclaiming the virtues of the school to which the successful candidate belonged. Examination successes were the criteria which, in the eyes of parents, distinguished the three-star schools from those whose results relegated them to lower gradings. Slowly and inexorably the chains of the examination system were being fastened on the educational body. Parents, pupils, teachers, all were enmeshed within it.

Since it was to the universities that many of the Senior Grade students turned on leaving school, the opinion of the College authorities on the question of the work done in the schools as judged by the answering of the candidates at College examinations, such as Matriculation, is of interest. The President of University College, Galway, saw the possibilities offered under the system for improving standards within the universities when he spoke in 1880 of the valuable results that had already appeared and his hopes that the Act 'will prove effective in raising the preparatory schools to a higher level of efficiency, and so augmenting the number of those qualified to take advantage of the higher course of instruction'.[7] A year later Dr J. L. Porter, President of Queen's College, Belfast, was able to say: 'The answering of candidates at the Matriculation and Scholarship Examinations, held in October, was on the whole more satisfactory than on any former occasion.'[8] The President of University College, Cork, was far less enthusiastic in his comments. He conceded that the system had 'stimulated schoolmasters to increased exertion and the adoption of better methods of teaching' and, in doing so, had improved the existing schools. But he saw the dangers that must beset a system in which examinations at three levels determine a year's work. In his eyes,

the schools are now attempting to adapt themselves to the scheme of examinations, and vie with each other in counting the honours of the pupils; and as if there were not already enough of prizes, rival schools found scholarships; school work is being reduced to an organized system of cramming the clever boys capable of winning prizes for themselves, and earning result fees for the school while the great majority who cannot do this receive little or no attention.[9]

J. P. Mahaffy, later to become Provost of Trinity College, at the same moment was warning of the dangers that would follow in the wake of the intermediate system. In his Report as an Inspector of Endowed Schools, dated 7 October 1880, he wrote:

The day will yet come when men will look back on the mania for competition in our legislation as the anxious blundering of honest reformers, who tried to cure the occasional abuse of favouritism, by substituting universal hardships, and to raise the tone of lower education by levelling down the higher, by substituting diversity for depth, and by destroying all that freedom and leisure in learning which are the true conditions of solid and lasting culture.

Within four years of the passing of the Act of 1878 the Standing

Committee of the two headmasters' associations presented a Memorial in which they made a concerted attack on the Board for what they held was 'a great departure from the scheme drawn up by the late Government and sanctioned by Parliament'. This was a reference to what they called 'the vast reduction in the scale of pecuniary awards both for students and schools'. The fact was that the Commissioners, encouraged by the results of the first few years, had raised the pass mark to 25 per cent for the examinations of 1882. They also had in mind the need for limiting in some way the number of candidates qualifying for exhibitions and prizes, since any improvement in the quality of the work and any increase in the number passing the examinations meant a proportionate increase in expenditure. And, working within a fixed income of £32,000 a year, which represented the interest accruing from the sum of £1,000,000, allowed the Board little scope for generous gestures either to students or schools. (Their own 'housekeeping' had already been questioned by O'Conor Don, who pointed out that '£11,315 were spent in distributing £12,000'!)

Receipt of the Memorial was acknowledged and on 24 January 1882 the Chief Secretary, Mr W. E. Forster, received a joint deputation from the two bodies. Dr Molloy, the Assistant Commissioner, who introduced the deputation, said that the bill was originally intended for boys only and that Earl Cairns had declared on 2 July 1878, and again on 4 July 1878, that 'should Parliament at any time be disposed to extend the system to them [girls] the financial arrangements would require enlargement'. The members of the deputation praised the working of the Act but warned that a reduction in prizes etc., would lead to the abandoning of the system by many schools. In replying to the deputation, Mr Forster showed himself determined not to commit the government to any additional expenditure and he seems to have relied on what could be interpreted as a legal quibble to do so. Referring to the implied assurance of Earl Cairns, he said that 'the House of Commons was the guardian of the public purse and voted money, and the Bill was passed in the House of Commons for boys and girls, with a certain sum fixed, and the House of Commons was, therefore, not pledged in any way in the House of Lords'.[10]

The schools were not slow to show their resentment at the reduction in the cash value of academic attainments. Table 3 shows the sharp decline in the number of examination candidates over the following five years.

Table 3

Year	Boys	Girls	TOTAL
1881	5,147	1,805	6,952
1882	5,153	1,461	6,614
1883	5,037	1,125	6,162
1884	4,413	1,091	5,504
1885	4,123	1,058	5,181

So acute, indeed, was the financial position that the Standing Committee of the Catholic Headmasters sent a letter to each member of that organisation

> requesting him to state whether the responsible authorities of the School or College, of which he was in charge, are prepared to continue the work of the Intermediate System, in the event of our failing to obtain from Parliament the funds requisite to enable the Board to continue the payment of Results' Fees, Prizes, etc., on substantially the same scale as heretofore.[11]

The Board, finding itself with an accumulated surplus of some £15,000 in 1883, averted the threatened crisis by deciding

> to increase the scale of the Results' Fees by about 33 per cent, and to restore the original proportion between the number of Prizes and Exhibitions and the number of students who pass, viz., one for every ten students, instead of one for every fifteen as in the year 1882 and 1883.

Few schools could survive without the money earned from examinations and by 1885, when the effect of the increased money for prizes and exhibitions was felt, the downwards trend shown in the table had been arrested. Other weaknesses in the system were then chosen as targets for attack and a member of the Schoolmasters' Association drew up a veritable inventory of the defects of the system which, without adducing any evidence, he attributed to the influence of the Christian Brothers. He held that the Commissioners had yielded too far to their demands and that, in consequence,

> in Classics and Mathematics higher scholarship is ruined; Modern Languages are learned by the eye alone; in English the love of literature is killed; the teaching of History is cramped; Drawing is most inadequately dealt with; and Natural Science limited to one or two experiments, and so treated as to be peculiarly open to cram.[12]

From another source came, not so much a criticism of the Intermediate Commissioners, as a criticism of a system of education which compelled the Christian Brothers to make use of monies earned by their pupils in intermediate schools to support both their primary and intermediate schools. The schools of the Christian Brothers had never been part of the primary system and,

> as the natural result of this exclusion, the Christian Brothers have to a great extent *substituted* Intermediate for Primary Education in their schools. All this has acted injuriously upon the Intermediate schools in Ireland, by absorbing, for the benefit of the schools that were founded mainly as schools of Primary Education, *a considerable amount of the limited public endowment now available for the purposes of Intermediate Education in Ireland.*[13]

The extent to which money intended for one section of the system was 'absorbed', in part at any rate, by the other, may be seen by reference to the Reports of the Commissioners. In one year, 1888, the number of boys who passed the examinations and in respect of whom results fees were paid was 1584. Of this number, no fewer than 913 were from the schools of the Christian Brothers. Seen in terms of money, this meant that

> The 'result fees' paid by the Intermediate Education Board to the Christian Brothers, as managers of these schools, amounted to £2,836 5s. 3d. − out of a total of £9,103 10s. 8d., paid by the Board to the managers of all the Schools in Ireland, Protestant or Catholic, from which boys had passed its examinations!

The Brothers were successful in what mattered most to those parents who entrusted boys to their care − examination success. The Superior-General of the Order, Brother Richard A. Maxwell, pointed this out in the course of a letter to the Board objecting to parts of the programme for 1892:

> I find by returns from our different intermediate schools throughout the country that in the examinations for the past three years 2,986 pupils of the prescribed age passed, of whom 157 won exhibitions and 205 prizes. Nearly 40 per cent of all that passed in Ireland were pupils of our schools, including 22 per cent of the exhibitions, 21 per cent of the prizes, and 17 per cent of the medals awarded.[14]

An average of 42.6 per cent of all students who presented, and of 48.5 per cent of all who passed for the three years were from the Christian Schools.

Table 4

Number of Students, of the prescribed age, from the Christian Schools, Presented, the Number Passed, and the Proportion per cent that Passed in the four Provinces at the Intermediate Examinations for the Years 1896, 1897 and 1898. (Source: *Intermediate Education (Ireland) Commission. Appendix to Final Report. Miscellaneous Documents*, Pt 2, p. 53.)

	1896			1897			1898		
	Pre-sented	Passed	Propor-tion %	Pre-sented	Passed	Propor-tion %	Pre-sented	Passed	Propor-tion %
Total Christian schools	2,578	1,779	69.0	2,595	1,899	73.2	2,582	1,851	71.7
Totals all other students	3,369	1,783	52.9	3,519	1,981	56.3	3,563	2,104	59.0
Totals all Ireland	5,947	3,562	59.9	6,114	3,880	63.5	6,145	3,955	64.3

The Commissioners were, of course, the prisoners of the Act of 1878 and had no power to prevent headmasters from developing the intermediate school even at the expense of the primary. What they could and did do, as we have already seen, was to continue to make more stringent the rules for obtaining a pass. Thus when the Rules for 1890 were published, it was found that candidates had to succeed in four and not in three subjects to pass the examination. What they do not appear to have done was to lessen administration costs, and ten years after O'Conor Don had drawn attention to expenditure under this heading we find that, taking the accounts for 1888, 'the total amount paid that year in "results fees" was only £12,045. The payments, for the same period, in salaries and other expenses of administration amounted to £12,229.'

During this period new schools were being built, almost entirely by religious bodies to whom the financial encouragement of results fees was a considerable inducement. And, as these bodies relieved the bishops of the necessity of providing schools, the bishops in turn were disposed to support their demands for adequate financial help. At the General Meeting of the hierarchy on 25 June 1889, a series of resolutions were adopted for submission to Parliament, 'through the leaders of Her Majesty's Government and of the Opposition, in both Houses of Parliament, and the Leader of the Irish Party in the House of Commons'. Resolution 2 dealt with intermediate education and urged

(a) That the amount of the Funds allotted by the State for the carrying out of the System, which is admitted on all sides to be entirely inadequate, should be largely increased. (b) That as the competition created by the System involves a large increase of schools expenses, the results fees obtained by schools should be increased.

The same Resolution expressed what it felt was a very general demand that 'girls, in so far as it is considered desirable for them to take part in the competition with boys, should compete for the same Prizes, and under the same Programmes'.

The phrase 'in so far as it is considered desirable' is revealing. There is evidence that Catholic schools for girls were less than enthusiastic about the intermediate system and, ten years after the passing of the Act of 1878, *only 207 girls* from Catholic schools passed the examinations of the Intermediate Board. This was all the more strange when it is remembered that girls were favoured both in the conditions for passing the examination and for gaining exhibitions. Opposition to the system was, however, based, not on academic grounds, but on the inherent dangers to what the editor of the *Irish Ecclesiastical Record* called 'maidenly modesty'. 'Girls', he said in an article written in 1883,

> have to travel sometimes to distant 'centres' to mingle with strangers; in fact, they must rough it for a week or more without adequate protection. Then the physical strain and nervous excitement is oftentimes decidedly and permanently injurious to the more susceptible temperament of females. If high culture can only be secured at the sacrifice of female delicacy, and the rewards of the Intermediate system can only be purchased by permanent injury to health, we think the nuns are quite right in preferring the maidenly modesty and healthy development of their pupils to the honours of the Intermediate Board.

While no general ecclesiastical direction seems to have been issued, Professor Dudley Edwards says,

> so far as girls were concerned, the Dublin Catholic Convents were discouraged by Cardinal McCabe, from taking part in public competition partly because of the potential dangers to modesty involved in entering examination centres remote from their schools.[15]

A different reason for the withdrawal of some convent schools from the system was advanced by Father William Delany, S.J., in his evidence before the Educational Endowments' (Ireland) Commission, when he said that 'people do not view with approval among Catholics, especially Catholic ecclesiastics who have the direction to a certain extent of the teaching, some of the subjects of the Intermediate Education Board's examinations as suitable for girls' education'. What the subjects were, he did not say. Bishop Nulty of Meath, however, was less reluctant to do so and in a pamphlet published in January 1884 he attacked the intermediate programme. To him it represented a concession to those who had raised the cry of the Rights of Women.

> What else [he wrote] could have made Greek and Latin - not to speak of Euclid or Algebra — leading subjects in an educational programme for girls, with 1,200 marks for each; while Domestic Economy was deemed worthy of only 500, and the various home industries which good house-keeping supposes, and which every good woman must at least understand, are not alluded to at all?[16]

Coming at the end of the Resolutions on Intermediate Education passed by the hierarchy in October 1895 was a reminder to the government of the need for power-sharing if the support of the Catholic Church was to be retained. In a reference to the composition of the Board, it said:

> As to the system of Intermediate Education, it is keenly felt as unfair to Catholics, that the Catholic members are in a minority on the Intermediate Education Board. This unequal treatment of the Catholic body is the more striking and the more obviously indefensible, inasmuch as the pupils of the Catholic schools have for many years carried off far more than 50 per cent of the Prizes, Exhibitions, and Medals awarded by the Intermediate Education Board.

That the balance of power should be with Protestants was all the more strange because it did not obtain on the National Education Board, where one half of the members were Catholic and one half Protestant. In fact it seemed to have been accepted at the time in Ireland that, in the case of 'mixed' public Boards where religious interests were concerned, the representation of the different religions on a Board should be as closely as possible in proportion to the numbers of the different religious denominations. In the eyes of J. P. Mahaffy this determination to avoid discrimination had its ludicrous aspects and he is quoted as having said of the Examiners that 'two Protestants are not to be trusted to examine Greek and Latin; there must be one Roman Catholic, whether he knows Greek or not'.[17]

A solution that was 'final', inasmuch as it lasted to the end of the Board's life, was found in 1901. In that year Mr Wyndham, Chief Secretary for Ireland, answering a question in the Commons, said:

> The number of members on the Board of Intermediate Education was fixed at seven by the Act of 1878. The Board then consisted of three Roman Catholics, three Church of Ireland, and one Presbyterian. In 1880 the number of Presbyterian members was increased to two, and the number of Church of Ireland reduced to two. This proportion was maintained down to the last year when the strength of the Board was increased by Act to twelve members. The Board now consists of six Roman Catholics, three Church of Ireland, and three Presbyterians.[18]

One of Wyndham's successors, Birrell, recognised the need to maintain this delicate balance between conflicting religious interests and when Mahaffy consulted him about a vacancy on the Intermediate Education Board, he explained his position:

> As I understand the ethics of the appointment, the new Assistant Commissioner must be a Roman Catholic, and ought to be a Classical Scholar, just as the next man must be a Protestant. I can assure you I shall not interfere with so nicely-calculated an arrangement.[19]

CHAPTER 5

THE EDUCATIONAL ENDOWMENTS' COMMISSION

Whatever may be said of Britain in regard to its management of Ireland, it never failed to set up a Commission or Committee of Inquiry when, by doing so, critical voices might be silenced and action deferred. As Hammond once said: 'Inquiries were incessant. Committees and Commissions were always investigating Irish problems.'[1] And, as Ireland's problems were many and, apparently, insoluble, so the Committees and Commissions were numerous and varied.

The Educational Endowments' Commission was but one of many set up to examine an educational problem. It was established in 1885 by Act of Parliament and provided for the appointment of two Commissioners and three Assistant Commissioners, two of whom 'shall be or have been Judges of the Supreme Court' and their three Assistants 'persons of experience in education'. The two Commissioners appointed were Lord Chief Justice Fitzgibbon and the Right Hon. John Naish, ex-Lord Chancellor, and they had as Assistant Commissioners, Professor Traill, Rev. J. B. Dougherty and Rev. Gerald Molloy. The composition of the Commission did not meet with the approval of Catholics, who considered Naish to be a 'Castle Catholic' and had heard Father Molloy described by Archbishop Croke as 'an unmitigated Whig and a jump Jim-Crow man in politics'.[2] The Catholic hierarchy, ever vigilant, as we have seen, in ensuring that undue representation was not given to Protestants, met in October 1885 and passed a resolution which read:

> That we call on the Government to reconsider the constitution of this Endowment Commission so as to give to Catholics their due proportion thereon; and we declare our opinion that if no action be taken to give effect to our claim, the Catholic Commissioners should at once resign.[3]

The government did nothing, feeling, no doubt, that they had gone some way towards conciliating Catholic sentiment by consulting the Cardinal on the appointment of one of the three Assistant Commissioners.

The objection of the Catholic hierachy ran deeper than the question of the relative numerical strength of Catholics and Protestants on the Commission. It was focused on the power of veto which was vested in each Judicial Commissioner. Admittedly, the Catholic

Commissioner could put an end to any scheme of redistribution of which he did not approve but, as the Cardinal was quick to point out, 'if the Catholic Commissioner can veto the Protestant scheme, and if the Catholic scheme is vetoed, the endowment remains with the Protestants'.

It is likely that both Protestants and Catholics saw in the Act of 1885 a wise and reasonable piece of legislation in which an anxiety was shown to give as wide a freedom as possible to those already in control of schools, to avoid undue interference with established rights and vested interests, and to ensure that any reorganisation necessary would not violate the spirit of the founder's intentions. With this in mind, the Commissioners announced: 'Any governing body, or governing bodies jointly may, within two months after the commencement of this Act, give notice in writing of their intention to submit a draft scheme for the consideration of the Commissioners.' The latter, doubtless, hoped that by expanding and extending the range of the endowments for the greater benefit of the people, the Act might do for Ireland what the Endowment Acts of 1869 and 1882 had done for England and Scotland. So ill-defined, however, were the powers of many school governors that for them there could be no question of expansion as long as they were insecure in their enjoyment of title. A number of them, including most of the schools under Presbyterian control, voluntarily applied to the Judicial Commissioners for legal authority to manage their schools and the property belonging to them.

One of the earliest tasks undertaken by the Commissioners was that of arranging for the better use of the endowments of the Royal Schools. Attendance at these schools had for some time been falling off and one of the causes appears to have been the belief that the disestablishment of the Protestant Church in Ireland was to be followed by the disendowment of the Royal Schools, whose headmasters were all ministers of that Church. The Commission decided against attempting to unite Protestant and Catholic schools under the same management. Instead, they prepared a draft scheme for the formation of two governing bodies, one representing the various Protestant denominations and the other exclusively Catholic. Each governing body was guaranteed a *minimum* annual grant from the endowment of its own locality sufficient to enable it to maintain at least one school, and it was for the Commissioners of Education to see to it that the school was efficiently conducted. The Commissioners expressed the hope, as early as 1887, that if the scheme for the Royal Schools was adopted, the very efficiency of the provision made for a definite district will strengthen the claim of the rest of Ireland to similar assistance from public sources. Even a moderate endowment judiciously applied would prove most useful and, with such a provision, we still believe that through the Educational Endowments Act, 1885, the arrangements for Intermediate Education throughout Ireland might now be placed on a satisfactory basis, but we are convinced that without it, the benefits expected from the work of our Commission will, in great measure, fail to be realised.

In May 1891 the scheme which the Commissioners had adopted for the administration of the Royal Schools was sanctioned by the Privy Council. Under the terms of this scheme it was stipulated that the endowments of the various Royal Schools be divided equally between Catholic and Protestant communities and while the lands attached to the school were to be retained for the use of the headmaster, both the Catholic and Protestant Boards agreed to sell the lands already let to tenants. This they were quite willing to do as it was believed that under the Land Acts they might be compelled to sell or accept a reduction in rents.

The Commissioners were able to deal far more speedily with the endowments of the Incorporated Society. These, they decided, were of private foundation and that, according to the spirit of the founders' intentions, they were intended for the benefit either of those who were members of the Established Church or of those who might be willing to conform to that Church. The Governing Body therefore was to consist exclusively of members of the Church of Ireland. So many endowments were restricted in this manner, being intended either for a particular religious denomination or for a particular locality and often making specific mention of boys, that girls' schools scarcely benefited at all even though Section 15 of the Act provided for extending to them the benefits of endowments. Dr Traill could say during his examination of witnesses before the Commission that 'in 1872, when I read a paper on the subject [i.e. women's education] before the Statistical Society in Dublin, there was absolutely no endowment for the secondary education of women at all'. One of the few schools to benefit was Alexandra School and College, Dublin, which was incorporated in 1887.

By the year 1890 when the Commissioners came to discuss the draft scheme for the administration of the Erasmus Smith Endowment, then worth something over £10,000 a year, one of the two Judicial Commissioners, Lord Justice Naish, had retired and had been replaced by Mr Justice O'Brien. It was this change which may well have barred the way to the ratification of the scheme which had been prepared by Professor Dougherty, a Presbyterian clergyman, and which had the support of the majority of the Commissioners. The other Judicial Commissioner, Lord Justice Fitzgibbon, held that as the founder's intentions were Protestant, his three schools must remain Protestant. Father Molloy thought that the endowments should not be treated as available exclusively for the benefit of Protestants but as intended primarily for the education of the children of the tenants upon the estates of Erasmus Smith. O'Brien favoured Molloy's plea but, according to Tim Healy, 'would not consult or discuss the matter with Fitzgibbon',[4] and the Act required that the two Judicial Commissioners must concur in approving a scheme. The disagreement between the two judges had far-reaching effects and, again to quote Healy,

> the Act became a nullity as far as the main endowment to be dealt with was concerned. Fitzgibbon confided to me (when we served together on the Trinity College Estates Commission) that if O'Brien had sought a compromise he would have awarded a generous share of the rentals to Catholic uses.[5]

Final agreement was not in fact reached until well over forty years later.

There was no other endowment comparable in value to that of the Erasmus Smith schools and, in the words of the Commissioners, 'The endowments available for Intermediate Education in Ireland are wholly inadequate, and are so unequally distributed that the majority of the people, in large districts of the country, are without adequate provision for higher instruction.' The Commissioners, conscious of their responsibility to respect the wishes of those whose charity had made available the original endowments, were equally conscious of the impossibility of providing anything like 'higher education' for those whom the well-established primary system had prepared for further educational advance. They realised the need of money to establish new schools in 'localities which are unprovided with Educational resources or in which these resources are scanty or precarious', and they believed that

> even a moderate amount of money applied as in the case of the Ulster Royal Schools, for the benefit of defined localities, under the control of a central body, and with an efficient system of inspection, would afford valuable assistance to many struggling institu-

tions and give a large impulse to Intermediate Education in Ireland.

It is arguable that more schools, located with regard to regional needs, might have contributed to stemming the movements towards the towns but even then, in the last decade of the nineteenth century, Ireland was beginning to show many of the signs characteristic of a country emerging from a period of cultural deprivation, and the newly founded intermediate schools were to hasten an already discernible drift from the land. As the Commissioners put it:

> ... the educational methods followed generally in Ireland are too exclusively devoted to that kind of intellectual training which is suited to lawyers, doctors, clergymen, teachers, civil servants, and all clerks of various grades, while the agricultural and industrial classes are left without any special preparation for their careers in life.

Their observations were largely if not totally ignored as the schools continued to chase results fees, and the pupils the exhibitions and prizes. The real value of their work lies in the fact that it is unlikely that a number of schools such as the Royal Schools would be flourishing today had the Commission never sat. It was at their suggestion that the endowments of the Kildare Place Society, which for many years were in the possession of the Church Education Society, were amalgamated with those of the Church of Ireland Training College and applied for the purpose of a training college in connection with the Commissioners of National Education. They removed many of the conditions which religious enthusiasm as much as religious intolerance had imposed, and, by 1894 when their work ended, they had completed and published 210 schemes. To see to the carrying-out of these schemes, a body called the Commissioners of Education in Ireland was set up. It consisted of ten Commissioners appointed by the Lord Lieutenant, ten Commissioners elected by the local Boards of Education, two Commissioners elected by the Council of the University of Dublin, two Commissioners elected by the Senate of the Royal University, two Commissioners elected by the Governing Body of the Institution known as the Catholic University of Ireland and two Commissioners elected by the Intermediate Education Board for Ireland.

Meanwhile the Commissioners of Intermediate Education were forced to adopt various strategies in an effort to live within their shrinking income. In 1889 they decided to await the result of each year's examinations and then to estimate the maximum amount that could be spent so as not to exceed an *a priori* figure, fixing 'the amounts of Exhibitions and Prizes upon the principle that the residue of the deficiency should be apportioned, as nearly as might be, rateably between the total sums awarded for "Rewards" and "Results Fees" respectively'. Such measures of economy were not to the liking of the schools which must have watched with dismay the drop in the money paid them. Figures for 1889 showed that the amount of results fees paid to managers of schools in that year was £10,093 13s. 9d., while a year later these payments had fallen to £8875 15s. 7d. In 1890 the government provided a new source of revenue for the hard-pressed Board. An additional income was created by allotting to the Board a proportion of the revenues collected in Ireland from Customs and from Excise duty on whiskey. The Local Taxation (Customs and Excise) Act of that year provided that, after a sum of £78,000 had been set aside for primary education, the residue should be given to the Intermediate Education Board for the payment of results fees and for prizes and exhibitions.

In 1891 the Commissioners received notification that the amount which would be payable as the Irish share of the Beer and Spirits Duties 1890-91 might be approximately placed at a minimum of £90,000 and, in fact, the proportion of the sum paid them was £39,042 6s. 11d. This enabled the Board to make considerable increases in results fees and prizes, etc. to students in 1892 which, in turn, encouraged pupils to stay on longer in the schools. Expenditure under the heading of Results Fees and Prizes rose quickly to £47,008 16s. 9d. in 1894 as opposed to £5,097 2s. 8d. three years earlier, before what became known as the 'whiskey money' had begun to affect the accounts. As a means of promoting education it had its critics, though it is difficult not to be somewhat sceptical of the truth of Mary Colum's observation that 'the convent girls entered the examination with mixed feelings, realising that young ladies could only succeed through the diligent intemperance of their alcoholicly minded fellow-countrymen'.[6]

By the end of the nineteenth century the intermediate education system was twenty years old. It had, in the course of those twenty years, encouraged, if indirectly, the founding of schools and, by doing so, provided an increasing number of pupils with a 'superior' education. The Census figures for the years 1881, 1891 and 1901 span, approximately, the twenty years in question and show how noticeable was the increase when set against a falling population.

Table 5

Number of Pupils in Superior Schools in each of the years 1881, 1891 and 1901, together with their Religious Profession

Attending superior establishments	1881	1891	1901
Catholics	12,064	15,430	25,647
Protestant Episcopalians	7,854	7,280	7,335
Presbyterians	3,063	3,342	3,638
Methodists	775	787	1,011
Other Denominations	937	930	934
TOTAL	24,693	27,769	38,565

The figures of the Census Commissioners are probably a better indication than those of the Intermediate Education Commissioners of the extent to which children were availing of 'Superior' education, because not all intermediate schools presented pupils for examination and many pupils were excluded from examination on such grounds as age and unsatisfactory attendance. Table 6 shows the numbers examined under the Intermediate Education Act.

Table 6

Year	Boys	Girls	TOTAL
1881	5,147	1,806	6,953
1891	3,856	1,300	5,156
1901	5,829	2,288	8,117

The numbers in the schools is a quantifiable factor, the quality of the work done is not. However, we do know that, as early as 1890, the Standing Committee of the Royal University had sought to harmonise 'the Programme of the Matriculation Examination in the Royal University and the Programme of the Intermediate Education Board'. Pupils from the senior classes presented and were successful in the Matriculation and, in 1900, Mungret College could boast in its prospectus that 'a large number of Students have obtained Honours and Exhibitions, and several have received the University Degree of Bachelor of Arts'. The Catholic University, which as early as 1874 had thirty-seven schools and colleges affiliated to it, appears, if we are to judge by the remarks of one writer, to have had some reason for being dissatisfied with the quality of the work in the intermediate schools. In an essay, entitled 'The Student Body', Professor James Meenan writes:

> Most of the schools from which the College now draws its students were established by the 1870's, but their curricula varied – varied so much that they send up 'gentlemen who have yet to learn such elementary truths as that Jerusalem is not in Africa, that the Helots did not live on the shores of the Red Sea, and that the patriarch Job lived and died before the Babylonian captivity'.[7]

CHAPTER 6

THE WORK OF
THE INTERMEDIATE EDUCATION COMMISSION

The system was almost twenty years old when, in January 1898, the Commissioners took the unexpected step of requesting an inquiry into the working of the Act of 1878. They did so by means of a resolution which they submitted to the Lord Lieutenant, the Right Hon. George Henry, Earl Cadogan:

> That this Board, as a result of their experience of the working of the system established by the Intermediate Education Act 1878, feel satisfied that there are many defects in the system, with several of the more serious of which they are powerless to deal under the existing statutes, and they therefore request His Excellency, the Lord Lieutenant, to constitute the Members of the Board, with such others (if any) as he may think fit, a Commission to enquire into the system and into its practical working, and to report whether any enlargement of the statutory powers of the Board is desirable with a view to the improvement of the system.[1]

The Lord Lieutenant, hoping that the inquiry would be 'short and inexpensive', gave his authority to the setting up of the Commission of Inquiry into intermediate education in Ireland by a letter of 29 April 1898.

A somewhat similar Commission, generally known as the Bryce Commission, had been set up in England in 1894 and as a result of its deliberations local education authorities had been established there. Rather surprisingly, the Commission set up in Ireland consisted of the seven members of the Board of Intermediate Education only. It was true that they had frequently criticised the Act of 1878 and were therefore most likely to be familiar with its defects, but at least one M.P. was later to voice his dissatisfaction with the constitution of the Commission. Speaking in the Commons in 1904, John Redmond said:

> Many of the Intermediate Education Board are eminent men, but none of them can be picked out as educational authorities or as qualified for the work upon which they are engaged. For twenty years the Intermediate Board had full control of intermediate education, and they carried on a system of cramming and payment by results to such an extent that they did irreparable

damage to the education of the youth of the country. But at last the people cried shame upon them, and they had to admit their failure. With a touch of true Gilbertian humour, they resolved themselves into a Commission to inquire into the defects of their own work.[2]

John Redmond was hardly being fair as it was not a question of defects in the work of the Commissioners but of defects in the Act itself. If it could be established that such defects existed, then new legislation might be necessary, but full information would first be needed both by the government and by the public. Only a Commission of Inquiry could obtain such information and present it in a convincing manner to the government.

The Commission had been requested to act 'with all convenient speed' and they appear to have done so. Within five weeks, i.e. on 4 July 1898, we find them sending a circular to the managers of Irish intermediate schools and, on the same date, a different circular to the 'Examiners under the Intermediate Education Board for Ireland and to others'. The 'others' included the archbishops and bishops of the Sees in Ireland, the Moderator of the General Assembly, the members of Parliament for Irish constituencies, the chairmen of municipal bodies as well as the Fellows and Professors of the Royal University and of the Queen's Colleges. No one could accuse the Commissioners of not having spread their net widely as, in addition to the circulars, they published advertisements in numerous newspapers and invited assistance from the English and Scottish Education Departments.

The problems which the Commissioners presented to those from whom they sought evidence centred on the system which made State aid to managers of intermediate schools depend on the results of one general examination of students held for the whole country. This, in turn, meant an examination not only of the system of payment by results in the abstract, but of that system as applied to intermediate education in Ireland, 'taking into consideration the effect which it necessarily has upon the admission or exclusion of *viva voce* questioning'. Had Irish schools not been so dependent on the results fees, the examinations might not have been so eagerly adopted by them. As it was, economic reasons made it difficult for schools to preserve their independence and the principle that the money did matter and that the reward of work was a money prize, deriving as it did from the highest educational authority in the State, pervaded the whole country and cannot have failed to influence the minds of the people. As one writer not unfairly put it: 'The formation of character, the cultivation of taste, the disinterested love of learning not being capable of being tested by examination, were disregarded in this sordid race for results fees.'[3]

Since the Commission recorded the written or oral testimony of some hundreds of persons, and since such testimony ranged over every aspect of the system, it is not possible to give more than an abstract of the views expressed. One of those who criticised the system in general terms was Miss Elizabeth Boyd of the Royal School, Raphoe, who gave it as her opinion that the system had failed in its avowed object

> to bring within the reach of the poorer people a cheap and accessible means of obtaining a better education than was to be obtained under the National System, one which would not only prepare for a University education, but qualify for commercial pursuits.

She pointed to the uneven distribution of schools and to the closing-down of schools in country districts which she attributed to 'the utterly mistaken manner in which money has been allocated', and also the failure 'to ameliorate the unfavourable conditions of the poorer and more remote districts, by placing them in a position to earn a fair share of the grant'. The first of these defects meant, she said, that instead of money being allocated so as to set up schools in remote country districts,

> the whole annual grant was thrown open in one undivided sum to all Ireland, and in such a way that schools in large centres of population — schools already not only self-supporting, but flourishing — got, as a matter of course, almost the entire grant, in virtue of the great number of pupils, leaving the very districts not within practical access of a good middle-class education as badly off as before.

Her suggested method of remedying the second defect, i.e. the unfavourable conditions in the poorer and more remote districts, showed her to be well ahead of her time in the matter of educational planning. She would make use of

> as much of the money allocated to a district, and not earned as results fees, in assisting to build and equip suitable school buildings and teachers' residences, the grants for such to be conditional on local contributions; secondly, by giving in addition to results fees, aid to teachers in the form of a capitation grant.

Support for her views came from Professor John England of Queen's College, Cork, who pointed to the number of people in the country

> whose means and position would naturally lead them to give their sons an education of a higher class than that given by the National Schools, but who may not aspire to a university education, nor would their means justify them in sending their children to expensive boarding schools.

He showed the difference in the earning power of large schools presenting big numbers for examination and the small schools putting forward but a few candidates in each Grade. Quoting from the Report of the Board for 1897, he said:

> a sum of nearly £9,000 was paid to about eight large schools, giving an average of about £1,100 to each, several of these being large boarding schools or colleges having considerable resources independent of the assistance derived from the Intermediate Education Board [while] nearly one-third of the entire number, received under £50 each — a sum evidently inadequate to much increase their efficiency.

This, in substance, was also the view of Dr Laffan of Cashel who, in his evidence before the Commission, said that the intermediate system had done nothing for the multiplication of local schools and that 'where a school could not live before it passed, it had not been able to live since'. Most probably, Dr Laffan had in mind the schools 'managed by Catholic gentlemen and Catholic ladies, where a good classical and general education was given'. Some of these had, it is true, died, but many others, unable or unwilling to compete with religious orders, had simply been taken over. I use the expression 'taken over' to convey that there was usually no break in continuity. Education in a country town might have been given for years by an individual who, having no one to whom to bequeath his school, would open negotiations with some religious body to take it over. The natural body to do so would be the Church authorities, for at the time only they, other than the State, had the continuity which was needed if secondary education were to proceed in any systematic way. Dr Houston, the headmaster of the Academical Institution in Coleraine, agreed with Dr Laffan that the small school, particularly in the more remote villages and towns, had received no encouragement under the Act but that, at the same time, there had been 'an abnormal and unnecessary increase in Intermediate schools'. He gave the number of intermediate schools then in existence as 324 and added: 'It seems to me that at least one-half of the 324 would be better occupied in providing a good technical and commercial education for boys and girls who do not intend either to enter the professional walks of life or to go to the university.'

It is not easy to say with certainty if, in fact, the figure 324 which Dr Houston quoted was quite accurate since the Commissioners of Intermediate Education and the Census Commissioners had each a different definition of a secondary school. For the former, it was a school in which the pupils followed the Board's syllabus and presented candidates for the Board's examinations. For the purpose of the Census, it was simply a school in which Latin, Greek, or one or more modern languages were taught. Colleges were not always tabulated with superior schools and, in 1891, such well-known schools as the Methodist College, Belfast, and Rockwell College, Cashel, with an aggregate of 470 students, did not appear under 'secondary schools'. The President of St Munchin's College, Limerick, Rev. Andrew Murphy, said in his evidence to the Commission that 'the pupils receiving superior instruction in primary schools have been tabulated both in 1891 and 1881, and pupils receiving primary instruction in superior establishments were eliminated'. The training colleges for primary teachers, of which there were five in Dublin and one in Waterford, were listed as 'superior schools' probably because they offered Greek and Latin as part of the curriculum. Table 7 shows the position over a period of thirty years.[4]

Table 7

Year	Male	Female	Mixed	TOTAL
1871	252	162	160	574
1881	205	117	166	488
1891	199	91	185	475
1901	197	111	182	490

A number of witnesses felt, as did Professor England, that some 'distinction ought to be drawn between Primary and Intermediate schools'. He was opposed to what was the ideal of the Christian Brothers, holding that 'any attempt to combine the two in one institution' was detrimental to both. (He claimed that the same opinion was strongly held by Dr Sullivan, the former President of Queen's College, Cork.) A certain amount of overlapping in the work of the higher classes of primary schools and the lower classes of secondary schools was inevitable, but the tendency of primary teachers to prepare pupils for the rewards of the Preparatory Grade was resented and may have been a factor in deciding the Commission to recommend the abolition of that Grade. The figures in the following table 8,[5] showing the disproportionately large number of pupils in the lower classes and the correspondingly large number of candidates for the Preparatory and Junior Grade examinations, point to where the Act was abused.

Table 8

Year	Number Examined				TOTAL
	Senior	Middle	Junior	Preparatory	
1892	287	710	2,942	1,820	5,579
1893	341	844	3,524	2,265	6,974
1894	364	971	3,693	2,654	7,682
1895	423	983	3,993	2,924	8,323
1896	438	1,109	4,110	3,062	8,719
1897	463	1,004	4,269	3,141	8,877
1898	404	1,109	4,396	3,164	9,073

This abuse meant a diversion to primary sections of intermediate schools of a large proportion of the income of the Intermediate Education Board. It was suggested that the Board could have effectively ended this abuse by altering Section 6 (Subsection 8) of the Act, which empowered the Board to make rules 'for prescribing and satisfying themselves as to the observance of the conditions upon which managers of schools may receive payment by result fees', and also by *expressly excluding national schools* from obtaining any payments under this heading.

Had this been done, it would possibly have ensured that the money for intermediate education could not flow into channels other than those for which it was intended, but it is questionable if it would have helped the number of those taking higher examinations. The Ireland of the time was still poor, and almost untouched by industrial development. It was a country in which the many small farmers and lowly paid labourers had need of the labour if not the earnings of their children, sometimes even before they reached the age at which they left the national school. As a writer in the *Synge Street Centenary Record* puts it, 'There are old Synge Street men alive today who tell how they got Exhibitions in Preparatory Grade or Junior Grade, and how their fathers took them from school and put them to work', adding that the Brothers called on the father and persuaded him to give the boy his chance. It is also true to say that only in the schools of the Christian Brothers was some effort made to co-ordinate primary and secondary education so that, 'when a child of ten or twelve years shows unusual ability, he is sent to one of their higher schools, where he is prepared for the Intermediate Examinations, and is enabled to commence an upward course'.[6] One result of this was that the proportion of those in the Brothers' schools who went from the primary department to the secondary 'was about one-fourth or one-fifth'.

Children of better-off parents who might have helped to swell the numbers in Middle and Senior Grade classes were often sent to school in England and we have seen that one headmaster, Maurice Hime, who gave evidence before the Commission, estimated that up to 1600 boys went there to school. While the figures given by Hime seem high, it must be remembered that Ireland in the nineteenth century had not begun to do more than loosen the chains binding it to England and the empire. To quote a writer of the time:

> The present Anglo-Irish landlord and his class, less patriotic than their forebears, send their sons to the English public schools, or, if their means are insufficient to do this, to some obscure private school, where they may unlearn their 'brogue' and acquire a genteel English accent.[7]

It may have been that the course of study offered pupils in the higher grades was too academic and did little to prepare them for a working life outside the professions. Dr Molloy, Rector of the Catholic University, described it as ' "grammar school education" which has come down from the universities and which is shaped with a view to prepare (*sic*) pupils for the universities'. This, he argued, was a grave defect in a system under which 'one-sixth only of those who pass through as students under the Board go to the learned professions'. Professor Kennedy of St Kieran's College, Kilkenny, shared the opinions of Dr Molloy and put forward the idea of two courses, 'a university and a non-university course, with approximately equal marks, the same advantages as to Results Fees, and offering in every respect the same attraction to both student and teacher'. This largely coincided with the view of the Association of the Intermediate and University Teachers who, in a written submission, recommended the abolition of 'the present Commercial course, in so far as it is engrafted on the ordinary or general course'. In its place they would substitute two courses, one of which 'should be so framed as to prepare the student for ordinary business life' and the other 'should be so framed as to be preparatory to a professional career'.

Mr Arnold Graves, Secretary of the Commission of Charitable Bequests, was in no doubt that it was the undue emphasis on courses suited to university requirements that caused most harm. In reply to a question of Baron Palles, asking if it had been his experience that the working of the Intermediate Education Act had hindered the industrial development of the country, he answered that it had hindered it considerably, 'by tempting the youth belonging to the agricultural and industrial classes away from their ordinary avocations to a university career'. He went on to quote figures from the previous Census returns which showed that while the number of those engaged in the learned professions was not more than 21,000, the number of those in commerce was 83,173; in industry, 656,410; and in agriculture, 936,759. Taking the figure of 21,000 for the learned professions, he estimated that, with an expectation of service of forty years dating from the year of entry into the profession, there would be an average of not more than 500 vacancies a year. Those for whom vacancies did not exist or who failed to complete their university course were the *Hungerkandidaten*. This was the word used by Dr Walter Starkie, the last Resident Commissioner for Education in Ireland, to describe the products of the intermediate schools

> whom [he said] they had withdrawn from industrial pursuits, and left derelict and *déclassés,* at the doors of what it would be flattery to call a university — unfit for political life, with no career open to them in the higher walks of literature, a class the creation of which every country in Europe now recognises as a 'national calamity of the first magnitude'.[8]

Support for these views came from other witnesses, many of whom particularly deplored the falling-off in the numbers taking practical science.

Among the many witnesses who expressed their views on the different courses and their content, few suggested that they might be framed with more consideration for the special needs of girls. Dr Kelly, Bishop of Ross, who criticised the system very severely, told the Commission of a pamphlet he wrote in 1889 calling attention to the fact that after the year 1880, thirty-one convent schools had withdrawn from the system and that there were then, i.e. in 1889, only '19 Catholic schools connected with the system'. He would have 'all the conditions of examinations, standards for prizes etc., identical for girls as for boys, just as in the Royal University, or else that there would be a totally distinct programme for girls which would be equally as attractive to Catholics as to Protestants'. His was almost a lone voice. In fact the only other witness who was prepared to offer any extensive criticism of the system in so far as it affected girls was Mr James Macken, who represented thirteen convent schools. Explaining why Catholic girls did not avail themselves of the intermediate system, he said:

> The reason is that a large number of parents of girls consider that the Intermediate system is not suitable for girls, and that if they entered into the competition they would not be trained in subjects and accomplishments which they regard as more fitted to form part of the education of girls. Others refused to allow their girls to go in for the examination on the ground that the work was too exhausting, and that the strain on them would be too severe.

The Commission was to hear little but praise of the system from the people who, after all, mattered most — the headmistresses. For Mrs Byers, Principal of the Victoria College, Belfast, the Act of 1878 had 'simply revolutionised girls' education in Ireland. The benefits can only be properly appreciated by those who remember, as I do, the condition of girls' schools generally some thirty or forty years ago.' Her remarks found an echo in a document submitted to the Commission by the Misses MacKillip of the Victoria High School, Londonderry, in which they said: 'The development of education through the working of the Intermediate system has been rapid and effective, and girls' schools have been completely revolutionised by it.' Twenty years was, evidently, too short a time for the convent schools to do more than make use of the Act of 1878 to consolidate the ground on which they had begun to build. In later years the mother superiors of convent schools were to prove themselves both able administrators and sharp critics of the system. But that time was not yet.

It is somewhat surprising to remark that in the course of the twenty-five days on which the Commission sat to take evidence, and in the course of the questioning of sixty-four witnesses, the problem of teachers' salaries was scarcely discussed. Miss E. Boyd of the Royal School in Raphoe, quoting from her own experience, said that she was offered '£40 non-resident to teach four and a half hours every day and prepare both advanced classes and junior classes', while another teacher criticised the Commissioners for allowing salaries to fall while at the same time grants to schools were rising. 'I am quite sure', said Hugh McNeill of University College, Dublin, 'that in the early years of the Intermediate system you never had a teacher employed by a school getting hundreds of pounds a year from your funds working from 9 o'clock till 3 for a remuneration of 12s. 6d. a week.' His contention was that the low salaries were of recent date and there is some confirmation for his belief in the relatively high figures of £140 and £150 a year paid to two lay teachers in St Patrick's College, Cavan, in 1874.[9] A suggested remedy was made by Mr James Comerton, the President of the Association of Inter- mediate and University Teachers, who recommended that teachers be 'properly paid, either directly by the Board itself, or indirectly, by results fees'. The Bishop of Kildare and Leighlin, Dr Foley, would go even further and he, in his evidence, advanced the idea of a minimum basic salary fixed by the Board with, in addition, a special allowance for teachers in small schools to which the Board might contribute or even pay in full.

Linked, of course, with any salary scale were such matters as qualifications, seniority, position in the school, etc., and the Com- mission heard a number of witnesses recommending the setting-up of a Registration Council for teachers. Mr John Thompson, Secretary of the Dublin and Central Irish Branch of the Teachers' Guild of Great Britain and Ireland, was one who believed it to be 'the most important reform that could be made in Intermediate education'. He found support in a distinguished quarter, as Archbishop Walsh expressed the belief that no one should be allowed to teach in a school receiving grants of public money unless the teacher was registered as a duly qualified, efficient teacher. Mr Comerton developed the idea of registration on lines which, many years later, formed a basis for the work of the first Registration Council.

While the Commission was hearing evidence bearing on the question of registration, the Board, which had to carry on with the day-to-day working of the system, considered a Memorial from the Teachers' Guild of Great Britain and Ireland (Dublin and Central Irish Branch), asking that any provision for registration of teachers in the bill dealing with secondary education, introduced in the House of Lords, should be extended to Ireland. The Board decided that the question was 'so large and important that, without a special inquiry into the subject, it would not be expedient for them to offer an opinion'. Almost twenty years were to go by before the registration of intermediate teachers became a reality.

If few witnesses expressed views on salaries, almost everyone had an opinion to offer on inspection, but before giving some idea of the views on inspection expressed before the Commission, it may be opportune to glance at the Memorandum sent by Michael Sadler, Director of Special Inquiries and Reports to the Committee of the Council of Education (England), in reply to queries put to him by the Commission. In it he made a sharp distinction between examination and inspection, both of which seemed to him to be essential but not to be confused:

> The less the inspection is mixed up with examination of individual scholars, the better for the schools and for the smooth working of the system. Would it not be possible to permit the schools to avail themselves from time to time, if they so prefer, of alternative university systems of examinations, approved by the Central Authority on the advice of the Consultative Committee?[10]

He then went on to comment on the situation generally in terms that are as relevant today as when they were made over three-quarters of a century ago.

> It is difficult [he wrote] to escape the conclusion that, in a country, which is distinguished by much and occasionally divergent activity of thought and aspiration, an ideal system of educational organisation would take the form of a national co-partnership between the Schools, the Universities, and the Educational Department of State.

One of those who advocated a restricted form of inspection was Dr J. J. Doherty, who had been Principal of the Training College in Marlborough Street for twenty-one years. He, like Michael Sadler, emphasised that inspectors should 'inspect not examine – except in some special cases'. He would, however, have them 'report upon the suitability of the school buildings and appliances, the teaching staff, the methods of teaching, and the educational training given in the school'. A professor of mathematics, Mr E. J. Dowling, favoured inspection but for reasons that were almost the opposite of those advanced by Doherty. He would have the inspectors concentrate on the teachers, the pupils and the classroom and, after the first few years, he would have them appointed from the ranks of serving teachers.

Not a few of the witnesses expressed strong opposition to the introduction of inspection. The Fullerton brothers, who shared the headmastership of the Academy in Ballymena, spoke of any approach to the national school system of inspection as 'being intolerable to teachers'. Father Devitt, S.J., who was then Rector of Clongowes

Wood College, found a rather unusual argument with which to oppose inspection. He believed that there would be no shortage of candidates as 'the failures in the teaching and every other profession would supply them', but he also felt that the establishment of a system of inspection 'would lead to general dissatisfaction, and at least to the suspicion of jobbery'. Father Carrigy, C.M., the Manager of St Patrick's College, Armagh, presented the case for and against inspection but, in the end, feared that if it was taken to mean 'a number of examiners sent to examine each Intermediate school in Ireland, then, in the present state of the country', he had to oppose it. He explained what he meant by 'the present state of the country' as referring to the absence of any body of trained teachers from whom inspectors might be selected and to the danger of religious prejudice showing itself in the attitude of inspectors to individual schools.

A far more positive approach to the problem was that of the Central Association of Irish Schoolmistresses who came down firmly in favour of inspection, even going so far as to suggest that 'Visits of inspection should be frequent and unexpected'! They found support in a distinguished quarter. Mahaffy would supplement the examination system by one of inspection, giving the inspectors power to prevent 'schools in a bad, unwholesome, or immoral state from competing at the examinations, or else stopping such result fees as would otherwise have been obtained'. Much more moderate in his enthusiasm for inspection which, nevertheless, he would have introduced, was Father Bodkin, C.M., the Prefect of Studies at St Vincent's College, Castleknock. In his eyes, inspection should be confined to the state of the school and the quality of the teaching, but he would not have criticism of the teachers themselves because 'Inspectors would not be qualified for such a task'. This, too, appeared to be the view of the Schoolmasters' Association who, at their annual meeting on 9 January 1899, unanimously resolved, 'That the principle of an annual written examination of the Intermediate Education Board be upheld, and that inspection be limited to inspection of buildings and apparatus, sanitation, and of school organisation and arrangements.'

Faced with the mass of evidence, forced to arbitrate between conflicting viewpoints and to decide what, if any, reforms or alternatives were needed, it would have been reasonable to expect the Report to be slow in appearing. This was not at all the case; the First Report of the Commission with an Appendix containing the answers to the circular letters appeared on 22 December 1898, and the Second or Final Report which contained a transcript of the evidence as well as the Recommendations of the Commissioners was presented to the Lord

Lieutenant on 11 August 1899. No less than eleven of the seventeen recommendations were devoted to the structure by which grants could be distributed to schools by the Board. If the Report appeared to approve of inspection, it was a very qualified approval, insisting 'that any power to this effect granted to the Board should be strictly limited, so as to secure that "the normal school grant" should always be estimated on the basis of the public general examination'. This, they hoped, would 'test true educational work' rather than 'the mere overloading of memory'. No suggestions were made as to how papers for such an examination were to be set and the Commission recommended that, in subjects which could not be tested adequately by written examination, the efficiency of the teaching ought to be assessed 'by the visit of an inspector, or *viva voce* examination in the school or at a common centre'. Further, the Board was to have the right of satisfying itself as to 'the sufficiency of the teaching staff' and 'the sanitary condition of the school', and it should be empowered to advance money to school managers for 'equipment and appliances for the teaching of Practical Science' on approved security.

These recommendations, while seeking to modify the payment by results system, left it almost unchanged. The money grants to the schools were still to be closely related to the success of the pupils at public examinations. The Commission held fast to the belief that in a competitive world those born into it must be prepared from an early age to compete, and if competition meant bringing pressure on pupils this, too, was needed 'in an age when competition in the race of life is so keen, and when success depends so largely on the result of competitive examinations'. As if to insist still further on all pupils following the same examination trail, it offered an additional financial inducement by basing the capitation rate for every school on 'the proportion borne by the number of students of the school who pass the public general examination to the total number of students on the "Intermediate School Roll" of the school'.

We have seen that the Report opened the way for an inspectorate, but it did not clarify and define the role which an inspectorate ought to play. The inspectorate was not to replace the examination system for grants purposes but was to supplement it, and even this supplementary role was not sufficiently clarified. In the Intermediate Education Act of 1900, which followed the Report of the Commission, specific mention is made of inspectors in Section 2 which states: 'The Board may, if they think fit, with the sanction of the Lord Lieutenant, and with the approval of the Treasury as to number and remuneration, appoint persons to act as inspectors in addition to, or instead of, the Assistant

Commissioners.' The stipulation that Treasury approval had to be given was to have serious consequences and the related questions of examinations and the function of the inspectorate was to be a matter of controversy and conflict for many years.

The content of the curriculum did receive attention and the Commission recognised the need for differentiation of school courses, 'so as to afford to each student the opportunity of selecting a course specially suited to the career which he may intend to pursue'. The members were aware

> that students in considerable numbers have been drawn away from studies more suitable to them, and induced to adopt what we have called the Grammar School course wherein the managers of schools find it easier to earn results fees, and the students to win exhibitions.

In an attempt to remedy the evil, the Commission recommended that there ought to be at least two distinct courses — the Grammar School Course and the Modern Course. The former was to be adapted to the needs of students entering the university or competing for the higher posts in the civil service. The Modern Course, with the emphasis on natural and experimental sciences and modern languages, was intended for students who hoped to make a career in industry or commercial life.

The Report, while it contains a vast amount of valuable comment on the nature and content of the courses and on a system of education which bred an intense concentration on an examination and on the results of that examination, was little more than a searchlight which shone for a time on the system, revealed the more glaring of its defects and then swept on. It failed, as Dr Starkie said, to detect 'the real root of the malady' which he regarded as payment on the results of an examination. It failed completely to identify the fundamental principles underlying intermediate education. The crucial element, i.e. the Senior, Middle and Junior Grade examinations, remained untouched; payment by results was to continue and while the subject of inspection was considered in some detail, it was not recommended for adoption with any enthusiasm. Strangest of all, in the light of twenty years' experience, was the failure of the Commissioners to ask for an increase in the money available for intermediate education.

It is tempting to ask if the Commission was not even then, at the end of the last century, beginning to feel the growing power of the Catholic Church in education and that it deliberately refrained from making positive recommendations on such matters as inspection and building grants for schools and so avoided a confrontation which would have been politically unwelcome to all parties. Despite the recommendations of a number of those who gave evidence that help should be given to 'young and struggling schools in districts where they are urgently needed', the Commission saw only the difficulties and so refused to ask Parliament for powers 'to enable the Board to give special grants in aid to schools so circumstanced'. No recommendation was made affecting salaries and conditions of employment because none could be made that would not have involved employed and employer in a struggle for which neither was ready. So it was that, a year later, Dr O'Dwyer, Bishop of Limerick, was able to say of the money that he received from the Intermediate Commissioners:

> I can do absolutely what I like with the money. I can build a Catholic Church with it; I can use it to send missionaries to any quarter of the globe; I can use it to establish a Chair of Catholic Theology in my own seminary. No one can even ask me what is done with the money.

CHAPTER 7

THE STRUGGLE TO INTRODUCE INSPECTION

Balfour moved promptly to give effect to the Report and introduced a bill on 15 May 1900 which, however, was withdrawn. A second bill was quickly prepared and this proved acceptable, probably because it did little to add to the powers of the Board. Among other trifling modifications of the Act of 1878, it raised the number of Commissioners from seven to twelve and empowered them to appoint inspectors. There is some evidence to show that Palles had at one time intended the Report to seek the introduction of amending legislation so as to increase the powers of the Commissioners. That as Chairman of the Commission of Inquiry he did not pursue the matter is regrettable, as an opportunity was then lost which was not to recur in the lifetime of the Board.

The new Rules came into force in 1902. In both the Grammar School Course and the Modern Course there were three grades, Junior, Middle and Senior. The Preparatory Grade was considered to be introductory to the other grades and, in order to lessen the pressure of competition, no honours, exhibitions or prizes were to be offered. As all subjects were allotted the same marks, Greek and Latin lost much of their importance. History and geography appeared for the first time as separate subjects and, in general, pupils were offered a wider range of subjects.

The most far-ranging changes were effected in the teaching of practical subjects and, in 1901, the newly-established Department of Agriculture and Technical Instruction issued a programme for the administration and distribution of grants for experimental science, drawing, manual instruction and domestic economy in secondary day schools, and a number of schools immediately adopted the programme. Following consultations between the Intermediate Board and the Department the Board decided to adopt, as from 1902 onwards, the Department's programme in science and drawing. The Department was also given power to allot an annual sum of money amounting to £55,000 to county and county borough councils for approved schemes intended to help the teaching of practical subjects. A number of councils availed of grants under this heading to award scholarships to boys from primary schools, tenable at intermediate schools where science and drawing were taught.

Inspection was the big issue both for the Commissioners and those in charge of the schools, and at a meeting held on 9 January 1899 the Schoolmasters' Association fired a warning salvo with the intention of making clear the position of its members. It took the form of a resolution which ran: 'That the principle of an annual written examination of the Intermediate Education Board be upheld, and that inspection be limited to inspection of buildings and apparatus, sanitation, and of school organisation and arrangements.' They must have thought it necessary to pass such a resolution as it did appear at the time as if the Commissioners would be given the powers they sought in respect of inspection. The Commissioners must have thought so too, as temporary inspectors were appointed in 1901 and, in the instructions given them, they were asked to report on such matters as the efficiency of the teaching, the sanitary condition of the school, the time-table, the appliances and equipment used for the teaching of practical subjects and the qualifications of the staff. The names of those first inspectors were Messrs Shuckburgh, Cassie, Steggall, Roberts, Mayfield and Brereton. Their reports for the school-year 1901-2 and 1902-3, together with their observations on schools and schoolmasters, are contained in five volumes. Many of their recommendations are of perennial interest; for instance, they anticipated by over half a century the efforts made later to close many small one- and two-teacher schools. Some of these they considered to be 'without resources sufficient to yield satisfactory results, and it is desirable that such small and inefficient schools should be combined so as to form one strong, fully equipped, and efficient school'. They seemed to have envisaged a regional plan for education, arguing:

> The frittering-away of the educational resources of the country and of the grants of the Board might be diminished if, in assigning money grants, the Board would consider the special needs of each district, keeping in view the various types and standards of education, and the main religious distinctions of the country.

Their remarks under the heading of 'Staff' made it clear that there was then no pool of qualified graduates from which to draw and that schools in country districts were particularly handicapped by the unavailability of specialist teachers. They instance five categories of teachers in the intermediate schools:

> Some had taken University degrees in honours, some in pass subjects, while many had not yet completed their University course. A considerable number held certificates from various boards for their respective subjects. A very large number had no qualifications except more or less experience.

And in the case of some teachers such 'experience' was not confined to the classroom, as instanced by the report of the inspector who visited the Academical Institution in Boyle, Co. Roscommon, in 1902:

> The Headmaster made the remarkable statement that 'for the last three months,' he has 'been in school for only one or two hours each day, having another matter in hand which is very pressing.' The 'matter' referred to is probably an electric light factory which he manages.

The urbanisation of the country must have been accelerated by the natural desire of parents to ensure competent teaching for their children and, as the inspectors point out, this, for subjects such as classics and modern languages,

> is only possible in large towns, where excellent teachers with good qualifications and practical experience can be obtained. In country districts, on the other hand, where such external help can but rarely be obtained, one teacher is compelled to give instruction in all the subjects of the curriculum, with the result that the teaching sometimes suffers, as the attainments of the teacher in one or other of the subjects is insufficient.

The temporary inspectors proved satisfactory and the Commissioners believed that their advice was of benefit to the schools. They acted on this belief and, by Rule 56B, sanctioned by the Lord Lieutenant Earl Cadogan in May 1902, 'presented bonuses of 10 per cent and 20 per cent respectively on the School Grant for schools which, upon the report of the inspectors, should appear to be "satisfactory" and "highly satisfactory" '. The granting of sanction for this Rule was of considerable importance because it thereby acquired the force of a statute, which made the introduction of inspection obligatory on the Board.

Inspection could, however, be either on a temporary or a permanent basis and in June 1902 a struggle began which was to last for six years between the Commissioners and the Lord Lieutenant over the appointment of inspectors on a permanent basis. It began with the sending of a straightforward request from the Commissioners to the Under-Secretary at Dublin Castle on 30 June 1902. In it they outlined the work of the six temporary inspectors and sought to obtain the sanction of the Lord Lieutenant and of the Treasury 'to the constitution under the Board of the offices of six Inspectors of Intermediate Schools'. The reply, dated 5 December 1902, informed the Board 'that the Lord Lieutenant thought it best that the Board's scheme for the establishment of a permanent staff of Inspectors should stand over till next year, to admit of its fullest consideration'.

The Treasury opposed inspection because the Commissioners did not propose to reduce the expenditure for examinations by an amount equivalent to that of the cost of inspection. That being so, it is difficult to see why the Commissioners did not ask for a separate grant. They must have been aware that in England and Wales, in Scotland, and in the Irish Department of Agriculture and Technical Instruction, and in the National Education system, inspection was provided for annually by a separate grant. They may not, of course, have wished to subject their policy to Parliamentary criticism as they would have had to do if they accepted an annual grant, but a letter from the Treasury, dated 11 December 1903, must have made it clear to them that the Treasury was concerned less with the educational advantages of inspection than with economy. In it the Treasury asked what saving could be effected were permanent inspectors appointed. Finally, a point was reached when the Board refused to make any further temporary appointments, giving as their reason that

> the appointment of temporary inspectors for another year would not answer their purpose, particularly as the school year was so far advanced; that it would do no more than continue a mode of administration of the funds at their disposal, which is contrary to the intentions of Parliament.

The Report of the Intermediate Commissioners for 1904 showed each side firmly defending the positions they already occupied. The Commissioners, already made aware that the cost of inspection should be met out of the expenditure on examinations, were informed that the question of establishing a system of inspection conducted by a staff of permanent civil servants would not be entertained until the parts which examination and inspection should play in the distribution of State aid in the schools had been settled. As this issue could not, in the opinion of the Commissioners, be dealt with other than by statute, their attitude remained unchanged. Neither side seemed disposed to move from its entrenched position and, in 1906, the Board summarised the history of what was referred to as 'the fruitless negotiations which have been carried on since 1902'. While all the evidence points to Treasury intransigence, Archbishop Walsh, in the course of a letter to *An Claidheamh Soluis* dated 23 April 1907, said: 'It is not a question of funds at all.' To him it was a question of increasing the powers of the Commissioners by authorising them to add the right of inspection to that of examination.

The Commissioners were hardly to be classed among the most impatient of men when it is seen that they continued to conduct conscientiously their normal business despite their long-standing differences with the government. Yet in 1908 it did appear as if they had no further reserves of patience on which to draw. The resolution which they sent to the Lord Lieutenant, The Right Hon. John Campbell, Earl of Aberdeen, in that year is a measure of their discontent. It ran:

> That in the opinion of the Board, the time has arrived when it is necessary for them to consider whether it is possible for them, in the interests of true education, to continue the administration of the funds entrusted to them for the promotion of Intermediate Education in Ireland in the absence of a system of inspection, the establishment of which was provided for by the legislature in the Amendment Act of 1900.

Whether as a result of the peremptory tone of the resolution or not, a favourable reply was not long delayed, and on 22 September 1908 the Board received word that the Treasury had sanctioned the appointment of six inspectors.

On 12 December 1908 the national press carried the advertisment for six posts as Permanent Inspectors of Intermediate Schools. The upper age limit was forty-five years and the notice concluded with the warning that 'canvassing, directly or indirectly, will be regarded as a disqualification'. The salary scales had been decided on by the Commissioners at their meeting of 30 September 1908 and approved by the Treasury. They were: Two inspectors at the scale of salary £700 - £20 – £800; two inspectors at the scale of salary £500 – £20 – £700; two inspectors at the scale of salary £350 – £20 – £700. There were over 400 applicants for the positions, and the appointments were made at a meeting of the Commissioners on 18 March 1909. The appointments had to be sanctioned by the Lord Lieutenant and approved by the Treasury before being made public on 1 April 1909. The first inspectors were Richard Charles Bolger Kerin, B.A., LOND.; Charles Edmund Wright, B.A., T.C.D.; Ernest Ensor, M.A., T.C.D.; Joseph O'Neill, M.A., R.U.I.; John Edward Maguire, B.A., R.U.I. and T.C.D.; Thomas Rea, M.A., R.U.I. Before beginning their work in October of that year, the successful applicants were given an opportunity of becoming acquainted with the systems of education in England and on the Continent.

A certain 'organised' antagonism to inspection showed itself almost at once when the Catholic Headmasters' Association and the heads of

Convent Intermediate Schools in Ireland met to define their position 'in reference to the scheme of inspection which is now being introduced by Commissioners of Intermediate Education'.[1] Two resolutions on inspection which were put to the meeting were carried unanimously. The resolutions were preceded by a lengthy statement setting out the position of the schools represented at the meeting, 'schools and colleges built without aid from the State, or from any public source', and this it was which made them adamant in their opposition to inspection and to any monetary payments to schools based on inspection. The first resolution stated:

> That while we are prepared to accept inspection as defined in paragraphs 11 to 14 of the 'General Summary' of the recommendations of the Viceregal Commission of 1898, we regard as outside the legal powers of the Board any extension of the scope of inspection so defined, and, in particular, the inspection of the residential departments of boarding schools, of the academic degrees, or diplomas, of teachers, and of the financial arrangements of the schools.

The second resolution did little more than affirm more strongly the terms of the first. It ran as follows:

> That pending the decision of the questions raised as to the legal extent and scope of inspection, information regarding the disputed points set out in the previous resolution, be withheld from the inspectors, and that even informal visits to the residential portions of boarding schools be not permitted.

While such statements may incline one to think that Catholic school authorities were being unreasonably intransigent, it is well to recall that, during the sittings of the 1898 Commission, the Catholic heads of schools came out in favour of a system of inspection which would supplement examination and that some years earlier the same authorities had readily given access to Messrs Dale and Stephens to visit their schools. Their objections may not have been to inspection as such but to the threat it posed to a system in which the basis of all monetary payments to schools was results, *unaffected and unaccompanied by inspection.*

The attitude of the Schoolmasters' Association, which represented Protestant teachers in intermediate schools, was much less hostile. At their meeting in September 1909 only one of eight resolutions passed referred to inspection and this, not without a certain deference, requested: 'That the Inspectors should make the situation, the method of teaching, and the qualifications of the staff matters of importance in their report, as well as the proficiency of the pupils in the several branches of learning.' This was sharply at variance with the attitude of the Catholic Headmasters' Association and of the Convent Intermediate Schools who had rather haughtily dismissed any implied criticism of the qualifications of their staff by saying: 'The education of the teachers employed in Catholic Intermediate Schools amply fits them for their work, and the Act of Parliament does not empower the Board to demand anything more.'

When inspection first began on a permanent basis in the autumn of 1909, it was usual for two inspectors to visit a school on the same day or days and their Reports on the classes visited were very detailed. Apart from class inspection, they were required to provide the Commissioners with information on a number of items, including lighting, heating, toilets, dormitories, punishments, qualifications of teachers and salaries. Their Reports on the schools were bound, printed and marked 'Confidential, Printed for members of the Board only'.

Almost the first thing one notices in reading these Reports is the bluntness of the criticism when it was necessary to criticise. The inspectors were independent-minded men reporting, it must be remembered, not to a government department with its sensitivity to the power of sectional interests, but to a Board of Commissioners not particularly concerned with holding office which, in any case, they held for reasons that were rarely exclusively educational. So it is that we find it said of the English compositions in the Middle Grade at Ballymena Academy that they 'were written in a kind of Hampton Court maze style', and a Report on the same subject in the Preparatory Grade of St Joseph's Seminary, Galway, credits the boys with distinguishing themselves 'by displaying complete ignorance of the elements of English grammar'. If at times the inspectors seem dismayed by the quality of the English teaching, they must have been positively distressed at the accent of many of the pupils taking French. The inspector who visited the Christian Brothers' School in Ennis did not seek any moderating euphemism for the sounds he heard but summarised them in one short sentence: 'The pronunciation of the pupils is atrocious.'

Information in relation to teacher qualifications and salaries seems to have been but reluctantly divulged and the entry 'Information Refused' occurs in the Reports of all the inspectors. When information was given, it revealed the modest range of qualifications even among permanent staff. Entries such as the following occur quite frequently under the heading 'Training and Experience': 'Ex Senior Honours student, Intermediate Board'; 'Undergraduate N.U.I.';

'Exhibitioner Junior Grade'; 'South Kensington Certificate'; 'Matriculation R.U.I.'. Obviously a profession which counted so few graduates had little bargaining power and it is clear that there was no accepted salary scale. Women teachers in general seem to have fared less well than men and the Madame de Prins College in Limerick was then, in 1909, paying £25 a year to an assistant mistress. That was certainly a below-average salary, but it serves to show the distance that had to be travelled before the profession of teaching could be made attractive to anyone except those who, *faute de mieux,* adopted it. As was to be expected, the wealthier Protestant schools did pay better salaries than their Catholic rivals, and two Belfast schools, Campbell College and the Royal Belfast Academical Institution, were then paying assistant masters over £250 a year, while the High School, Dublin, was paying them £200 a year.

It is entirely true to say that the causes of low salaries to which the Molony Report was later to draw attention remained unchanged during the entire lifetime of the Board. That Report summarised them as follows:

> In many schools the pupils were drawn from the poorer classes, and in these the fees charged were of necessity low, and often merely nominal. The grants from the Intermediate Education Board fluctuated from year to year owing to the operation of the results system, and were never adequate. No assistance was received from local rates. Indeed many of the schools could not have existed at all but for Diocesan collections and private bene factors.[2]

CHAPTER 8

THE REPORT OF DALE AND STEPHENS

While the Commissioners of Intermediate Education were seeking sanction for the appointment of permanent inspectors in Ireland, the government invited two inspectors of the English Board of Education, Messrs Dale and Stephens, to conduct a survey of Irish intermediate schools. The extent of their brief was made known to the Commissioners in a letter from the Chief Secretary, George Wyndham, dated 3 May 1904. They were asked that their Report should deal with the following points:

(i) Co-ordination of intermediate education with primary, technical, and university education.

(ii) Staffing, equipment, sanitary conditions, &c., of schools receiving grants from the Intermediate Board.

(iii) (a) Allocation of the funds of the Intermediate Board; (b) Possibility of allocating the school grant in the form of grants to selected schools; (c) To what extent, if any, inspection might take the place of examinations conducted by the Intermediate Board.

(iv) Possibility of establishing a profession of intermediate teachers analogous to that of elementary teachers – (a) Training of intermediate teachers. (b) Salaries. (c) Proper staffing of schools. (d) Registration of schools.

Their brief was far-ranging, their stay was short, but their Report could hardly have been more thorough even if there must have been some misgivings among heads of schools about the purpose of their coming. For W. J. M. Starkie there was no mystery about that:

> Messrs. Dale and Stephens were sent for three weeks to Ireland, ostensibly to report on the organisation of secondary education, but really for the purpose of blocking our legal demand for inspectors, in the interest of some great scheme for the reformation of Irish education which was in the minds of the government of that day, but which was destined never to materialise.[1]

What truth there is to Starkie's remarks on inspection is hardly borne out by the facts, but it is true that some 'scheme for the reformation of Irish education' was in the mind of the government at the time and will be referred to in the next chapter.

There were, according to the Census figures of 1901, 475 intermediate schools in Ireland at that time, 80 of which were visited by the inspectors. They had completed their inspection by the end of 1904 and their Report was forwarded to the government on 15 February 1905. At the outset they summarised educational provision at second level as it then existed in Ireland:

> The bulk of the supply of Intermediate Education is furnished by the schools in connection with the Board of Intermediate Education, and it is to be particularly noticed that these schools undoubtedly include nearly all the large and important institutions providing Higher Education for scholars from 13 to 19 years of age. There are, it is true, large institutions similar in essential respects as to size, equipment and aims of their pupils to those in connection with the Board which have refused to come into the system. Two examples may be found in Mungret College, near Limerick, and the St. Joseph's Convent of Mercy, Charleville, both of which we visited.

They concluded that the number of such schools was 'comparatively insignificant' and they were satisfied that the difference between the Census figure of 475 schools and that of the Board, i.e. 262 schools in 1903, was due to the considerable number of schools which did not 'fall within the system of Intermediate Education as aided by the State'. These were grinding establishments for the preparation of candidates for lower grades of the civil service or for admission to the training colleges and also the many small private schools for girls. For instance, according to Dale and Stephens there were only eleven private girls' or mixed schools receiving aid from the Intermediate Education Board, whereas according to the Census of 1901 there were fifty-three schools in the province.

While the number of intermediate schools may have seemed reasonably adequate having regard to the number of children in the age-group thirteen to nineteen who could afford secondary education, the number of those who derived full benefit from their schooling was small. Dale and Stephens found that no more than one pupil in ten went through the intermediate system from Preparatory to Senior Grade, so that, in their words:

> the Intermediate system has failed to secure the complete and continuous course of study which is contemplated in its programme for the majority of Intermediate students, or that the full benefit of the system is reaped by only a very small fraction of the population.

They found it difficult to understand how two Boards of Commissioners, one for primary or national schools and the other for post-primary or intermediate schools, could carry on their work in complete isolation from one another. This they remarked upon when they found that there was no generally accepted age for transfer from the national school to the intermediate school, adding that 'the pupils were retained in the lower school far too long'. The Intermediate Commissioners could justify their apparent lack of concern, at least in this matter, by stating that not many of the 741,795 pupils then in national schools would ever enter intermediate schools. Whatever the reason for the lack of co-ordination, the inspectors were totally correct in the summing-up of the position when they wrote:

> There is no relation between the two Boards for the purpose of administration. . . . The syllabus and regulations of each Board are drawn up independently, without reference or consultation with the other. The line of demarcation may in short be described as absolute.

A year earlier the attention of the Chief Secretary had been drawn to the matter when the Under-Secretary, Sir Antony MacDonnell, wrote to him on certain administrative problems which he wished to have dealt with. Paragraph four of his letter is devoted to the question of control and in it he said:

> I am impressed with the want of connection between Primary and Intermediate Education in Ireland, and of the waste of power involved in having two separate Boards to do the work which should naturally fall to one. Primary and Secondary Education are parts of the same subject, and they should be controlled, both centrally and locally, by the same authority. If the system of School Boards could be at once introduced into Ireland as it has been into England, I should advocate the abolition of both the National Education and Intermediate Boards, and the creation of a Department of Public Instruction.[2]

He goes on to develop briefly his 'conception of a single Board' which should consist partly of elected and partly of nominated members. He would have the elected members 'represent three interests (a) the ratepayers, (b) the School Managers and (c) the Teachers'.[3] He may not have realised it at the time that to propose the setting-up of a body in which two units, such as 'a' and 'c', could outvote the single unit 'b' was totally unacceptable. The letter was filed, nothing was done, the problem remains.

Whatever efforts had been made to effect some measure of co-operation between the two branches of the educational system appear to have been made by Protestants, and even here the links were far from strong. Provision had been made by the Endowed Schools' Commission for scholarships tenable by Protestants (and Catholics) in schools in the towns of Armagh, Cavan, Dungannon, Enniskillen, Letterkenny and Monaghan. These were for day boys only and, in consequence, the scholarships were effectively confined to boys living within easy distance of the town. The Society for the Promotion of Protestant Schools in Ireland gave twenty full scholarships and ten assisted scholarships for boys to the schools of the Society at Athlone, Kilkenny, Dundalk and Sligo. The main defect in both these schemes was that the scholarships were not available to Presbyterian, Methodist or other denomination. The same was true of the Society's scholarships for girls which were tenable at Ranelagh, Celbridge, and Victoria High School.

They also found, though less surprisingly, that there was no direct connection between the universities and the Board, though university professors had acted as members of the Board and, in addition, lecturers and tutors had acted as examiners at the examinations of the Board. This led them to regret that the Senior Grade examination was not accepted for university entrance, with the result that many pupils were often engaged upon two courses in the one year. To remedy this, they recommended that the four-grade examination system should be replaced by two certificate examinations, called the Lower School Certificate Examination and the Higher School Certificate Examination. The first of these would, they hoped, serve two purposes. It would serve as a guarantee to the successful candidate, his parents and the school 'that a proper degree of efficiency had been attained' and, in addition, permit the Board to award a certain number of scholarships enabling pupils to continue at school or study at 'one of the larger schools which occupy themselves more particularly with preparing scholars for institutions of university rank'. It was their hope that the Higher Certificate would be accepted by the universities as the equivalent of their own Matriculation and that they would make use of it, as had been suggested by Trinity College, for nominating a certain number of exhibitions in the Senior Grade or sizarships or scholarships of a similar nature.[4]

In their Report they commented on 'the rigid uniformity of aim' in the schools which, indeed, they might have accepted as inevitable in a country where they all belonged either to a religious body or were controlled by governors elected on a sectarian basis. There were very few schools outside the large boroughs and towns, nor was there any local authority charged with the duty of considering the needs of the various levels of education in its area. In considering the spread of educational provision in the country, they found that there were good schools in Ulster for the well-to-do, no matter to what religion they belonged, but that there was 'an almost complete absence of Intermediate schools to serve the needs of the poorer boys'. Connacht was, academically speaking, little better than a barren waste in which there were only 728 pupils in intermediate schools out of a total population of 646,932.[5] The greatest concentration of schools, outside the Dublin area, was to be found in the province of Munster where, in such counties as Limerick and Clare, the tradition of the hedge school had lived on to the end of the nineteenth century. In this context, it is of interest to notice that the schools of the Christian Brothers were more numerous in Munster and Leinster than elsewhere, probably because the bishops in those provinces had been in much closer contact with the founder, Ignatius Rice, than those in Ulster and Connacht. This pattern was to change somewhat as bishops throughout the country became doubtful of some of the provisions of the Board of National Education and invited the Brothers to open schools, many of which developed intermediate departments.

The part played by numbers in the prosperity of schools was clear from their reference to the unsatisfactory conditions in the smaller ones. Endowments had helped to preserve schools in areas where otherwise they would have decayed, but lack of endowments as well as poverty and emigration meant that too many schools would be always pitifully poor and ill-equipped. Such schools were to be found existing as 'a single room over a shop, or behind a chapel, in a dilapidated farm-house, in a low wooden shed attached to a dwelling-house'. However, as long as a school contained ten pupils who had made not less than one hundred attendances during the year, as defined in the Act, it was entitled to present candidates for the examinations of the Board, and to receive result fees in the event of their being successful. The inspectors inclined to the view that a minimum of fifteen pupils should be required for purposes of recognition and, in general reference to unsatisfactory schools, they said that 'a system under which the Central Office had not the power to refuse any grant of public money to such institutions appears to us to stand self-condemned'.

When they came to consider the question of the staffing of the schools, they found that only 11.5 per cent of the male Catholic teachers were graduates of a university and 8 per cent of the women

Catholic teachers. The Christian Brothers, of whom 145 were at that time teaching in intermediate schools, had almost certainly no more than the two years' training they received in their college at Marino. The proportion of graduates in the Catholic diocesan colleges was probably quite high and it is likely that most of the eighty-four graduate Catholic male teachers referred to by Dale and Stephens as being employed in the schools were 'Maynooth men'. Yet even these, if we are to accept the word of Most Rev. Dr O'Dwyer, Bishop of Limerick, in evidence before the Irish University Commission of 1901-2, were not adequately educated.

> There are [he said] about 4,000 boys taught all over Ireland by a number of priests who have no higher education than I have got. These young priests are clever men; many of them have great natural ability. Their philosophical and logical training in Maynooth is first-rate. They come out of Maynooth with very clear intellects, and very great logical power, but they are absolutely deficient in that indefinable thing that is not knowledge but culture — the character of the man that is formed when he goes through the process of a real University education — something that you cannot put your hands on, a something which cultivates a sense of honour, and right judgement with regard to the affairs of life. If our priests had such an education, they would be totally different teachers to what they are now. They would have a true equipment and training for their office, not a mere book-knowledge of Classics and Mathematics, which by themselves are quite equal to all the requirements of the Intermediate system.[6]

Protestant schools, longer established, often well endowed and drawing support from a wealthier section of the community, were well staffed, many of them by graduates drawn from universities throughout Great Britain and Ireland. The proportion of male graduates was 55.8 per cent and these came from Trinity College (82 per cent), the Royal University (75 per cent), other universities (66 per cent). The women teachers in Protestant schools numbered 425, of whom 131, or 30 per cent, were graduates — '110 of these having obtained their degree at the Royal University'.

Dale and Stephens found that many of those engaged in teaching had no intention of adopting the profession permanently. This they had no hesitation in attributing to the low salaries, absence of pension schemes and insecurity of tenure, saying in support of the last statement that 'the assistant-master may be dismissed at a quarter's or term's notice without any cause'. While they had not anything like complete returns for the whole country, they had ascertained 'that in the year 1903 the average salary in 70 Intermediate schools was £48 2. 7.'. Referring to these figures, Hanna Sheehy Skeffington, herself a practising teacher, said:

> From my own experience I would fix the latter sum at a considerably lower figure for the ordinary convent school-teacher. I have known University graduates — exhibitioners, scholars, gold medallists — accept salaries which a competent cook would have scorned.[7]

On the question of salaries, the official organisation of inter-mediate teachers accepted the figures given in the Dale and Stephens Report and placed the blame for such unsatisfactory salaries on the Intermediate Commissioners who, they said, 'could do much if they liked, to alleviate the hardships of teachers'.[8] What the organisation must have known was that, as long as the Commissioners failed to insist on certain minimum qualifications for teachers employed in the intermediate schools, no demand could be made on the schools to pay a minimum wage. The Commissioners did not insist and, if we are to believe Dr Starkie, 'any man or woman, no matter how incompetent, may be appointed to a position in a secondary school'. The teachers, conscious perhaps of the modest academic attainments of many of those who at least had found employment in the schools, preferred to fight the salaries battle on ground of their choosing. They criticised the principle on which the sum of approximately £50,000 was paid in result fees to the managers of secondary schools, arguing that not alone was it possible that those schools which needed it least received the most, but that there was no 'guarantee whatever that the money received is really spent on Education. It may go into the Headmaster's purse, or it may be used for any purpose whatever by the Corporation managing the school.' How dependent the assistant teachers were on their employers is underlined by what the Com-missioners then went on to say:

> For the Commissioners to insist that the Assistant teachers should receive a share of the result fees would be useless, as the amount might simply be deducted from the present salary. In fact, some Headmasters actually threatened to do so, should the Com-missioners insist on such a course.

The solution offered by the Association was that 'Every school wishing to benefit by the Intermediate Grant should supply the

Commissioners with a properly audited balance sheet, showing income, expenditure, salaries paid to masters etc.'

This was the expression of an ideal increasingly far from attainment in a country where the growing number of schools under clerical control ensured that their power was unlikely to be questioned by a professional class largely dependent on them for employment. Messrs Dale and Stephens had not failed to observe how the amount paid in results fees had grown, enriching the schools but not the teachers. They showed, for comparative purposes, the figures for 1879 and 1903, set out in table 9.

Table 9

Year	Amount of school grant in results fees	Number of students who passed	Number of schools receiving results fees
1879	£ 5,778 0. 0.	2,332	239
1903	£57,318 0. 0.	4,910	294

They commented on the amount paid to the manager of a school for the success of an individual student which, in the year 1903, ranged from £5 16. 0. for a pass in the Preparatory Grade to the 'astonishing sum of £39 3s. for a pass with honours in the Senior Grade'. In their words, these 'results fees had completely failed to test or to recognise, the work of the school as a whole' and, they might have added, most schools were satisfied that it should be so.

When the two inspectors came to discuss the question of teacher training, they were extremely circumspect because of what they called 'the special conditions of Intermediate Schools in Ireland'. This simply meant that it would be unwise to demand a graduate teaching-body while the Catholic Church controlled so many of the intermediate schools. They did, however, comment on the training courses peculiar to the different religious communities

which had adopted teaching as their main work long prior to the latter half of the nineteenth century, which first saw the growth of the movement in the State-organised system of Education in Germany. Wherever students had passed through a prolonged course of study in Philosophy and were teaching in schools in which their work was supervised by superiors who were scholars, trained observers, and experienced teachers, the essentials of a teacher's training were to be found.

While they do not mention any particular religious order, they must have been impressed by the method adopted in all the schools of the Christian Brothers where shared classrooms were the rule; the experienced teacher taught at one end and a younger colleague at the other.

If a number of male religious orders had made an effort to prepare for the work of teaching before the end of the nineteenth century, it was not until much later that we find positive action being taken to train women 'who have adopted, or intend to adopt, teaching as their profession'.[9] A letter sent to 'the Provost and Senior Fellows of Trinity College, Dublin' about 1869 asked that an examination be held for women and that certificates be awarded 'to such candidates as shall be judged to deserve them'.[10] This was done and for the next five years Junior and Senior Certificates were awarded to successful candidates. This 'hesitating step', as Bailey describes it in his *History of Trinity College,* cannot have had great impact and nothing further was done until 1896 when the Board of Trinity College 'agreed to the holding in 1897 of a trial examination in methods of teaching with George Francis Fitzgerald, Louis Claude Purser and John Isaac Beare as examiners'.[11] This does not seem to have led to any permanent arrangement but we do know that at the first examination, held in January 1898, 'three candidates, all English teachers, presented themselves'.[12] Neither Bailey in his *History of Trinity College* nor Balfour in his study of the *Educational Systems of Great Britain and Ireland* throws any light on developments in the next few years, though the College Calendar for 1901-2 gives the 'Rules Respecting Examinations in the Theory, History and Practice of Education'. Successful candidates in these examinations were awarded a diploma.

Queen's University, while it had opened its doors to women students as early as 1882, was slow to accord them equal status with male students. The first step, i.e. to gain admission to the university, was taken by the Belfast Ladies' Institute in 1873. This was unsuccessful, but when in 1882 they tried again they were in a stronger position as the Royal University was open to women, a number of Belfast girls had already matriculated, and the president supported their request. 'The council agreed (21 October 1882) rather cautiously to admit women to arts classes, and a dozen of them attended the college during the session 1882-3 without serious mishap.'[13]

In 1897 the Senate of the Royal University instituted the Diploma in Teaching open to graduates in arts of the university and, in the same year, the Ursuline Convent in Waterford set up its own training college to prepare candidates for the Teacher's Certificate of the Cambridge Syndicate. The Dominican Convent at 19 Eccles Street, Dublin, set up a similar training college in 1908 for graduate teachers, to enable them to 'qualify for the Secondary Teachers' Diploma, granted by the Cambridge University'. Alexandra College established a separate department in 1905 'for the Training of Secondary Teachers, which is carried on in connection with the Department for the Training of Teachers established in Trinity College'. Queen's University was slow to give formal recognition to teacher training but when the Chair of Education was founded in 1914, it immediately established the Higher Diploma Course in Education. Teacher training followed the establishment of the Chairs of Education in University College, Dublin (1912), University College, Galway (1914), and University College, Cork (1936).

If there had been a compulsory course in the Theory and Practice of Education for intermediate teachers, it would have been possible to compile a register of teachers whose competence was guaranteed. As matters stood, the difficulties in the way of setting up a register of intermediate teachers seemed enormous. As a prerequisite there was the need for giving recognition to the school as an intermediate school. Otherwise recognition might not be given to those employed within it. That posed the problem of inspection of the school, but there was then no permanent inspectorate in Ireland. Non-graduate teachers, who had taught under the intermediate system with success for many years, found themselves on the same level of salary as students who returned to teach in schools after passing the Senior Grade. Graduate teachers with honours degrees were often little better off. In an Appendix to their Report, Dale and Stephens gave the regulations 'for the formation of a Register of Teachers established by the Schedule to the Order in Council of 6 March, 1902'. If we are to judge by the deferential tone of the following resolution, passed at a general meeting of the Association of Intermediate and University Teachers, the Commissioners were under no great pressure to tackle the question. The resolution read:

> That the Association of Intermediate and University Teachers respectfully requests the Intermediate Board controlling, as they do, the disbursement of public funds for educational purposes in Ireland, to establish a register of properly qualified teachers, as has been done in England. The Association desires to express the firm belief that such a course is absolutely essential to the interests of Irish Secondary education.[14]

The work of Dale and Stephens was perhaps the most complete appraisal of education in a united Ireland; it was a searchlight from which almost nothing of value to the educationist was hidden. Their visits to schools throughout the country left them in no doubt 'that the desire for higher education is in Ireland felt more keenly than in England by the large body of people belonging to what may be roughly described as the lower middle class of society'. They were satisfied that, in general, the schools were providing a good education but they listed what they called 'grave educational defects' which lessened their efficiency. In their eyes, the system did not permit of any initiative on the teacher's part and all was subordinated to the requirements of an external examination. This they considered to be the cause of the lack of differentiation of schools which 'is an essential principle in the educational organisation of other countries', and which meant that courses for girls and boys should not be uniformly alike nor would they impose 'the same general programme or examination tests on town and country schools'. Finally, they saw monetary rewards held before the pupils for examination as the highest incentive to study, with too little regard for the level of work throughout the whole school.

CHAPTER 9

THE IRISH COUNCILS BILL

During 1904 there were rumours that the government was dissatisfied with the system whereby separate Boards, the members of which were nominated by the government, were responsible for education. Such rumours may have stemmed from the remarks of Sir John Gorst, member for Cambridge University, in the Commons on 16 March 1904, when he expressed the hope that the 'system adopted in England and Scotland of entrusting the obligation of providing education for the children to the local authorities would be extended to Ireland'. Whether or not that was the case, encouragement for further speculation came a month later when a motion, in the name of Mr Nanetti, member for Dublin, College Green, that 'in the opinion of this House, the system of primary education in Ireland is fundamentally defective, and has proved injurious in its operation', was the subject of a long debate.

Gorst again propounded views which, while they may have been acceptable to Parliament, were certainly far too radical for a people who had little reason to be dissatisfied with the educational advances which the religious orders had helped to achieve. Referring to the principle on which Irish education should be conducted, he said that the first thing was 'to bring it under popular control' and, developing this theme, he proposed that

> the responsibility for the organisation and administration of elementary education should be entrusted to some Irish body either elected by, or representative of, the people, with responsibility in the first instance to the Irish Education Department, and therefore to the House, and in the second place to the people of the locality out of which it was chosen.

The Chief Secretary, Mr George Wyndham, was thinking on similar lines when, in referring to the different ways in which education might be helped, he spoke of seeking 'to co-ordinate technical instruction and intermediate education' and 'to develop local control and rate-aid'. He was clearly seeking some means by which reforms could be effected without confining education to some unwanted central agency when he said of the difficulties facing them, that it was for Parliament to go 'over them, through them or round them, and in any case to get beyond them'.

Wyndham had earlier shown his interest in education and in a letter, dated 20 December 1902, he referred to what he called 'the defective provision for education in Ireland' which he attributed largely to the poverty of the country and 'the very small proportion which local contributions bear to its total cost'.[1] He felt that what the Irish system lacked was 'both the stimulus of local interest and the efficiency of State control'. He realised that the causes for this lay in the history of the country but he was not disposed to go on believing that this should present a permanent obstacle to change, and he suggested that it was a matter for consideration 'whether those causes are still operative to such an extent as to necessitate the continuance of the present unsatisfactory system'. He gave it as the view of the Irish government that the local authorities should be encouraged 'to enlarge their responsibilities' though he counselled that any advance should be made 'gradually and with caution'.

Any feelings of optimism aroused by the statements of Gorst and Wyndham were quickly dispelled when John Redmond, member for Wexford, intervened in the debate to make clear that any move to set up a Department solely responsible, as it would be under the existing system of government, to English opinion, would be resented. His remarks were intended, he said, 'so that there might be no misconception on this point, and that the Chief Secretary might know that this scheme for creating a new Department in Ireland was not one that they approved, and that they would resist that proposal'. T. P. O'Connor, member for Liverpool, was much more menacing. He told the House that if popular control in Ireland were granted, 'he was sure a tempest would arise in that country which the right hon. Gentleman, with all his sweetness of temper, would not be able to withstand'.

The Catholic hierarchy remained silent, while the parochial clergy conducted what David Miller describes as 'an all-out campaign against "reform" of primary and secondary education'.[2] When the hierarchy did meet at Maynooth on 22 June 1904, in the course of a statement issued to the press, they gave their reasons for opposing the abolition of the Boards:

> On the Boards we have, at any rate, an assurance for the independence of our schools and colleges, and for fair play and equality of Catholics. We have no intention of exchanging these advantages for the control of a Department. The personnel of such a body would be sure to be objectionable. Its Protestant members might be Protestants, but we fear that its Catholic members would

be chosen to represent Government rather than Catholic interests.
. . . A Department of Education may be well enough in England,
where society is socially and politically in a normal condition, but
in Ireland it would mean another bulwark of Dublin Castle and
further opportunity for political ascendancy for a favoured sect.

The statement went on to attack what it believed was an attempt to
laicise the schools:

We regard with mistrust this new-found zeal for educational
reform and the importation of English secularists to propagate
their views and are satisfied that its purpose is not the improve
ment of our schools, but the elimination from them of the religious
influence of the Church.

Whether because of such criticisms or not is difficult to say, but
nothing further was heard of the matter.

A little over a year later Michael Davitt made a strong plea for the
setting-up of such a Department, arguing that absolute popular
control makes for greater efficiency and that schools so managed are
therefore to be preferred to schools which are only partly or not at all
under popular control.

Popular control [he said] stands for a higher payment of teachers,
for a better standard of secular teaching and, more important still,
for such attention to sanitation and to the comfort and health of
children as tend to make their education an easier task for
teachers, with an assurance of more efficient results for their
labours.[3]

Davitt's statement was a refutation of the arguments of Dr
O'Dwyer, Bishop of Limerick, who had urged that all Catholic-
controlled schools should receive public monies whereas, for Davitt,
the expenditure of any public money on schools should mean
publicly-controlled schools for all citizens, irrespective of religion.

At this time when Ireland's land problems were well on the way to
solution and when it appeared as if her educational grievances were at
least being given a sympathetic hearing, it was unfortunate that the
Irish Councils Bill, introduced by the Liberal government in 1907,
proved unacceptable to the Irish Parliamentary Party or, rather, that
the Party should have been influenced into considering it as unacceptable. Birrell, who prepared it, had been President of the Board of
Education in England, and the measure was an attempt to do, among
other things, for Ireland what the Balfour Education Act of 1902 had

done for England and Wales, i.e. give rate aid to denominational
schools. It did no more than propose the transfer of certain depart
ments — local government, agricultural and technical instruction,
national and intermediate education, reformatory and industrial
schools — to a representative Irish council which was to be started on
its career with a bonus of £650,000 from the imperial exchequer.

When the bill had its first reading, the leader-writer in *An
Claidheamh Soluis,* which could hardly be accused of favouring the
government, said of the proposals:

If they, or anything like them, reached the Statute Book, we shall
be on the eve of the greatest and most beneficent revolution in the
modern history of Ireland. THE SCHOOLS WILL BE OURS.
The shadow of Death and the Nightmare Death-in-Life will have
passed away from the Irish landscape.

He saw the bill as giving to Ireland 'an education authority
representative of the people of Ireland, answerable to Irish public
opinion, and free from the domination of the British Treasury'.[4] *The
Irish Times* saw it as a prelude to Home Rule and warned that 'its
adoption will be followed by Separation as surely as the night follows
the day'. Of the education clauses in the bill, it said: 'The National
and Intermediate Boards are to be swamped in a new Department of
Education, whose operation the Roman Catholic Church will either
dominate absolutely or resist absolutely — there is no possible alternative.'[5]

The Irish Times was right, the Catholic Church did resist it —
absolutely. Bodies such as the Munster Council of Catholic Clerical
Managers had no wish to be subject to popularly elected councils and
to have to furnish accounts to laymen or even to have money distributed to them by laymen, and so they denounced the educational
provisions of the bill as being 'entirely unsatisfactory'. Individual
bishops, notably Bishop O'Dwyer and Bishop Foley, attacked it in
more specific terms. To the former, it represented an attack 'upon the
position of religion in our schools'.[6] He claimed that all classes of
Irishmen were satisfied with 'our splendid educational systems' and
called upon the people to reject the 'perfidious gift offered to them by
men to whom secularism is dearer than Home Rule'. Dr Foley seems
to have based his opposition to it on his own unsupported statement
that no Catholic clergyman would be allowed to serve on the
Council's Education Committee.[7] At the heart of their fears was the
word 'control' and they did not hesitate to invoke nationalist senti-

ment to kill the idea of a Department which they held would be unresponsive to Irish opinion.

The full story of the rejection of the bill by the Nationalists has yet to be told, as has the reason for what Dillon, in a letter to Redmond, described as 'an explosion of dissatisfaction and anger'[8] with regard to the bill. When the bill was introduced in the Commons, Redmond deferred judgment until he and his colleagues had time 'to consider every portion of the scheme'. Birrell must have consulted him before he decided on having the bill drafted and it is likely that Redmond was confident that he could ensure its adoption by his party. The dilemma then facing him as he stood up in the House of Commons was to gauge its effect not only on the members of his party but on those among his followers whose acceptance of constitutional methods was a qualified one. It was a positive disadvantage that the scheme, according to Redmond's biographer, Denis Gwynn,

> bore every trace of having been devised by Sir Antony MacDonnell on the lines of provincial governments in India. But to reject it off-hand might well mean the loss of all further prospect of reforming Dublin Castle while the new Parliament lasted. Its acceptance, if it were really put forward as a first instalment of Home Rule, would certainly make the establishment of a real Irish Parliament much less difficult, if the Liberals could return to power in the following Parliament.[9]

He therefore approached each clause cautiously as though his political antennae were issuing warnings of possible hostile reaction in Ireland. He expressed moderate disappointment with 'the nominated element in the Council', preferring the Education Board to a 'new Department responsible to an English House of Commons and an English Government'. Having, as it were, assured his lines of retreat, Redmond encouraged the House in the belief that his party might support the bill when he went on to say:

> We should shrink from the responsibility of rejecting anything which, after that full consideration which the Bill will receive, seems to our deliberate judgment calculated to relieve the sufferings of Ireland and hasten the day of her full national convalescence.[10]

And he marched into the lobby with the 'Ayes' when the vote to introduce the bill was carried by 417 votes to 121.

A fortnight later the National Convention of the United Irish League, called to consider the bill, listened to statements condemning it. Redmond delayed his intervention in the debate but when he did speak it was to show that he had accurately judged the strength of the hostility to the measure and he moved its rejection. He proposed,

> that, having considered the Irish Councils Bill introduced by the Government, we declare that it is utterly inadequate in its scope, and unsatisfactory in its details, and should be rejected by the Irish nation, and we regard the introduction of such a measure by a British government pledged to Home Rule as confirmation of the position we have always taken up, that any attempt to settle the Irish problem by half-measure would be entirely unsuccessful.

The proposal was carried unanimously.

To those present, and they represented the Irish from the United States, Britain and Australia, what was offered them was 'too little and in any case too dangerous for the cause of ultimate Home Rule'. When, some weeks later, Redmond spoke in the Commons, it was to express astonishment that members of the House could believe 'that the defeat of the Bill, in Irish public opinion, was due to clerical interference and influence'.[12] He seems to have been at considerable pains to exonerate the Catholic Church which, in the eyes of many, had effectively killed the bill, and he assured the members that 'there never was a decision in the field of Irish politics which was less influenced by any clerical considerations whatever'; rather was its rejection, he said, due to a 'spontaneous outburst of public opinion'. This scarcely deceived anyone, certainly not the leader-writer in the *Church of Ireland Gazette* who saw in it the triumph of 'the Roman Catholic priests' who 'proved once again that religion is more to them than nationality'.[13]

If the rejection of the bill was a disappointment to those who saw in it a means of reconciling conflicting political opinions, it was a tragedy to those who had hoped it would help to free education from clerical control. Strauss refers to the defeat of the bill as

> perhaps the most spectacular political event brought about by the direct political intervention of the clergy. . . . The Bill was the first fruit of Campbell-Bannerman's step-by-step policy and the creation of an All-Irish administrative council, though far from revolutionary, might have been an important step forward in handing over Irish affairs to the Irish middle classes.[14]

But Redmond, crushed by the coalition of the priests and the Ancient Order of Hibernians, was unable to assert his authority, 'thereby acknowledging his impotence as a leader in the face of the combined hostility of the Church and the party machine'.[15] Birrell was so upset by the absolute rejection of the bill that he was prepared to resign and told the Prime Minister, Campbell-Bannerman, that he would do so if the Prime Minister thought he should. In the event he did not.

CHAPTER 10

MOVES TO FORM A TEACHING PROFESSION

The Commissioners were never completely satisfied with their financial position. They had succeeded for a period of thirty years in working within their income only by alternately nibbling at their capital and reducing the amounts for exhibitions and prizes. Initially, the sole income of the Commissioners was the interest on £1,000,000 from the funds obtained by the disestablishment of the Church of Ireland. These bonds had been exchanged in 1897 for something over a million pounds worth of Irish Land Guaranteed $2\frac{3}{4}$% Stock, and the income from this source was £30,898 17s. 6d. At about the same time serious financial difficulties began to embarrass the Commissioners, but it was then too late for them to do more than express dissatisfaction with a situation which might more properly have been dealt with in 1888 when an Act was passed providing for the payment of money from the imperial exchequer for the relief of local taxation. The funds were to be divided on the basis of 80 per cent for England, 11 per cent for Scotland and 9 per cent for Ireland. The basis of contribution was originated by Mr Goschen, Chancellor of the Exchequer from 1886 to 1892, 'and was stated by him to depend upon the amount of the assumed contribution of each country to the Revenue for Common purposes'.[1] The income of the Commissioners from this source varied but, no matter what the amount contributed in taxation, it was reduced each year by a fixed sum of £78,000 which had to be paid to the Department of Agriculture and Technical Instruction.

This money became known as the 'Equivalent Grant' which, to quote Lord St Aldwyn, the former Sir Michael Hicks-Beach, meant that 'when a grant was made for a particular purpose to England they were obliged to make a proportionate grant to Ireland and to Scotland, quite irrespective of whether they needed it or not'. In fact what appeared to be a reasonably equitable system of apportioning money to the three countries concerned was, in reality, far from being so. The population of the countries did not appear to matter, nor did their educational needs. The population of Ireland was greater than that of Scotland, yet Scotland got 11 per cent of the money to Ireland's 9 per cent; Dale and Stephens showed that Ireland had proportionately more pupils receiving education in the secondary sector than England, yet the ratio of 80:9 showed little recognition of this.

When the Chief Secretary, John Morley, was later confronted in the House of Commons with the question of the injustice being done to Irish education by the 'Equivalent Grant', he indicated that he was himself uncertain of the correct legal interpretation of the Act.[2]

Whatever the purpose of the framers of the Act, it had the effect of impoverishing Ireland and impeding educational advance for a period of over thirty years. Its legality was called in question by Arthur Samuels, K.C., who held that the 'Equivalent Grant' was

> entirely contrary to constitutional right under the Union and which, not only in its practical operation, is effectively used as a basis for cutting grants to Irish needs, but is also employed through a new method of Treasury book-keeping for advertising her in blue books and finance accounts and almanacs and returns, as a bedraggled entity, contributing year by year less and less to the Empire, though in fact she is taxed, year by year, higher and higher, and year by year her falling population pays more and more into the Exchequer.[3]

Asquith, baffled no doubt by the complexity of the method employed to calculate the grant, a complexity admitted by its author,[4] said of it that 'a more confused and illogical condition of things is impossible to imagine'.[5]

As if to compound the financial problems of the Commissioners, the income from 'whiskey money' was declining and, as a result, 'the more sober Ireland became, the less she got for Education', and this was reflected in the monetary awards for exhibitions and prizes. In the ten years up to 1910 the money awarded to students under this heading fell from £18,000 to £7,000 and the number of exhibitions fell from 700 in 1900 to 294 in 1909, although there was an increase of over one thousand candidates in the interval. Table 10 gives a picture of the mounting crisis in the years from 1900 to 1910.

The financial position was acting as a brake on all educational development, but this was especially true in the secondary sector which, catering for pupils beyond the compulsory school-leaving age, needed the inducement and encouragement of financial support. The Christian Brothers, whose fees were lowest of all, communicated their views by letter to the Commissioners through their Educational Committee at the end of 1908.[6] In the course of it they said that they viewed with concern

> the steady and serious diminution of the funds available for distribution by the Board. The average capitation paid on the pupils on

Table 10

Income of the Intermediate Education Board in the Decennial period, 1900-1910

Amount received under Local Taxation Act	Total income from all sources	Face value of Capital Reserve Fund	Withdrawls from the Reserve Fund	Year
£71,400 2s. 5d.	£103,527 14s. 3d.	£103,171 7s. 3d.	£ 3,695 9s. 0d.	1900
£64,730 16s. 2d.	£ 96,968 6s. 10d.	£ 99,171 7s. 3d.	£ 4,610 10s. 6d.	1901
£56,583 14s. 10d.	£ 88,868 2s. 4d.	£ 99,171 7s. 3d.	-	1902
£59,430 14s. 0d.	£ 91,835 10s. 11d.	£108,127 13s. 7d.		1903
£56,156 3s 4d.	£ 88,573 5s. 10d.	£108,127 13s. 7d.	-	1904
£50,385 6s. 10d.	£ 83,030 1s. 10d.	£108,127 13s. 7d.	-	1905
£48,255 19s. 6d.	£ 81,474 8s. 6d.	£103,560 0s. 0d.	£ 2,013 12s. 1d.	1906
£49,916 17s. 6d.	£ 78,140 19s. 2d.	£ 98,440 0s. 0d.	£ 4,217 11s. 0d.	1907
£49,504 7s. 1d.	£ 85,721 4s. 8d.	£ 98,440 0s. 0d.	-	1908
£46,566 15s. 5d.	£ 82,791 17s. 5d.	£ 92,040 0s. 0d.	£ 4,500 8s. 0d.	1909
£16,998 14s. 6d.	£ 53,006 8s. 11d.	£ 54,040 0s. 0d.	£29,925 17s. 6d.	1910

the rolls of Irish Intermediate Schools is only £3 15s. 6d., while in England Secondary Schools receive a grant of £5 a head for all pupils between the ages of 12 and 18, to which is added a grant from the local authority of £2 10s. 0d. or more.

The poverty of the country and the scattered nature of the population made the existence of small schools especially precarious, yet, as the letter points out, 'the lowering of the Preparatory Grade capitation rate has injuriously affected the smaller Intermediate schools especially', and they appealed to the Commissioners 'not to allow them to be sacrificed in the interests of larger establishments which are not so dependent on the aid they receive from the Board'.

The Christian Brothers went on to make a case for the poor parents of intelligent children who wished them to have a secondary education and they deplored the lowering of the Preparatory Grade fund which was a loss 'to the very class that stood most in need of help'. They instanced the efforts of the London County Council to enable such children to obtain a secondary education and which spent more than £100,000 a year in scholarships which were 'awarded to pupils of from ten to twelve years of age, and increased when the holders reach the age of 14'. The weakness of the Irish system as they saw it lay in the fact that 'each year only a certain sum is available for distribution among the schools, so that success in one direction must mean failure in another'. They might have added that the Irish system was also the only one in the United Kingdom 'that was not financed by the Treasury for administration, inspection and examination purposes'.

At the time when the Christian Brothers were deploring the lack of scholarship provision to enable students to benefit from secondary education, some criticism was levelled at Trinity College for offering valuable Entrance Scholarships 'as the result of the Intermediate Examinations, without further test'.[7] The writer clearly implied that the authorities of Trinity College were unduly eager to attract promising material, remarking:

> These new scholarships, be it noted, are offered not only to Exhibitioners of the Senior Grade, but also to those of Middle Grade; that is, to boys of sixteen and not infrequently of fifteen years of age, who have not yet completed the ordinary school course.

When some years later an opportunity was offered the Intermediate Commissioners, under the terms of the 1908 Act, 'to assist, by means of exhibitions, scholarships, bursaries, payment of fees, or otherwise, students or intending students at any university in Ireland', they did not do so.

Money was needed to fund scholarships, money was needed to increase capitation grants, but, most of all, money was needed to improve the salaries of those on whom ultimately the success or failure of the system rested — the teachers. Yet there has been little mention of them in this record up to now and anyone reading of the development of secondary education during the first thirty years of the life of the Commissioners might well have believed that the system was automatic. The annual Reports which they presented to the government recorded the number of schools, the failure and pass rate in each subject of examination, the grants given, the prizes and exhibitions awarded, but one might ask if there were any teachers and, if so, whether they were a dominant force in shaping the structure of education and in asserting their rights as a professional class.

There were in fact about 1700 assistant teachers, clerical and lay, in regular employment in 1908 and it must at once be said that they were neither dominant nor assertive. Without contracts of employment, security of tenure or pension rights, it could scarcely have been otherwise. Any murmurs of discontent among lay teachers seemed to have been muted either through fear of dismissal or through tacit acceptance of a position in which there was no hope of advancement. In 1909 a meeting took place which gave hope of better things. A joint committee representing the headmasters of secondary schools of all denominations met and asked for grants from the exchequer for Irish intermediate education, to cover 'the whole cost of administration, inspection and examination' as well as a sum of £74,000 which they considered to be the proportional equivalent of the grant of £657,000 to England and Wales. The Catholic hierarchy approved heartily of such a demand made, not on the resources of the Church, but on those of the government and, at a meeting held on 21 June 1910, they passed the following resolution:

> While the State provides all parts of the United Kingdom with grants for secondary education out of the local Taxation Account, further large grants in aid of secondary education are made by the Treasury through the Annual Estimates to England, Scotland and Wales, without any equivalent being given to Ireland. . . . If the inequality and present unfairness in the distribution of Treasury Grants were amended, the additional fund would be sufficient to enable the Board of Intermediate Education to meet, *inter alia,* the reasonable demands of lay teachers in the secondary schools of Ireland.

Support for the claims of teachers grew and at a mass meeting held in the Mansion House, Dublin, in December 1910, the headmaster of St Vincent's College, Castleknock, said how much he would welcome 'the proper provision of status, salaries and pensions of the teachers in these [secondary] schools'.

By spring of the following year, when nothing had been done, the tone of educational discussion hardened and John Dillon voiced the mood of disillusionment when he spoke in the budget debate in the Commons on the amount of money spent on education in England where, 'in addition to its share of the whisky money, there is a grant on the Estimates of £650,000 a year, a vote which is rapidly increasing. As against that vote we in Ireland get not a farthing.'[8] He pointed out that for ten years his party had been asking that a vote should be put on the Estimates which would have enabled the House to discuss the system of intermediate education in Ireland. This had never been done and no grant proportionate to its population had ever been given to Ireland. The saving to the Treasury was obvious because in any distribution of money on the same proportion as the 'Whiskey money', 'the Irish proportion would be £74,000 per annum, as against £650,000 for English Intermediate Education' but, in the event, Ireland got nothing.

Birrell did not intervene in the budget debate but chose, at a later date on 23 May 1911 in the House of Commons, to speak generally on the claims of secondary education in Ireland. Ireland, he said, had a strong case, 'one of the strongest cases that it is possible for anyone to make, because it simply has not anything — nothing at all'. One of the remedies he had in mind was the introduction of a system of scholarships by means of which pupils might pass from primary to secondary schools and then to the university. He also hoped to raise the status of the schools which he felt could only be done by raising the status of the teacher whom he, a man little given to exaggeration, saw leading a life that he called 'detestable', on an 'inadequate' salary and 'with no tenure of office at all'. He went on to treat in more detail some of the uncertainties of a teacher's life:

> He is very often engaged in September for six months, and then the whole tenure and term of his employment may, or may not, be continued on. It is no use bolstering up any Scheme of Secondary Education which has so rocky a foundation as that, and the first task and object, I think, of all persons either engaged in the profession themselves or desirous of seeing it occupying the position of repute that it ought to do, would be to raise the standard of the secondary teacher in Ireland.

For all the concern he professed for the teachers, Birrell, when he did decide to act, dealt first with the provision of scholarships. He could, however, be said to have justified his action when, in his speech outlining what he proposed to do, he said:

> It was his desire to introduce a system of Scholarships whereby suitable pupils might pass from the primary schools into the secondary schools, and ultimately to the University, and also to raise the status of the Secondary schools, which, in his opinion, could only be done by raising the present status of the teachers in these schools.

The Board of Intermediate Education was asked to draw up, in co-operation with the Board of National Education, a scholarship plan on the lines he had indicated. The Schoolmasters' Association met to discuss this plan, but when they did so it was to pass unanimously the following resolution:

> That we do not consider the scholarships the most urgent of these questions. That inasmuch as the demand for a Treasury Grant was chiefly based upon the necessity for improving the position of the Secondary Teacher, we think the possible cost of (a) providing for an increase in Teachers' salaries and (b) providing a Pension Fund should be inquired into before embarking upon the question of Scholarships.

The plan was not proceeded with; what killed it, however, was not the opposition of teachers but the strangely truncated nature of the scheme proposed and the efforts of the Commissioners to extend it. The Board understood that it was the desire of the Chief Secretary that the scheme should be designed solely for the purpose of completing the university scheme, and that it be drawn up accordingly. The Board did not approve of this limitation and suggested the extension of the scheme so as to provide increased facilities for agricultural and technical training, and to allow the poor man's son to take advantage of these facilities, either in advanced primary, or at trade, preparatory, technical or agricultural schools. The Treasury refused to give sanction to such a scheme and nothing further was heard of the matter.

Even if Treasury sanction had been forthcoming, it is very unlikely that the scheme in its original form, i.e. without the Board's suggested extension, would have been accepted. This was largely if not entirely due to the hostility of a little-known but influential body, the Irish County Council's General Council. Their opposition was to the threat that scheme represented to their control over university education. At the October meeting in 1912 of the Executive Committee the members thanked Birrell 'for his successful efforts to provide a system of higher education acceptable to the great majority of the Irish people'. (This was a reference to the Irish Universities Act of 1908.) But they were completely opposed on educational grounds to the proposal

> to award to children of tender years upon the results of an examination based chiefly upon personal estimates of their natural intelligence scholarships tenable at Intermediate schools linked with the extraordinary condition that at the conclusion of a three years' course they are to possess, subject only to the veto of their own preceptors, an inalienable right to demand from the Council of their county the provision of £240 of the ratepayers' money to defray the cost of a University course, subject to no control by the Council in its award or expenditure, subject to no examination to determine whether the original estimate of the child's intelligence has been fully justified, or whether the youth's present intelligence and acquirements point to a material advantage to be derived by him from University education, and conditional upon a mere pass matriculation.

Nor were the financial conditions which accompanied the proposals any more acceptable, as 'for each £10,000 of free grants the Councils must convenant to provide £20,000'.

The educational arguments which they advanced were cogent and reasonable, but it is possible that what weighed more with the County Councils was the question of control and on this they made it clear that 'the effect of the acceptance of this scheme would be a relinquishment by the County Councils of the measure of control over University education placed in their hands by Parliament, and its transfer to a body of an unrepresentative character'. It was evident that they had no wish to hand over £60 a year for four years to students who would select their own university and choose their own course of study at that university.

If the early years of Mr Birrell's Chief-Secretaryship had been uneventful — he was, after all, in the country for five years when, in 1911, he gave the House the benefit of his views on education — he was to know many difficulties in the years that followed. On 31 July 1912 he outlined the conditions for a proposed grant of £40,000 for intermediate education. The draft scheme for the distribution of the grant made it a condition of payment that

> each boys' school is to have not less than one registered lay assistant teacher, at a minimum salary of £120 a year for each forty pupils on the roll, and each girls' school is to have not less than one lay assistant teacher, at a minimum salary of £80 a year, for the same number of pupils on the roll.

He also proposed to establish a register of secondary teachers and he explained to the House his reasons for doing so:

> But for my purpose and the purpose of the House, I am considering raising the status of the lay teacher. The status of the clergyman — the status of the man in religious orders — does not need to be raised. He has his status by virtue of the dedicating of his life to religious purposes.

The idea of a register had been mentioned in the 1899 Report of the Commission on Intermediate Education, but as the Commissioners had considered the question of such an issue to be outside their terms of reference, nothing had been done.

Opposition to Birrell's proposals was quickly organised and on 12 September 1912 a statement on behalf of the Catholic Headmasters' Association and the Committee representing convent schools was issued to the press. The statement made it clear that the suggested regulation that every school should employ a prescribed number of lay teachers was entirely unacceptable to them. As the statement pointed out, the number of lay teachers actually employed in Catholic schools was considerably greater than would be required by the regulation. There were then about 12,800 pupils on the rolls of their schools and, 'Allowing one lay teacher for each 40 pupils, that would give 320 lay teachers, while the actual number employed is 368.'

Answering a question in the House on 30 June 1913, the Chief Secretary gave, as the most recent figures available to him, those showing the number of teachers employed in the school year ending July 1910, given in table 11.

Table 11

Lay assistant teachers regularly employed

| | Women | | | Men | | |
Catholic Schools	Protestant Schools	TOTAL	Catholic Schools	Protestant Schools	TOTAL	Gross
75	328	403	293	249	542	945

Clerical assistant teachers regularly employed

Nuns	Men	TOTAL
435	371	806

Assistant teachers occasionally employed (lay)

| | Women | | | Men | | |
Catholic Schools	Protestant Schools	TOTAL	Catholic Schools	Protestant Schools	TOTAL	Gross
86	102	188	123	82	205	393

Clerical assistant teachers occasionally employed

Nuns	Men	TOTAL
22	18	40

Initially at any rate the Catholic hierarchy appeared as if not at all anxious to embitter the dispute that was already building up between the Catholic teaching orders and lay teachers. Indeed, in a statement issued to the press, it affected to be equally concerned with the welfare of each, observing: 'In the allocation of a proposed grant for Intermediate Education, we must protest against the discrimination between lay and clerical teachers whose services the interests of education demand, whether laymen or clerics.' Frank Hugh O'Donnell, who, however, cannot be considered as an impartial observer of the educational scene, would insist that the lay teacher was being positively discriminated against, not by the State but by religious teaching orders. In the year before Birrell made his plea for the lay teacher, he had written: 'In the female world alone, every corner of English civilisation is full of poor Irish governesses who are crowded out of every teaching-post in their native land, except the most menial, by the organised armies of teaching sisterhoods.'[9] His views seem to have been largely shared by one prominent teacher who, sensitive to the extent of Church influence in the country, gave warning that such innovations as the Chief Secretary was proposing would prove unacceptable. Hanna Sheehy Skeffington, who was then teaching in Alexandra College, wrote an article in which she expressed doubts that Birrell's scheme had arrived in time to save the profession. In her opinion, 'The prospect of a minimum £120 for men, £80 (a still wilder dream) for women with the same or higher qualifications, steady, if laborious work, and the certainty of half a year's notice' were all propositions 'startlingly revolutionary in character'. So she expressed no surprise 'that the vested interests are up in arms, that the headmasters and the clerical representatives of the convent schools are clamouring', and she appealed for public support 'to range itself behind Mr Birrell and insist that his scheme for the betterment of a sorely aggrieved class be helped to a realisation'.[10]

The Protestant schools seemed well satisfied with his proposals, reaffirming their resolutions of 1912 when they met in 1913, and asking only 'that special consideration be given to the circumstances of small schools, which will find it difficult to comply with all the conditions'. They also stated that they believed that 'six months' notice' of dismissal would prove to be unworkable and suggested instead 'three months' notice'. For Protestant teachers the issue was uncomplicated: money was being given to be divided among them - the practitioners in the field of education. For the religious who controlled almost all Catholic schools the issue was far different. They had provided schools and worked in the schools, employing lay teachers unwillingly and only when no religious were available. And a register, which insisted on certain qualifications, might not accept the training given to nuns and monks and clerics in their own novitiates and training colleges. The elements of the conflict that was to follow were already present when the bishops issued a statement on the question, in the course of which they said:

> In Ireland the difficulties (of registration) are not unreal, but as far as we are concerned we are quite ready to agree to the formation

of a Register on condition that we are satisfied as to the persons who are to make it, the principles on which they are to proceed, and that due allowance is made for the special circumstances of our nuns and other religious teachers.[11]

Five years were to elapse before these conditions were satisfactorily met and a register compiled.

Meanwhile the lines of battle were drawn for the inevitable confrontation between teachers and their employers over the Teachers' Salaries Grant. The government stipulation of 'one registered lay assistant on a minimum salary of £120 a year for each 40 pupils on the roll' was not in itself objectionable. What was objectionable was the claim of the government to decide the exact number of lay teachers in Catholic schools, as this seemed to imply 'that priests and religious do not possess the same rights as laymen to earn their own livelihood'.[12]

The Secretary of the Catholic Headmaster's Association was a Father Murphy from Limerick, who saw in Birrell's claim to decide the proportion of lay teachers in a school owned by religious a threat to the very existence of such schools. 'In plain words', he wrote in *The Irish Educational Review* which he edited,

> this demand logically involves the claim to seize the schools built and maintained by the Bishops and Religious Orders for the Catholic people of Ireland, and turn them into Government schools. We are unable to see that such a claim differs from the claim of the governments of France and Portugal to the right of forcible confiscation.[13]

His Association made the important distinction that the grant should be made for Irish intermediate schools generally and not based on the number *in each individual* school. To the government claim that the Protestant schools had raised no objection, the Association replied that to insist on one lay teacher for forty pupils in Protestant schools meant nothing since the staff were almost entirely lay.

A lengthy correspondence followed between Birrell and Father Murphy which was terminated by Birrell when he saw that no progress was being made. The correspondence was laid on the Table of the House and later published in *The Irish Educational Review*. It would be wrong to think that the controversy was confined exclusively to the Chief Secretary and the Catholic Headmasters' Association. The Association of Secondary Teachers (Ireland) made known its views in its official organ, *The Irish Journal of Education*.

This journal was far more representative of what might be called the trade union or professional viewpoint than *The Irish Educational Review,* and it constantly drew attention to the arbitrary dismissal of lay teachers whom it claimed were 'being ruthlessly driven out of certain schools'.

The government was, however, wise enough to see that the field of education was ill-chosen as a battle-ground when ranged against it was a Catholic Church resolutely adhering to its core principle of retaining power within the schools where, one bishop did concede, 'There are, and always will be, a certain number of lay teachers, but they are comparatively few, and whoever attempts to deal with Irish education should keep that fact before his mind.'[14] Birrell did, apparently, keep it before his mind and he withdrew his insistence that the stated proportion of lay teachers should be maintained in *each* school. The struggle was over and on 10 August 1914 'the Bill to amend the law relating to Intermediate Education and for other purposes connected therewith' became law. It was welcomed by lay teachers who saw in the clause which provided for the setting-up of a Registration Council a major step towards attaining the status of a learned profession. It was welcomed by the Catholic hierarchy as a justification of their stand for non-interference with the schools under Catholic control. And it must have been a considerable rebuff for Birrell who, as President of the Board of Education in England, had successfully opposed denominational interest in education and prepared the scheme for the setting-up of local rate-aided school boards. If, before coming to Ireland, he confessed to knowing little of the country save as a tourist, the years of protracted negotiation with the Catholic hierarchy must have taught him something of the power of the Church in a country still lacking a native ruling class.

CHAPTER 11

THE COMMISSIONERS CRITICISE THE SYSTEM

The Rules for the application of the Teachers' Salaries Grant were made by the Lord Lieutenant with the approval of the Treasury on 25 January 1915. According to these Rules, the grant was intended to promote the employment of an adequate number of duly qualified *lay* teachers in intermediate schools. Many years later, a Dáil deputy, Professor Magennis, was to refer to the imprecision of the language used in the Act and the failure of the Parliamentary draftsman to define the word 'lay'. Speaking in the course of a debate on education, he pointed to the confusion which arose from this failure and its effect on the Salaries Grant.[1] What he did not do, probably because it was not relevant to his purpose, was to draw attention to the hostility it caused between layman and cleric in a country where religion pervades the daily content of living and where labels such as 'lay' and 'cleric' have always had an exaggerated importance. He began by asking the question, 'What is a lay-teacher?' and to his own question he gave the answer:

> The ordinary man in the street would answer readily, 'Anyone not in Holy Orders is a layman and I suppose a lay-teacher is a teacher not in Holy Orders.' The intention of Mr. Birrell and his advisers was to define as a lay-teacher the ordinary layman as contrasted with a member of a Religious Order. Now there are various Religious Orders which under their regulations have not the priestly character. Nuns, for example, are, strictly speaking, lay-teachers. The Presentation Brothers, the Christian Brothers, although wearing the frock of the monk, and living under monastic rule are — in the strictly legal interpretation — laymen, and when you compute the number of lay teachers employed in a group of Catholic Schools you are obliged according to the legal effect of the rule I cited to count the numbers of these Religious Orders as among the lay-teachers for the purpose of this distribution.

He then referred to financial loss suffered by 'genuine' lay teachers through extending the benefits of the Act to members of religious orders:

> It is [he said] one of the grievances, I understand, of the genuine lay-teacher that the provision in aid of his meagre income is not given to him fully because of the deficiency of the English

language, and because of the inability, so to speak, of the draftsman, to make it clear. Thus the sum intended for the ordinary lay-teacher is made to depend upon the way you interpret the rule!

The Association of Secondary Teachers (Ireland) had sought legal advice in an attempt to remedy what appeared to be an injustice to members of the profession, but without success. In a pamphlet published many years later, they blamed the Lord Lieutenant for his failure to act when it was in his power to do so:

> In every year from 1917-18 onwards a note in the Annual Report on the distribution of the Birrell Grant, furnished by the Intermediate Education Board, stated that there were several 'nuns and members of brotherhoods' who claimed to be lay teachers, and pointed out that a decision as to whether these were lay teachers under the Rules rested with the Lord Lieutenant.[2]

The Association contended that the Lord Lieutenant had power to discontinue the method of distribution and to prescribe a new method, where the conditions of Rule 3 had not been carried out, but that he did not do so, 'even though the failure of the Catholic group to comply with the conditions was pointed out to him'. Counsel's opinion was that 'the Association has no legal redress for the failure of the Catholic group to obey the Rules, and that the only course open was for the Lord Lieutenant to use his power to alter the Rules'.

When in 1915 the Rules for the application of the Teachers' Salaries Grant came into effect, it was estimated that £23,000 of the £40,000 voted for the benefit of their assistants would go to the superiors of religious schools. This figure was based on the known number, 19,000 boys and girls, on the intermediate school rolls, and the 900 men and women lay teachers then in regular employment. From 1915 onwards the Commissioners presented a separate Report on the application of the grant and these show the gradual change from an unqualified or partly qualified teaching force to a more fully qualified one. In 1914 there were no more than 282 'duly qualified teachers' in the intermediate schools of Ireland. (This figure did not include '202 nuns and 36 members of brotherhoods who claim to be lay teachers and who satisfy the conditions as to salary and tenure necessary for duly qualified lay teachers'.) In the Report for 1921, the last for a united Ireland, the figure for 'duly qualified teachers' had grown to 2609. While these figures did reflect an improvement in the conditions of employment of 'duly qualified teachers', they were not to be considered excessively generous. The Rules simply provided for salaries of not less than £140 for non-resident men and £90 for non-resident women teachers, and the Commissioners could say, in their Report for 1916, that not forty assistant teachers in the country had an annual salary of £200 or over.

While the first meeting of the Registration Council took place on 15 November 1915, regulations for the Register did not come into force until 31 July 1918. Even then, a transition period of seven years was allowed, at the end of which intermediate teachers had to have a university degree, a diploma in teacher training and three years' experience before they could be registered. In 1919 additional regulations were issued recognising the Certificate in the Practice and Theory of Education of the Royal College of Science for Ireland and that of Clongowes Wood College, Co. Kildare. Recognition of the Certificate of the Royal College of Science was made retrospective but that of Clongowes Wood College was 'deemed to be approved for a period of three years from 1 August 1920'. The Clongowes Wood College Certificate finally expired on 1 August 1971 and no application has since been made for the renewal of recognition. That of the College of Science was terminated on 7 May 1926 when all functions relating to the college were transferred to the National University of Ireland.

The Commissioners may have been wearied by the years they had spent wrestling with obdurate Treasury officials, they may have been subject to the indefinable despair which we are told invades at times the heart of *fonctionnaires* in all countries. Whatever the reason, in their Report for 1916 they asked for nothing less than the complete reconstruction of the educational system in Ireland. The members of the Board showed themselves aware of the defects of a system which they and their predecessors had administered conscientiously for thirty-seven years. They had seen it fail to establish the idea of the school as a training-ground of mind and character in which to form men and women worthy to fulfil their stations in life but, instead, it had put before them 'a single examination in the year as the sole criterion of educational efficiency'. The system, to quote their own words, did not

> give sufficient freedom to teachers to develop their own powers and ideas. It attempts to force all schools into the same mould, by making all submit to the same regulations, and bringing them into undue competition with one another — a competition which is naturally injurious to the best interests of secondary education.

The Commissioners found themselves unable to help to extend the benefits of intermediate education to districts where intermediate schools did not exist, nor could they give assistance to schools whose existence was threatened because of the poverty of the locality. Their opinion was that 'In a country such as Ireland, especially, small and struggling schools in backward districts are often of the highest advantage to the community as a whole, yet they are inevitably condemned to the scantiest of grants.' Nor could the Board 'encourage the establishment of schools in places where they are needed nor attempt to meet the special requirements of any given locality'. To help to remedy some of the defects, the Commissioners recommended that 'the school grant should be a capitation grant, paid to schools which satisfy the required conditions, on all pupils between certain prescribed ages who have been in regular attendance throughout the year'. The 'required conditions' were (1) that the Board should be satisfied as to the efficiency of the school; (2) that a reasonable proportion of the pupils should pass the certificate examinations; (3) that the teachers should possess qualifications to be approved by the Board; (4) that the capitation grant should be greater for students between the ages of sixteen and eighteen than for those under sixteen years of age.

They unreservedly recommended the abolition of the existing examinations and the introduction of two new examinations to which they gave names which were to become familiar to later generations of pupils, 'Intermediate Certificate' and 'Leaving Certificate'. The Commissioners were thinking of a separate certificate for those not proposing to go to university and shaped the leaving certificate 'for those who go through the complete course of secondary education'. At the time the prestige enjoyed by the Senior Grade examination was so high that all the Irish universities had accepted a recommendation from the Board of Studies that 'a Pass in the Intermediate Senior Grade, in subjects recognised for Matriculation, be accepted as equivalent to a Pass in the Matriculation Examination'.[3] Three years later the Senate of the Queen's University decided to bring

> the prescribed courses into line with those for the examinations conducted by the Board of Intermediate Education, thus facilitating the preparation of candidates, especially in the smaller schools; the conditions on which the Intermediate examination would be accepted as equivalent to the matriculation were also somewhat eased.[4]

Trinity College admitted all those who had passed the Senior

Grade without entrance examination, 'except in subjects which they had not presented at the Intermediate examination'.[5]

In the years during which the intermediate system was in operation the teachers, rather like the stokers of a ship confined to the boiler-room, had little knowledge of what was going on up on deck. The meetings of the Commissioners were private, Parliamentary debates on education infrequent and the headmasters of schools, for the most part, dutifully concerned with such trivia as pass lists, prize winners, exhibitionists, school grants, etc. So it must have come as a surprise when, on 24 May 1917, the Schoolmasters' Association sent a Memorial outlining their grievances to the Chief Secretary. This was supplemented, at the request of the Chief Secretary, by a statement forwarded on 9 July containing 'explanatory remarks and arguments in support of the claim urged in the Memorial'. Much of what they said echoed the earlier recommendations of Dale and Stephens. They called for the appointment of a Minister of Irish Education, presiding over three separate departments of primary, secondary and technical education. Each department would be organised by a permanent paid Secretary or Commissioner who would have the advice of an Advisory Board on which there would be representatives of the schools served by the Department. Such departments would, it was hoped, help to correlate the work of the schools between which there were no links. What was, perhaps, most striking in their proposals was the clear intention to have substituted for the Board a paid official and to have teachers sharing responsibility for the development and improvement of the schools of the country.

When one considers the uneven distribution of secondary schools in Ireland, even at the present time, it is interesting to find the Association, while favouring inspection of schools, recommending that there should be 'some control in the direction of determining the number and kind of Schools required in a given town or district, of deciding the need of new Schools, and of encouraging different varieties of Secondary Schools'. The financial basis of support for these schools should be a capitation grant payable to schools satisfying certain conditions as to building, staff, and number of pupils presented for examination. They showed themselves to be ahead of their time in the matter of examinations, favouring two, not three examinations, with some choice of syllabus left to the staff who might also, with the aid of an external examining body, monitor the tests. We know that a deputation from the Association was received by the Chief Secretary on 12 October of that year. The rest is silence.

Dissatisfaction did, however, express itself elsewhere. Ireland and its educational problems was the subject of a day-long debate in the Commons on 4 March 1918 when the government introduced a proposal to grant £50,000 for the purposes of intermediate education in Ireland. This money was to be paid 'during the year ending on March 31, 1918, for Intermediate Education in Ireland, including the Teachers' Salaries Grant'. What seemed a measure intended to benefit all teachers met with considerable opposition chiefly among the younger men. A circular, issued by the Incorporated Association of Assistant Teachers and quoted in the course of the debate, made it clear that the manner in which it was proposed to distribute the money had aroused 'universal opposition from the Intermediate teachers'. The lay teachers who were employed as assistants were most in need, but the circular estimated that 'the benefit accruing to assistants will be practically negligible'. Yet the grant sought to give special assistance to schools in which assistant teachers were paid *more* than the minimum prescribed under the 1914 Act. This money was in fact a capitation grant payable to managers of schools 'in respect of all pupils between the ages of twelve and nineteen who shall have made 100 attendances between those ages during the educational year'. A further clause made clear that the measure was intended to help the teachers:

> For each complete forty pupils upon whom the Capitation Grant is payable and for each twenty or more such pupils in excess of a multiple of forty there shall be employed in the school at least one teacher recognized by the Board, such teacher to be in receipt of a salary of at least £20 per annum more than the minimum stated 'for a duly qualified teacher' in the Rules governing the Teachers' Salaries Grant (1915), and to have the security of tenure required for a duly qualified teacher under those rules.

Sir Edward Carson, speaking in the debate, revealed something of the financial position of teachers at the time. Out of 350 schools in the country, 'only twelve pay salaries of £200 or over'. These were the élite of the profession but, as he pointed out, 'there are not forty assistants altogether who receive such salaries, 35 per cent of the whole number receive less than £100 a year non-resident'. The extent to which schools either could not or did not wish to pay salaries above the minimum is shown in the further figures given by him on the occasion: 'Two hundred of those qualified lay assistants receive above the minimum, but 140 of these come from thirteen schools, and the remaining 337 schools contribute only sixty between them;

about 170 lay assistant qualified teachers received the actual minimum.'

The figures available show that many schools, particularly those in the control of Catholic religious bodies, were not fulfilling the conditions attached to the 1914 Act and, in consequence, were forfeiting money they could have had. This may have been because of a sufficiency of qualified religious or because of a scarcity of qualified lay teachers or it may have been part of a deliberate policy not to employ lay teachers. Whatever the reason, the figures given by Mr Samuel, M.P., Solicitor General for Ireland, did little to lessen the dissatisfaction of the teachers. He analysed the figures for the three years, 1914, 1915 and 1916.

In 1914 there were only forty-six certified registered teachers in the Roman Catholic Schools. That number rose to 125 in 1915 and to 164 in 1916. That shows a certain amount of progression. When we come to deal with the number of pupils in the schools we find that they have risen from 12,000 to 13,200 in three years. If you divide the 164 teachers into 13,200 pupils, you will find that the quota of 330 has not been nearly fulfilled, and then these 166 lay registered teachers, deficient, if I may say so, in the Roman Catholic Group of schools — that is practically to say that they are 50 per cent below what the proper quota should be in order to get the full advantage of the Birrell Grant. On the other hand, the second group of schools — the Protestant schools — had 237 certified teachers in 1914 and 295 in 1916, while their pupils had risen from 5,500 to 5,900, so that they have 100 per cent more than the necessary quota to get the Grant.

The only member of the House to protest against the capitation grant was Sir Edward Carson, who described it as the 'most illogical and most mischievous method of financing the needs of Ireland that can possibly be conceived'. On the day the money was voted Mr Samuel wound up the debate with some words of encouragement by which, doubtless, he hoped to dispel the fears raised by the words of Carson:

In this matter I would like to say that Ireland should be treated by the Treasury as a cheerful giver. We have, however, a sum of £50,000 given to us, and, as you see by the Vote, it is an Equivalent Grant. That at once implies that it is not a stereotyped Grant. I have had the advantage of consulting the Financial Secretary to the Treasury, who assured me that it is what is called an Equivalent Grant, and that it will vary from time to time if this system of Equivalent Grants is continued, according to the amount that may be paid for English education.

Then, in the manner of a patient teacher dealing with a rather backward class, he went on to say that he wished to 'remove a mis-apprehension that may possibly exist'. He praised the former Chief Secretary, Mr Birrell, who had, he said, done all that he could 'to push the interests of Irish education' and whose name 'is very honourably associated with what is called the "Birrell Grant" '. Then he added: 'That is a stereotyped sum of £40,000. This grant is not a stereotyped sum.'

How the Equivalent Grant 'varied' is best seen from the figures given by the Commissioners: 'In 1917-18 we received £50,000 for the first time; in 1918-19 we received the same sum: and again for the year 1919-20 the same sum appears in the estimates.'[6] In fact it remained unchanged at £50,000 for 1920-21, the last year of the Intermediate Education Board. So we will never know how much longer that grant which was to vary 'from time to time' would have remained unvaried.

CHAPTER 12

THE VICE-REGAL COMMITTEE OF 1918

The inadequacy of the financial provision that had initially been made for intermediate education was to limit its development to the end. Problems arose in the internal working of the system, but most of these could have been solved if enough money had been available. The Commissioners showed considerable skill in devising methods whereby on a fixed income they could meet increasing expenses but, unless they were to reduce the results fees which were, in effect, a type of concealed schools grant, there was no effective measure they could take to achieve financial stability. They must, then, have been glad to see that the terms under which a Vice-Regal Committee was appointed in 1918 had specific reference to the financing of schools and the payment of teachers.

The Vice-Regal Committee was appointed by the Lord Lieutenant

to inquire and report as to any improvements which may appear desirable to be made in the conditions of service and in the methods of remuneration of teachers in Intermediate schools in Ireland; and in the distribution of the grants made from public funds for Intermediate Education, and as to the best means in the public interest of effecting such improvements.

The members of the Committee, which was presided over by the Rt Hon. T. F. Molony, Lord Chief Justice, were: Rt Hon. W. J. Starkie, Sir Joseph Larmor, Rev. Canon Marshall, Rev. T. Corcoran, Brother Hennessy, Professor R. M. Henry, J. Thompson, Miss A. M. White, Miss A. McHugh, Mr C. R. Beavan, Professor W. J. Williams, Miss E. Steel, M. F. Headlam, G. Fletcher, E. Ensor.

The Committee met on thirty days and examined twenty witnesses. These included officials of the Intermediate Education Board for Ireland, the Board of Education for England and Wales, the Scottish Education Department, representatives of the Catholic Head masters' Association, the Schoolmasters' Association, the Central Association of Irish Schoolmistresses, the Association of Secondary Teachers (Ireland) and the Incorporated Association of Assistant Masters (Ireland Branch). Other witnesses examined included a number of individual teachers who came forward to give evidence in response to an invitation issued through the press at the commencement of the Inquiry.

The Report of the Committee which was sent to the Lord Lieutenant on 4 March 1919 is in substance an unequivocal statement on the unsatisfactory nature of the system of intermediate education and on the need for early remedial legislation. The Commissioners of Intermediate Education commented on it in terms which, while guarded, were favourable. In their Report for 1918 they devoted a paragraph to it in which they said: 'While some members of the Board make reservations with regard to certain specific points we find ourselves in general agreement with the recommendations of the Committee.' In fact the Committee had itself dealt extensively with the work of the Intermediate Commissioners before going on to express their views on teachers, their conditions of service, remuneration, etc.

In their appraisal of the system they listed a number of defects, the most serious of which were:

(i)   The great and urgent need of improvement in the salaries and security of tenure of intermediate teachers and the necessity for the provision of pensions.

(ii) The absence of an organised Central Authority for primary, intermediate and technical education.

(iii) The insufficiency of the correlation between primary, intermediate and technical schools.

(iv) The dependence of the school grant exclusively on the results of examination.

(v)   The rigidity of the examination system, and the tendency it exerts towards over-pressure.

(vi) The inadequacy of the financial provision from public funds.

(vii) The inelasticity of the grants.

(viii)The cost of administration is not, as it is in England and Scotland, borne by the Treasury.

The Report advised the setting-up of a salary scale for all teachers and the fixing of a minimum salary payable by the school. While the members agreed on the necessity for the payments of increments by a central authority, they would not have the increment vary on the ground either of special ability as a teacher or of specially high academic qualifications. They showed themselves rather in advance of their time in recommending similar salaries for men and women. They agreed with the principle underlying the 1914 bill which stipulated one fully registered teacher for each forty recognised pupils and asked that pension rights be guaranteed such teachers. They expressed concern that certain conditions 'had not been fulfilled in the case of the group of schools under Roman Catholic management'.

The members were also concerned that, to quote their own Report, 'a teacher is still liable to dismissal for no fault of his own, and has no redress'. With a view to remedying this grievance, they recommended that there should be no dismissal during good conduct and efficiency, that a contract of employment terminable only on three months' notice in writing, on either side, should be given to each teacher, and that such a contract should set out the conditions of work and also the body to which the teacher could appeal in the case of alleged wrongful dismissal.

The constitution of 'the body to which the teacher could appeal' divided the members as between supporters of Church and State. Father T. Corcoran, S.J., Professor of Education at University College, Dublin, explained, in a Note to the Report, his interpretation of what constituted an Appeal against Notice of Dismissal. He believed that teachers should have the right of appeal but that the right of appeal 'must be reasonably in accord with the nature of the school and its work'. He insisted that Catholic schools had received their existence and commission to educate from the Catholic Church alone. Their origins, above all in Ireland, as well as their past and present scope of work, precluded any 'but a strictly limited relation with the State'. As long as the State intended 'promoting' intermediate education there would be no difficulty, but once it tried to 'control' the education given, then issues of principle would arise. 'The most essential issue in the Catholic nature of Catholic schools is', he contended, 'full Catholic control of the choice of teacher, retention of teachers, and removal of teachers.' Such a statement was so absolute that it allowed for no compromise and it was clear that Catholic schools could not, in his view, accept an appellate authority that was not in full conformity with Catholic principles on issues intimate to the running of the school and the conduct of teachers. To hammer home the point, he ended his *Note on Appeal against Notice of Dismissal* by saying: 'The imposition on Catholic schools of a State tribunal of appeal would be a denial of their essential principle, and would produce evils incomparably worse than the defects which may call for remedy.'

It was with the viewpoint expressed in this Note that the three signatories of the Minority Report, R. M. Henry, W. J. Williams and Annie McHugh, did not agree. They did not believe 'that a Catholic teacher's right of appeal to a publicly constituted tribunal against arbitrary dismissal is likely to interfere with the efficiency, dignity or freedom of Catholic schools'. On the contrary, they considered that such a tribunal would ensure public confidence and act as a guarantee that a teacher is not, because of the arbitrary decision of an individual headmaster, deprived of a livelihood provided for him out of public funds. They drew attention to the evidence before the Committee that a lay teacher could lose his post in a Catholic school to a member of a religious order, not because of inefficiency or misconduct, but because 'such power of dismissal was regarded by some Catholic heads of schools as an inalienable prerogative of their position'. Such exercise of authority the signatories of the Minority Report charac terised as 'scandalous'. They held that if the State is justified in taking steps to ensure that the education for which it provides the funds is of a proper standard, it is equally justified in ensuring that the teachers paid out of public funds are not deprived of their positions without a public inquiry into the cause.

In the event, the Minority Report was ignored and arbitrary dismissals continued until 1937 when a form of agreement was drawn up between Religious Superiors and the Association of Secondary Teachers (Ireland) which provided for three months' notice of dismissal *to be preceded by a month's notice of such intention.*

An important recommendation of the Vice-Regal Committee, that there should be 'a single authority responsible for education (Primary, Secondary and Technical)', was linked with the suggestion that an advisory council on educational policy with defined statutory powers should be established to assist the authority.

The Committee appeared to be somewhat uncertain as to the importance of examinations as a factor in determining the efficiency of a school, but they were in no doubt that they would have them subordinate to inspection. They foreshadowed the present form of examination in recommending that there should be no more than two examinations, i.e., one for an 'Intermediate Certificate' and the other for a 'Leaving Certificate'. Their comments on what they considered to be the purpose of each examination are worth quoting. Of the first they said that it 'should be on a general course which should allow the widest possible liberty to schools in the selection of texts to be read', while the Leaving Certificate should be recognised 'as equivalent to the entrance to university and other places of higher education'. They condemned the system of payment by results and would abolish the monetary rewards that had come to be associated with success in examination, replacing these by a flat capitation rate. They saw that this might be a serious disadvantage to a school in an area of small and declining population and, to ensure that a small rural community would not be deprived of a secondary school through falling numbers etc., the Report put forward the idea of empowering the Central Authority to make up the grant earned by small schools in such areas to a certain specified sum. It is likely that almost any source of revenue, provided that it was permanent, would have been welcomed by the schools which had watched the money spent in exhibitions and prizes fall very much below that spent under the same headings in earlier years. 'In 1886, the amount so allotted was £12,330; in 1895, £15,445; in 1900, £19,312; and in 1901, £20,406. During the period 1901-1910, the amount gradually fell, but since 1910 it has remained fairly constant at almost £6,500 a year.'

Table 12

Number and value of the exhibitions awarded in 1900 (*Report of the Vice-Regal Committee on Intermediate Education (Ireland), 1919* (Cmd. 66), XXI, p. 28)

	Senior Grade	Middle Grade, £30 a year, tenable for two years	Junior Grade, £20 a year, tenable for three years	Preparatory Grade, £20 a year, tenable for one year	TOTAL
Boys	20	60	190	84	354
Girls	11	24	83	24	142
GROSS TOTAL	31	24	273	108	496

Table 13

Number and value of the exhibitions awarded in 1917 (*Report of the Vice-Regal Committee on Intermediate Education (Ireland), 1919* (Cmd. 66), XXI, p. 28)

	Senior Grade		Middle Grade		Junior Grade		TOTAL
	1st Class £30	2nd Class £20	1st Class £20	2nd Class £15	1st Class £15	2nd Class £10	
Boys	16	24	24	32	42	61	199
Girls	8	16	13	27	24	33	121
GROSS TOTAL	24	40	37	59	66	94	320

Remarking upon the fall in class numbers between the first and final year, the Committee hoped that by means of scholarships more pupils would be encouraged to remain at school. They recommended that money should be provided from public funds for three types of scholarship:

(a) Burses from primary and other schools giving elementary education to intermediate schools, to be offered for pupils at the age of 11 or 12, but not later, and to be tenable until the age for taking the 'Intermediate Certificate' examination;

(b) Burses tenable in intermediate schools by students who have passed the examination for the 'Intermediate Certificate';

(c) Burses tenable in the university or other places of higher education to be awarded to students who have passed the examination for the 'Leaving Certificate'.

They would delegate to the Central Authority such matters as the number and value of the awards while leaving to those responsible for primary and intermediate education, respectively, the selection of scholarship holders under (a). The awards under (b) and (c) were to be made by the schools, but with money provided by the Central Authority on the results of the general examination.

When they came to consider the financial underpinning of the Board, they prefaced the rather revolutionary changes they desired by saying: 'No country if it wishes to maintain an influential position in the community of nations, can afford to neglect the means of giving its children a liberal education.' Sentiments as valid today as when they were then expressed. Indeed, to read one of the last 'Recommendations' of that Vice-Regal Committee is to make one regret that the swift-flowing tide of political events gave no chance of ever giving it legislative sanction. It read:

A flat rate should be levied over the whole country and paid to the account of the Central authority, who should spend it impartially for the benefit of education throughout Ireland. We recommend that there should be an Advisory Committee, representative of the various localities, which should meet in Dublin at stated periods to discuss educational matters with the heads of the Central Authority.

In their view, a national rate would have helped towards reinforcing the central control which was very desirable in a small country like Ireland with, in many parts, a population so sparse as to make the proceeds of a local rate for education inadequate. Again, to suggest local rather than central control would, they believed, in the case of Ireland, lessen efficiency and induce something approaching chaos by a multiplication of small committees with widely different aims and ideas.

CHAPTER 13

THE CATHOLIC CHURCH ASSERTS CONTROL

The government set up a departmental committee to draft a bill embodying the recommendations of the Vice-Regal Committee and also those of a Committee on Primary Education which had met under the chairmanship of Lord Killanin. It was a committee of five, small, but composed of men of proven ability in education who had the advantage of having a wealth of well-documented information to draw upon. Not only had they the Molony and Killanin reports but also the Dale and Stephens Report, many of whose recommendations were still very apropos, as well as statements from the teaching bodies such as the I.N.T.O. and the A.S.T.I. Their names were: Mr Bonaparte Wyse, Chairman; Mr Butler, Assistant Commissioner of the Intermediate Board, Mr Fletcher, Administrative head of the Technical Branch of the Department of Agriculture and Technical Instruction, Mr Alexander, Assistant Secretary of the Scottish Education Department, and Mr Bennett, former Chief Inspector of the English Board of Education.

Their work resulted in a bill, generally referred to as the MacPherson Bill, 'to make further provision with respect to Education in Ireland; and for other purposes connected therewith'. Under its terms, it was proposed to create a Department of Education for Ireland consisting of the Chief Secretary, the Vice-President of the Department of Agriculture and Technical Instruction, and a permanent member, to be appointed by the Lord Lieutenant. It was further proposed to establish an Advisory Board of Education of fifty-one persons (including, *ex-officio*, the members of the Department of Education) to advise on educational matters and to formulate policy. There was to be a county education committee for each county, to make provision for maintaining, repairing and equipping national schools in the county or county borough. Powers relating to compulsory school attendance, school books, school transport, continuation classes, etc., were all contained in the bill. It had its first reading on 24 November and was published on 29 November 1919.

Ireland may have been outside the theatre of war in the years 1914-18, but it was to experience some of the effects of 'the restless, half-formed educational demands engendered by the war'.[1] In England, Fisher, who was appointed Minister of Education in December 1916 under Lloyd George and remained a member of the

Cabinet until 1922, had done so much of value for education generally and in particular for teachers that Ireland could not remain untouched by his achievements. He had procured a superannuation scheme for teachers, had appointed the committee under Lord Burnham which raised and standardised teachers' salaries, and had seen to it that objective, external standards of examination were set for all secondary schools. The climate in political circles was favourable to reform and the MacPherson Bill did incorporate a concensus of educational views as distinct from views which derived as much from religious conviction as from educational expertise. Unfortunately for Ireland, the Church was less ready for a measure of reform which could only lessen its power. Miller in his book, *Church, State, and Nation in Ireland*, inclines to the view that MacPherson underestimated the strength of Church opposition, and imagined

> that a clause in the Bill guaranteeing continuation of 'the principles and practices which at the time of the passing of this Act govern religious instruction in national schools' would allay episcopal fears. If so, he was soon to be disabused of the notion.[2]

The Standing Committee of the Catholic hierarchy met on 9 December 1919 and denounced the bill, invoking the most extreme chauvinistic feelings as a weapon with which to attack it. It condemned in particular the central department which would be set up 'at the instigation of an intolerant minority in one angle of the country', and warned that 'the people of this country will set their faces against the appointment of any minister or combination of ministers who, as foreigners, are absolutely unfit to guide the intellectual destinies of Ireland'.

No less explicit was the protest of the Central Council of the Catholic Clerical School Managers which met on 21 January 1920 and, in a press statement, said:

> We offer our firm and united protest against the new Education Bill . . . [and] we consider it necessary at the present juncture to declare as a fundamental principle that the only satisfactory education system for Catholics is that wherein Catholic children are taught in Catholic schools, by Catholic teachers, under Catholic control.

Many of the same Catholic teachers were not unfavourable to the bill. The Central Executive Committee of the Irish National Teachers' Organisation met on 10 January 1920 and issued a circular to be sent to all the branches of the organisation. The circular spoke of the many proposals in the bill 'which, in our opinion, either effect vast and much needed improvements in the present position of Irish education or contain within them the possibilities of such improvements' and advised 'the teachers and such of the public as may be influenced by our advice to co-operate in framing amend ments which may make it more acceptable to all concerned'. The Central Executive Council of the Association of Secondary Teachers in Ireland met in the course of the same month and appointed a committee to draft amendments to the bill, the enactment of which they expected and, with reservations on the issue of a teacher's security of tenure, favoured. On the other hand, the Standing Council of the Irish Technical Instruction Association felt that the bill might, by altering the existing system of technical instruction, impair its efficiency.

The strongest support for the proposed measure came, not altogether unexpectedly, from two predominantly Protestant profes sional organisations. The Schoolmasters' Association approved unreservedly of the contents of the bill and urged that 'in the interests of Irish Education . . . legislative effect should be given to the Committee's recommendations without delay'. The Association convened a special meeting 'to consider the Irish Education Bill in detail and to take such steps as it may think proper to support it and to secure such amendments as may appear to it to be in the interests of education'. The views of the Association were presented to a deputation of the English Labour Party on 20 January 1920, who 'expressed sympathy with the claims put forward'. The Committee of the Central Association of Irish Schoolmistresses cordially welcomed the introduction into Parliament of the Education Bill (Ireland) and desired 'to express its approval of the main principles embodied in the Bill'. It might have been expected that Sinn Féin would express support for the bill as it did appear to be a concession to its conception of an Ireland in which, ultimately, native-controlled institutions would be responsible for the government of the country. The Parliamentary elections of 1918 had given the party influence and power. Yet in all the controversy that followed the introduction of the bill, the party remained silent, as Miller writes in *Church, State and Nation in Ireland*,

> in the same spirit that its leaders a year earlier had deleted from the Democratic Programme that sentence which would have committed the nation 'to encourage by every reasonable means the most capable and sympathetic men and women to devote their talents to the education of the young'.[3]

Their silence was politically, at least, prudent. They had seen the Irish Party humbled by the weight of Church power in 1907; they had no wish to be the target in 1920.

In any event, it would have been difficult for them to support it when, in a statement issued from Maynooth, the Catholic arch bishops and bishops made clear what card they were going to play by referring to the bill as 'the most denationalising scheme since the Act of Union'. It was, in their opinion, 'an attempt on the part of the British Government to grip the mind of the people of Ireland, and form it according to its own wishes' and, should the bill become law, they warned that it would be their duty 'to issue instructions to Catholic parents in reference to the education of the children in such a deplorable crisis'. Many saw control of the schools as being crucial to retention of power by the Church and, in the carefully chosen words of the bishops, such control was 'necessary for that religious training of the young which Leo XIII declared to be a chief part in the care of souls'. Once again the duel of Church versus State was seen in its primary colours; each seeking an extension of its own influ ence and authority.

In the months that followed, individual members of the hierarchy attacked the bill which they seemed to present to their flock as consti tuting a greater danger to their national identity than to their spiritual welfare. By far the most vehement critic was Dr Foley, Bishop of Kildare and Leighlin, who, in a letter read in all the churches of the diocese, appealed to the people to resist

> this latest brazen-faced attempt of a hostile Government to impose on the mind and soul of an intensely devoted Catholic people the deadly grip of the foreign fetters with which they are gravely threatened; but which, if we be only true to ourselves, and prepared to make the necessary sacrifices, we can, and we shall defeat.

Well aware of the feelings of the congregations to which his words were addressed, he went on to emphasise the 'foreign' nature of a measure which would impose

> a British Department of Education with a British Minister at its head and responsible solely to an alien Parliament for the discharge of the enormous powers with which he is to be invested, over not merely paupers and lunatics, or seeds and manures, or the breeding of cattle and horses, but over the very mind and heart and soul of the Irish nation.

When he presided at a meeting of the County Carlow Agricultural and Technical Instruction Committee, he returned to the attack. A motion proposed by him sought to record the protest of the members against a bill

> which proposes to bind in foreign fetters the mind and soul of the Irish nation by the establishment of a Department of Education, consisting of three members of whom one is unknown and the other two Presbyterian Scotchmen, who were political party hacks and devoid of any vestige of qualifications of an educational character.[4]

Rev. Canon Ridgeway voted against the motion but he was a lone voice, indicative, in its way, of public opinion generally, which showed no desire to oppose the directives of the Church.

Another bishop who made martial noises was Dr Fogarty, Bishop of Killaloe, who, in his reply to a resolution sent him by the King's County County Council, wrote that Mr MacPherson 'hopes to accomplish through this "infamous" bill what his tanks have failed to effect — the destruction of Ireland's self-consciousness as a Catholic nation'.[5]

After such pronouncements from prominent members of the hierarchy it was unlikely that any organisation would challenge the authority of the Catholic Church to safeguard what it considered to be the educational welfare of its flock. It could, in any case, always rely on the unqualified support of the aggressively nationalistic Ancient Order of Hibernians. This was, then as now, an almost self-contained society largely made up of land-owners and businessmen whose greatest strength in Ireland lay in the border counties of Monaghan, Cavan, Armagh and Down. The influence of this organisation in promoting opposition to the bill was an important factor in its rejection. An extract from the speech of the Derry County Secretary of the Order well conveys the sentiments of the members, ever content to equate the best interests of the country with those of the Catholic Church. In support of a resolution condemning the bill, Brother Shields said that

> when they had to fight such a nefarious Bill they could not but deplore the fact that they had not such a strong Irish party in the House of Commons as heretofore. . . . However, apparently, from all they could learn it was MacPherson's intention to pass the Bill into law by force of numbers behind him in the English Parliament. Bills had been passed into Acts before in Ireland but a

united and determined people had made them inoperative. The present Bill might reach the Statute Book, but in view of the hostility of the people it was dead already. The Government might pass the Bill, but as Hibernians, whose motto was Faith and Fatherland, they told all whom it might concern that not all the armed forces at present in Ireland could enforce it.[6]

The influential Irish County Councils' General Council also threw their weight behind the opponents of the bill, which they condemned as 'placing supreme control in an alien triumvirate opposed to Irish public opinion and interests'.

Support for the bill came from the Protestant bishops and from the General Assembly of the Presbyterian Church. The Education Board of the latter body unanimously resolved:

> as the Irish Education Bill co-ordinates Primary, Secondary and Technical Education, makes increased provision for the salaries and pensions of teachers and for the building and upkeep of schools, provides for a measure of popular control, and gives effect generally to the recommendations of the recent reports on Primary and Intermediate Education, this Board considers that the Bill should be read a second time in the House of Commons

It was never to be read a second time. The rump of the Irish Parliamentary Party saw to that. A few members of the Party had survived the General Election of 1918 and when, on 16 December 1919, the bill was set down for a second reading, these M.P.s — Devlin, Kelly and Redmond — introduced a 'filibuster'. They spoke at length on the Air Estimates which preceded the Education Bill on the Order Paper for the day and, by doing so, prevented the bill being read before the end of the session. Six days later Mr Bonar Law answered 'in the affirmative' when questioned as to whether he proposed to re-introduce the Education (Ireland) Bill. He reckoned without the power of the Catholic Church. Cardinal Logue proclaimed a National Novena to avert 'the threatened calamity', the bishops were instructed to invite the fathers of families 'to register their protest against a measure which trenches on their parental rights' and, on Passion Sunday 1920, a statement by the Catholic hierarchy condemning the bill was read in all the churches. That was in the month of April and, on 13 May 1920, Mr Henry said in the house: 'It is not possible at present to name a date for the Second Reading. . . .' The bill which was to be cited as the 'Education (Ireland) Act, 1919' was almost dead. It was finally withdrawn on 13 December 1920.

Commenting on the decision to drop the bill, the Irish correspondent of *The Times Educational Supplement* wrote:

The first disservice done by the government to the country was the dropping of the Education Bill, a disservice recognised as such by nine-tenths of the lay teachers. But the majority of the Irish people, following most uncritically the leading of the Catholic clerics, damned the Bill, and, in face of that opposition it would probably have been as futile for the Government to force the measure on the country as the attempt to force conscription proved.[7]

The determined nature of the opposition shown by the Catholic Church to the bill made clear that, as always, the response of the Church to British educational offerings depended on the extent to which these helped or hindered the interests of that Church. In this case they chose, in the words of Dr Walter McDonald,

the politician's way; objecting apparently to the fact that in the proposed new arrangement, two out of three of the supreme rulers of the schools will be non-Catholics and non-Irish. As if their lordships would welcome a board of three Irish Catholic laymen![8]

The Church had won a victory but, in doing so, helped at a crucial time in history to defeat the cause of a united Ireland. In a reference to the possibility of setting up two Parliaments for Ireland in the proposed Home Rule Bill, *The Belfast Newsletter* commented:

We are not in a position to say what the Parliament for the rest of Ireland would do with Mr. MacPherson's Education Bill, though we rather think it would give it short shrift and legislate for a cast-iron system of clerical control over education. We do know that here in Ulster the demand would be instant for the introduction of full popular representative control in all its development as is now in force in Great Britain.[9]

Speaking in very similar terms, Sir Edward Carson considered the defeat of the bill as

one more unanswerable argument in support of the extreme courses which I have taken in the past to prevent the placing of Ulster under an Ireland Parliament. Such a Parliament would be dominated by the influences which have killed the Education Bill, and under it we should find it impossible to obtain a measure enabling us to give the children proper instruction and to pay the teachers as they ought to be paid.[10]

Looking back on the history of that first quarter of the twentieth century, it is not difficult to believe that, at a crucial moment, the Irish people allowed themselves to be deflected from the main path of political advance which, had they but realised it, would at some stage have led to a confrontation with the cult of Church power. The people failed to see or did not wish to see that the Church was seeking to defend its own interests in the control and management of schools rather than broadening and extending the range of education. Had the Irish Nationalist Party been stronger it might have sought a compromise solution by reconciling the legitimate aim of the Church to retain a measure of control with the equally legitimate aim of the State to expand the education service and, had the bill become law before the Government of Ireland Act was passed, it might have survived any such change and the existence of a common adminis-trative structure might have helped to draw the two parts of Ireland together. Is it an exaggeration to say that of all those who in different ways gave service to Irish interests in the early years of this century, Carson came closest to understanding the importance of education when he said, 'This Education Bill, to my mind, is a thousand times more important than your Home Rule Bill'?[11]

CHAPTER 14

THE LAST YEARS

The Commissioners did not comment on the MacPherson Bill. They had, as it happened, their own very grave problems. In their Report of 1919 they spoke of the threat of 'a very serious breakdown throughout the country' and the necessity of taking immediate steps 'if disaster is to be avoided'. They referred to the fact that 'a strike of teachers in certain Irish Secondary schools for a living wage has actually occurred' and that 'out of 1,349 lay teachers, only 100 are in receipt of a salary of £200 per annum, and of these 31 are heads of schools; whilst about 30 per cent of the whole number of lay teachers are in receipt of salaries of less than £100 per annum'. They again pressed the Lord Lieutenant to request His Majesty's Government for a Parliamentary grant in aid sufficient to meet all the administrative expenses of the Board. They emphasised that in the post-war world there would be a vastly increased demand for education and they deplored that, in such circumstances, 'the educational system in Ireland, far from having a chance of improvement, is at the present moment face to face with ruin'.

New forces were, in fact, already beginning to threaten the educational edifice that seemed so securely set on the twin pillars of Church and State. One of these forces was the teachers and, in March 1920, the Association of Secondary Teachers (Ireland) demanded an immediate increase of 140 per cent on pre-war salaries. In a circular letter issued by the Association, the average salaries were given as non-Catholic (*sic*) men £180 and women £140; Catholic men £139 and women £97. Their demand was ignored probably because of the inability of headmasters to pay such an increase. A series of strikes followed. Members of the Association in Cork, Dublin, Tralee, Letterkenny, Galway and Sligo withdrew their labour until, at a conference of representatives of the Catholic Headmasters' Association and the A.S.T.I. held on 10 May, the strike was settled. The terms of the settlement were that a flat bonus of £75 would be paid on the basic salaries of £160 and £110 to full-time, non-resident men and women, and a similar bonus of £40 would be paid on the basic salaries of £130 and £90 to full-time resident men and women.

The settlement was not binding on all the Catholic secondary schools, since convent schools and the schools of the Christian Brothers were not members of the Catholic Headmasters' Association. In addition, internal differences in that Association led to a refusal by the headmasters of the secondary schools in Limerick to be bound by the terms of the settlement. This resulted in a very confused situation which meant that six of seven Cork schools, three Limerick schools and, in all, 'nearly 30 of the Colleges refused to be bound'. Agreement was, however, reached between the various parties in dispute before the summer vacation of 1920. The strike had achieved something more than an improved salary scale. It had added stature to the A.S.T.I. and it was significant of the growing spirit of co-operation between the lay members of the teaching profession that the following motion was adopted unanimously at a meeting of the I.N.T.O. in the spring of that year: 'That £1000 be placed at the disposal of the Strike Committee of the A.S.T.I. immediately.'

It should not be thought that salary demands concerned only the Catholic teachers. Most Protestant teachers were members of the Union of Assistant Masters or the Incorporated Association of Assistant Masters, and these bodies were not in dispute with their headmasters. But the Protestant schools were not spared the financial difficulties that beset those in Catholic control and, in November 1920 at the Annual Prize-Giving in the High School, Dublin, the headmaster, Mr J. Thompson, issued a warning that if some solution were not found 'before next summer, there would be a serious collapse of Protestant education in Ireland'.

Protestant and Catholic education alike were threatened as the inadequacy of the provision made for an expanding system of education became apparent. The germs of despair if not of decay seem to have begun to gnaw at the hearts of those most concerned and it must have been with relief that the Chief Secretary, Sir Hamar Greenwood, replied to a question in the House as to what steps the government proposed to take to remedy the situation. His answer was pointedly brief: 'Under the Government of Ireland Act, 1920, questions of Secondary and other education pass under the jurisdiction of the Irish parliaments, to which the final solution of these questions must now be left.'[1]

In 1920 the Commissioners wrote what was, in effect, both an apologia for their work and, at the same time, an acknowledgement of their final failure:

Looking back over the period of 42 years which have elapsed since we, as a Corporate body, were established by Parliament, and remembering the innumerable difficulties which have had to be faced and overcome before the various educational interests in this country came to recognise and accept our scheme as an absolutely impartial effort to promote the true interests of secondary education; remembering also the scanty funds with which our admittedly successful efforts were achieved, it is difficult for us at this juncture — when the whole edifice of secondary education in Ireland is toppling to destruction — to refer to these matters in language of moderation and restraint. Of one thing, however, we feel quite certain, and that is that if something is not done immediately to place Irish Secondary education in the position of financial equality with that of Great Britain, it is impossible to see how the complete disruption of the system can be avoided.

Members of the Board and members of Parliament, administrators and legislators, were all of a mind that education was in a sorry state. Teachers were practical enough to realise that money would have to be injected into the system if it was not to collapse and that a possible solution lay in achieving 'financial equality' with teachers in Great Britain. So, for the first time, all sections of intermediate teachers — heads and assistants, men and women, Catholic and Protestant, North and South — met at the invitation of the Intermediate Board on 5 January 1921. They presented a lengthy Report, 'consisting of a series of resolutions passed unanimously prefaced by an explanatory statement', to the Chief Secretary, Sir Hamar Greenwood. In substance, what they asked for was the application of the Burnham Scale of salaries to Ireland and that the costs of administration, inspection and examination be a charge on the Treasury. By the time the Report had been received at Dublin Castle, the process by which Ireland was to be given a measure of Home Rule had begun and those teachers, 'North and South', who had met for the first time, were not to meet again.

The downfall of the 'edifice of secondary education' was, in fact, near. The Government of Ireland Act contemplated the division of the Board into an Intermediate Education Board for Southern Ireland and an Intermediate Education Board for Northern Ireland. The Commissioners sent their last report on intermediate education in an undivided Ireland to the Lord Lieutenant on 27 June 1921. It was their forty-second Report and it bore the signatures of W. F. Butler and W. A. Houston, Assistant Commissioners. In the same month an Order in Council made by His Majesty, George V, provided for the setting-up of an Intermediate Education Board for Northern Ireland in accordance with the provisions of Section 63 of the Government of Ireland Act. The Northern Parliament, however, rejected this

142 *Secondary Education in Ireland 1870-1921*

proposal and vested all the powers of the Commissioners as regards Northern Ireland in the Northern Ministry of Education created by an Order in Council of 7 June 1921.

On 30 November 1921 the Commissioners received a letter from the Secretary to the Ministry of Education in Northern Ireland asking the Commissioners to conduct the examinations for 1922 in Northern Ireland. They agreed to do so but in the meantime the Irish Free State was set up and a Provisional Government had taken over Dublin Castle and the administration of the affairs of twenty-six of the thirty-two counties. The Northern Ministry then decided against having the examinations conducted by the Commissioners. The position became very confused when 864 pupils in Northern Ireland who had notified the Commissioners of their intention to present for examination decided to exercise their right to do so. Accordingly, twenty-two centres were constituted in Northern Ireland and 738 candidates were examined.

In the Report for 1921 is set out the number of schools under the jurisdiction of the educational authorities in Northern Ireland and in the Irish Free State as well as the number of pupils between the ages of twelve and nineteen on 1 October 1920 on the rolls of the schools on that date. The figures are given in table 14.

Table 14

Northern Ireland	Number of Schools		Number of Schools	
		Boys	Girls	TOTAL
Boys	20	2197		2197
Girls	31		1610	1610
Mixed	27	1054	1221	2275
	78	3251	2831	6082
Southern Ireland				
Boys	136	11930		11930
Girls	116		7842	7842
Mixed	26	491	547	1038
	278	12421	8389	20810
TOTAL	356	15672	11220	26892

Statistics for Northern Ireland and for the Irish Free State were being given in the same Report for the last time and the occasion was availed of by the Commissioners to say that progress could only be made on the lines pointed out by them, i.e. 'the provision of sufficient funds for Secondary Education, proper salaries, increments and pensions for teachers, with due security of tenure, and the abolition of payment of results fees dependent on the examination results of individual students'. The legal separation of the educational services in the two states was fixed for 1 February 1922. (The date came in the middle of the school year and was the cause of some confusion as some 738 candidates from Northern Ireland preferred to sit the examinations of the Intermediate Board rather than those conducted under the authority of the Minister of Education in Northern Ireland, Lord Londonderry.) By the end of the same year the financial settlement was completed with the transfer to the government of Northern Ireland of the following amounts:

£247,191 0. 3.   Guaranteed $2\frac{3}{4}$ per cent Stock (No. 1 Ac.)

£14,300 0. 0.   War 5 per cent Stock, 1927-47 (No. 1 Ac.)

£315 0. 0.   5 per cent National War Bonds, 1929 – 4th Series (Registration Council, Capital Ac.)

£90 0. 0.   5 per cent Stock, 1929-1947 (Registration Council, Capital Ac.)

£345 7. 0. $2\frac{1}{2}$ per cent Consolidated Stock (No. 2 Ac.)

The division of the country was by then completed and it remained only for the government of the Irish Free State to decide what to do with the Commissioners. By an order of the Executive Council a Board of Commissioners was established,

to exercise in *Saorstát Éireann* all the functions which were on the 6th day of December, 1921, exerciseable in the area now comprised in *Saorstát Éireann* by the Intermediate Education Board for Ireland. The Irish Education Commissioners were to consist of two Commissioners to be appointed by the President of the Executive Council. In pursuance of this Order the President of the Executive Council on June 18th, 1923, appointed Seosamh O'Neill and Proinnsias Ó Dubhthaigh to be Irish Education Commissioners. The old Board was thus dissolved after an existence of 45 years.

It is, I think, worth giving the names of the members of the old Board at the time of its dissolution. They were: Rev. T. A. Finlay, S.J., M.A., Thomas Patrick Gill, Esq., The Right Hon. T. F. Malony, Lord Chief Justice of Ireland, The Most Rev. John A. F. Gregg, D.D., Archbishop of Dublin, William Kennedy, Esq., M.A.,

F.T.C.D., The Right Hon. and Most Rev. J. H. Bernard, D.D., Provost, Trinity College, Dublin, Douglas L. Savory, Esq., M.A., The Rev. Major-General John Simms, C.B., C.M.G., D.D., Professor William Magennis. Of the two Assistant Commissioners in office at the time of the Treaty, W. A. Houston opted to serve the government in Belfast while W. F. Butler continued to work with the newly formed Department of Education until his death in 1929.

It must not be thought that the Intermediate Education Board was the only educational body to be dissolved. The Commissioners of National Education who administered the system of primary education, the Commissioners of Education in Ireland who administered the scheme for endowed schools, the Department of Agriculture and Technical Instruction which administered technical education, all these were dissolved but continued to live under different names. Any study of the development of local government or education immediately reveals a continuity barely touched by the coming of the new State. In consequence, independence for Ireland did not precipitate the problems that have beset many of the more recently independent states of Africa and Asia. What change there was lay in the centralisation of authority in the hands of a Minister for Education with Cabinet responsibility, and a Department of Education staffed in great part by civil servants who were themselves the products of the intermediate system. Today the importance of our educational inheritance can be better appreciated as the difficulties of countries that have achieved freedom but lacked a body of educated and skilled administrators are clearly seen.

With the passing of the Ministers and Secretaries Act, the reformatory and industrial schools were also brought under the control of the Minister for Education, thus fulfilling part of Pearse's dream which he had entitled 'When we are Free' and in which he had written that

> when an Irish Government is constituted there will be an Irish Minister of Education responsible to the Irish Parliament; that under him Irish education will be drawn into a homogeneous whole — an organic unity will replace a composite freak in which the various members are not only not directed by a single intelligence but are often mutually antagonistic, and sometimes engaged in open warfare with one another, like the preposterous donkey in the pantomime whose head is in perpetual strife with his heels because they belong to different individuals.[2]

What Pearse could not have anticipated was that the *first* Parliament of the Republic of Ireland did not, in fact, appoint a Minister for Education. A resolution of the Ard-Fheis of the Gaelic League in 1919 seeking the appointment of a Minister for the Irish language was read to the Dáil by the Ceann Comhairle on 27 October 1919. Cathal Brugha spoke on the subject and said that he thought the appointment of a Minister for Education should await the return of Mr de Valera from the United States but that, in the meantime, it was essential that the authority of Dáil Éireann should be placed behind the Gaelic League. He thought, therefore, that pending the return of the President, a Minister for Irish should be appointed. The proposal was agreed to and a Minister was appointed. This meant that there was a Minister for Irish before a Minister for Education was appointed. It was not until 26 August 1921 that the Dáil accepted Seán Ó Ceallaigh as the first Minister for Education.

CHAPTER 15

AN ANALYSIS OF THE SYSTEM

'Irish education has scarcely ever been considered as a purely Irish problem with its own difficulties and its own aim altogether distinct from anything H. G. Wells or the English reformers wrote of.'[1] What, then, was the overall aim of the men who shaped the Act of 1878? Was it to give the people of Ireland an opportunity, even though a limited one, to acquire the knowledge which would enable them to take advantage of opportunities offered in Britain's expanding empire? Was it to silence the protesting voices of the Catholics, largely unendowed and underprivileged? Was it to conciliate the Irish Parliamentary Party then beginning to show its political teeth? Whatever the aims, the fact that the nation made notable advances during the years following 1878 is indisputable. Indeed, the social and political advance which is probably traceable to education seems less in dispute than its more strictly intellectual results on the national mind. Irish issues precipitated events of social, political and religious change in Great Britain which might otherwise have been long delayed. National education, Disestablishment of the Church and, above all, State intervention in the sphere of land economy made effective appearance in Ireland long before they did in Great Britain. Rural ways of thought were merged with new urban ways of life and sought expression in a literary renaissance which drew strength from a generation of school-leavers most of whom had passed through the intermediate system.

One of these was Patrick Pearse who in *The Murder Machine*, published in 1912, characterised the intermediate system as 'the most evil thing that Ireland has ever known'. His thesis was that the system was repressive, hostile to all individualism and fatal to that freedom which he felt should stimulate the efforts of the pupil and characterise all aspects of the educational process. *The Murder Machine* represents the terminal point of his educational writings and emphasised his conviction that Ireland needed educational reform as much as it needed political freedom. It synthesised his deeply rooted attachment to the social institutions of Celtic Ireland with which he would replace the stultifying uniformity of the intermediate system which to him was 'murderous' in its disregard of basic educational concepts and unconcern for national aspirations.

He was almost alone among Irishmen of his time in having studied at first hand the system of education in Wales and also in Belgium, where the existence of two rival languages gave a sharp edge to all educational discussions. Bilingualism was to him not just a national issue but also a pedagogical one, and he treats of each in a series of articles which first appeared in *An Claidheamh Soluis*. He was later to test the efficacy of the teaching methods he had seen employed when he opened St Enda's. He may have been unduly optimistic in his hopes of a great cultural revival in Ireland when he wrote that 'The Gaelic tongue stands for the intellectual independence of Ireland', but he remained steadfast in his belief that only a national culture could 'restore manhood to a race that has been deprived of it'.

His own contribution to education was a positive one: he founded a school, staffed it with teachers of distinction, sought to encourage drama and art, fostered traditional games and advocated the use of the Irish language. But the experiment, for such it was, proved, like his own life, to be short-lived. Had he lived he would have seen that one of the first acts of a native government was to implement his plan for a central authority in which the National Board, the Intermediate Board and the Technical Department were united under a single Minister of State. Probably his most radical suggestions were to recommend the abolition of public examinations and that teachers would not alone teach but administer the system.

At a period when the work of the various bodies of Commissioners was slowing to a halt, there was an acceleration of interest in education. The setting-up of a Registration Council, the reports of the Killanin and of the Malony Commission, the MacPherson Bill, the strike movement among secondary teachers – all pointed to something other than the 'Death and the nightmare Death-in-Life' which Douglas Hyde quoted to describe education under the National and Intermediate Boards. But, if it would be wrong to attribute these stirrings directly to the writings of Pearse, it would be equally wrong to dismiss the influence that he exercised among those of his generation and which the manner of his death was but to strengthen.

And it was to those who had passed through the system that, in the view of Professor Michael Tierney, later to be President of University College, Dublin, the nation owed much of its advance. To him it was clear proof 'of the inevitable connection between higher education, of whatever kind, and the power of democracy, that only in the era when intermediate and university education was thrown open to the people, has the ideal of a free Gaelic Ireland been first clearly adopted by the nation'.[2] As he saw it, education was the mainspring of the various cultural movements that had made the Ireland of his youth a place of quickening ideas and passionate enthusiasms, much of which he would attribute to 'the immense part that has been taken by University graduates and old Intermediate boys in the political regeneration of the past few years'. Like Helvetius, he, too, believed that *l'éducation peut tout* and that 'once given knowledge and capacity for assimilating ideas, the full assertion of his rights and the full recognition of his duties is inevitable to the average healthy citizen'.

That views very contrary to those of Professor Tierney were held is certain. We have seen that it required something of an effort to have recognition given to Irish language and literature on the examination syllabus; in the opinion of at least one M.P., Mr Dolan of Leitrim, the Intermediate Board 'were undoubtedly animated by ideas which were entirely foreign to the spirit which animated the young generation of Irishmen'.[3] If the impact of the system on the national consciousness is a matter of debate, what is not is the financial benefit it brought to schools. It was inevitable that whatever Act was passed it would have to give some financial aid to existing schools and that, if it were to succeed, religious contention would have to be avoided. The Act of 1878 did give financial aid, it did avoid contention but, it is also entirely true to say, that it was more concerned with instruction than with education. As Dr Kelly, Bishop of Ross, was later to say in evidence before the Intermediate Education Commission: 'there has been wider diffusion of knowledge, but the wider diffusion of knowledge does not necessarily imply education'. In its determination not to offend the religious susceptibilities of anyone, it resolutely adhered to a rigid programme in which examinations and the results of examinations and the prizes and exhibitions were all-important. 'Love of excelling, not the love of excellence' appeared to be the motive of study and what were derisively called the 'Hume Street Hurdles' attracted annually more and more competitors 'in this sordid race for results fees'.

Some writers, in an attempt to explain the worship of examinations in Victorian times, have suggested that lack of success imputed moral failure to those who had not done well and that material advance waited on the virtuous. This extreme of worship was never reached in Ireland, but there is little doubt that the schools welcomed a system which rewarded able pupils, linked the payment of grants to the success of these pupils and controlled, if imperfectly, the work done in the schools. On the latter point, it is worth noting that precious little information did filter through on the efficiency or otherwise of the schools. The system tested only about one-third of all the pupils in the school, i.e. those only who presented for examination. As no information was given which would identify the school of the candidates who failed (usually between 30 and 40 per cent of the total number of candidates), those about whom satisfactory evidence was given were less than 5000, or about one-fifth of the whole.

Yet, despite its imperfections, the examinations system did offer an outlet, some would say an escape, to the successful ones. And if boys seized the opportunity so, too, did girls, even though, as we have seen, it was only a late amendment that enabled them to do so. When the intermediate examinations were first held, few girls were entered for a test for which many schools considered them unsuited. However, early successes gave them confidence and table 15 shows the striking increase over a period of forty years in participation rates for girls, especially in Senior Grade.

Table 15

	Junior	Middle	Senior
1879	2,163 candidates 521 girls or 24.08%	682 candidates 156 girls or 22.87%	373 candidates 59 girls or 15.82%
1921	7,491 candidates 3,232 girls or 43.14%	3,336 candidates 1,310 girls or 39.27%	1,593 candidates 578 girls or 36.28%

One critic of the intermediate system to whom these figures must have brought little joy was Frank Hugh O'Donnell, who accused the convents of having 'found a means of utilising these young brains in the accursed chase of the Result Fee, with results even more calamitous than in the case of the young victims of the other sex'. To him the pupils of intermediate schools were little more than *'fee-earning machines for irresponsible and unsupervised communities* which never publish accounts nor are asked for any . . .'.[4]

More reasoned and reasonable criticism, while aware of blemishes in the system, believed that these were chiefly due to erratic attendance at school, a low school-leaving age and the uneven and often indifferent quality of the teaching. School attendance always tends to be lower in a farming community than in a non-farming one and, in our uncertain climate seasonal absences are even more marked than elsewhere. As far back as 1910 one of the newly appointed inspectors referred to this when he visited the Christian Brothers' School in Charleville:

Generally the masters are handicapped by irregular attendance. There is a labour famine round Charleville, and the tendency grows stronger to keep the boys from school that they may work on the land, drive the milk to the creamery, etc. When work is slack in mid-winter, then bad weather keeps the boys away. This may be distressing to the teachers, but the simple truth is that boys doing farming have no need of secondary education, do not profit by it, and should be let alone. The number of Intermediate boys at this school is falling rapidly and it is not such a bad sign as the teachers think.[5]

Nor was there any easy solution to the problem of school atten dance as the Catholic hierarchy was at all times opposed in principle to compulsory attendance as an infringement of parental rights and expressed their disapproval of it. It may have been because of this that a bill dealing with compulsory school attendance which was introduced in Parliament in 1885 was not proceeded with and that the Irish Education Act of 1892 limited the application of the Act to places under corporate control.

The question of a low school-leaving age can only with difficulty be separated from that of costs and benefits. School fees, except for boarding-schools, when paid at all were extremely low, but where poverty existed the earnings even of a child could make a difference to the income of a poor family. According to the Census of 1911, the last before the Intermediate Education Board was dissolved, the number of pupils in secondary schools was 40,841 out of a total school-going population of 704,807. Commenting on these figures, F. S. L. Lyons says: 'A system which allows only one in seventeen of its children to proceed beyond the primary stage provides its own effective condemnation.'[6]

The system did, however, succeed in attracting more pupils 'to proceed beyond the primary stage' even if, as a percentage of the total in national schools, this percentage remained small. In the first-ever examinations under the Intermediate Board, 3954 pupils were examined. By 1921 this number had increased to 12,419. Judged on these figures, the Board had, at least, won the support of schools for the annual examinations. And this, despite the fact that the failure rate was always high, that is if we compare it with the failure rate in the present-day Intermediate and Leaving Certificate examinations. Table 16 shows the pass rate in the four decennial periods that spanned the life of the Intermediate Board.

Table 16

1879	The Report did not present the results in the form followed in subsequent years but simply said: 'Of those examined, the number of those examined who came up to the standard fixed by the rules on the schedule, as the lowest for obtaining the payment of results fees, was 2,327, viz., 1,845 boys and 482 girls, or nearly 60 *per cent* of those who presented for examination' (p. iv of Report of I.E.B.).		

	Boys	Girls	TOTAL
1889	58.7	69.2	61.5 (p. v of Report of I.E.B.)
1899	69.3	70.4	69.6 (p. ix of Report of I.E.B.)
1909	55.5	55	55.3 (p. v of Report of I.E.B.)
1919	52.2	48.7	50.8 (p. v of Report of I.E.B.)

There was no statutory age for the transfer of pupils from the national to the intermediate schools and the clever pupils were often retained far too long in the lower schools. This had as one result the fact that pupils did not always benefit to the full from an intermediate course based on study at three levels, Junior, Middle, and Senior, and many left school without taking the Senior Grade examination. The 'retention rate' over a period of forty years may be seen from table 17.

Table 17

	Number of pupils who presented				Number who presented in Senior Grade			
	Boys	Girls	TOTAL		Boys	Girls	TOTAL	
1879	3,218	736	3,954	p. iv	397	63	460	p. vii
1889	4,838	1,695	6,533	p. iii	284	135	419	p. x
1899	5,726	2,042	7,768	p. vi	368	147	515	p. xiv
1909	7,676	3,656	11,332	p. iv	436	244	680	p. vi
1919	7,316	4,803	12,119	p. iv	605	267	872	p. vi

The absence of any link between the Board of National Education and the Board of Intermediate Education was so marked that only after 1900 was 'a uniform educational year' introduced. To this lack of co-ordination the schools of the Christian Brothers were an exception and Starkie attributes much of their success to the close association of their primary and intermediate schools, 'whereby clever pupils in the 5th standard are removed, at 11 or 12, to the higher school'.[7] A possible solution would have been to establish what were later known as 'secondary tops' in the national schools, but this was never done. It is unlikely that such a development would have found favour with the Board of Intermediate Education whose concern was to increase the number of intermediate schools.

Wide differences must have existed in the quality of the work done within the schools, even if the declining value of endowments compelled many of the older schools to abandon their more distinctive customs and teaching in order to accept what Denis Gwynn called 'the lamentably unimaginative programme of the old Intermediate Board'.[8] Before condemning the Commissioners for their apparent failure to appreciate the work done in individual schools, it is well to remember that, in their own words, they had 'no power to look upon the school as a unit, but can treat it only as a collection of individual pupils', nor had they power 'to withhold recognition from a school'. It must also be borne in mind that headmasters were free to decide how the Board's programme should be taught, that no inspector crossed the threshold of an intermediate school in the first twenty-four years of the Board's life and that staff were recruited, not always on qualifications, but on their willingness to accept small salaries and work long hours.

The course set for the various grades were excessively literary and, in this respect, the Commissioners were doing no more than following the hedge-school tradition which favoured literary and, to an extent, mathematical knowledge rather than expertise in manual skills. The programme of studies prepared pupils adequately for clerkships and similar work of a routine nature while setting before them the learned professions as the highest goal in life. At least one educationist, J. P. Mahaffy, was under no illusion as to what the system was doing to the country when he wrote: 'to become a lawyer, a doctor, a schoolmaster, any sort of bookman, is regarded as far more dignified than cultivating the fields or working manual industries'. As he saw it, a country whose wealth was the land was abandoning the tilling of that land 'to the idle, the ignorant, the worthless, while the clever brothers of the same family are spending all their energies and wasting their time in learning the grammar of languages they will never use or enjoy, in learning abstract sciences they will never use or apply'. He saw them qualifying for professions which would release them 'from the imagined degradation of manual labour, and leave the land to be the prey for the ragwood and the thistles which disgrace the face of Ireland'.[9] Harsh words, but more than justified by a Church-inspired disdain for education for trades which meant that it was left to Technical Schools and Mechanics Institutes to provide courses in practical subjects. Nor was advantage taken of such Acts as the Technical Instruction Act of 1850 which empowered the local authorities throughout Ireland 'to tax themselves for the purposes of Technical Education and though this power has existed for some years, it has hardly been availed of by the Irish Municipalities'.[10]

The 'clever brothers' of whom Mahaffy speaks did escape from 'the imagined degradation of manual labour', many of them to go on to the university. The author of a pamphlet entitled 'Irish University Education' traces the academic career of the hundred Senior Grade students who won the first ten places in each of the ten years, 1889 to 1898. Of these students, twenty-five entered University College, Dublin, nineteen entered Trinity College, Dublin, eighteen entered Queen's College, Belfast, three entered Queen's College, Cork, and two entered Queen's College, Galway. 'We find', he wrote, 'that of the 10 students who obtained the First Place in each of the 10 years, eight entered University College.'[11]

These clever pupils were absorbed, many by the professions and some by the priesthood, while those for whom vacancies did not exist or who failed to complete their university course became, in the words of Dr Starkie, the *hungerkandidaten* who were left derelict and *déclassés*. Every extension of education and scholarship seemed to increase the prestige of the professions while it lessened the worth of all other forms of labour.

> Were it not [wrote Father Cahill, S.J.] for the necessity of providing a priesthood and securing the existence of a profes-sional class (and these, be it remembered, were not wanting in Ireland before the Intermediate Act was passed) it were better for Ireland if the whole Intermediate system was swept back into the Irish sea.[12]

Nor was 'the priesthood' uniformly satisfied with a system which one Catholic bishop, Dr Hallinan of Limerick, characterised as 'un-religious, un-Irish, unproductive'. He felt that it put 'a premium on secular knowledge; lavished prestige, honours, prizes, and other rewards upon it, to the detriment of religion'. The charge that it was 'un-Irish' is not easily refuted if we consider the content of the curriculum in the early years but, by the turn of the century, 'th~

currents which would settle the nation's destiny within two decades were already beginning to run' and, even in the schools, Ireland, its language and traditions, came to be more widely and sympathetically studied. The Irish language had long been popular with many clergymen of the Church of Ireland, mostly Fellows of Trinity College, who were often more anxious to preserve the culture of the historic Irish nation than to restore the spoken tongue. The attitude of the Catholic clergy was more ambivalent; many priests were prominent in the Gaelic League but there were many others, particularly those in control of schools, who favoured the study of English language and literature if only to enable the pupils to make the most of the opportunities afforded them in the post-penal age.

The subject 'Irish Literature and Language' only appeared on the curriculum after O'Conor Don, M.P. for Roscommon, had pleaded for its inclusion during the debate on the Intermediate Education Bill and, for the first few years, the interest shown in it was hardly encouraging. Figures for 1882 show that eighty boys presented in the subject for Junior Grade of whom twenty-seven passed, thirty presented for Middle Grade of whom eighteen passed and eight presented for Senior Grade with six passing. The subject was largely ignored in girls' schools and we find that only one girl presented Celtic for Junior Grade and she, as it happened, failed. There was but one candidate in the subject for Middle Grade and she was successful, while none presented for Senior Grade.

Difficulty in recruiting teachers, difficulty in getting suitable textbooks, and, above all, the low marks allotted to it (600 as against 1200 for English, Greek and Latin), contributed to make it unpopular with parents and teachers. And as if to reduce the importance of the language still further, this mark was lowered by 100 in 1882. A resolution was at once sent to the Board by the Society for the Preservation of the Irish Language, 'deprecating the reduction of the maximum mark in Celtic from 600 to 500', but to no avail. An intemperate attack was made on it by Mahaffy and Atkinson, both professors at Trinity College, during the hearings of the 1898 Commission, but it was splendidly defended by Douglas Hyde. The revival movement failed to influence the Commissioners in any way and they seemed quite content to retain the language as a subject for written examination and no more. Despite this 'neutral' stance, *An Claidheamh Soluis* could say in 1907: 'We are not sure that, when all is said, the most valuable work that has so far been done for Irish in the schools, has not been done in the domain of secondary education.' By 1912 over 60 per cent of the boys and almost 45 per cent of the girls were taking Irish in the examinations and, by 1920, despite the decline in the number of people who were still Irish speaking and despite the fact that it was not a compulsory subject, Irish was being taken by almost 80 per cent of the examination candidates. Table 18 shows the popularity of the language as an examination subject in 1921.

Table 18
Total number examined in Irish*

Junior	Boys Middle	Senior	Junior	Girls Middle	Senior
2,908	1,367	739	2,148	773	340
(4,259)	(2,025)	(1,015)	(3,232)	(1,310)	(573)
		Number who passed			
Junior	Middle	Senior	Junior	Middle	Senior
1,880	804	431	1,131	348	340

*Number who presented themselves in a range of subjects in parentheses.

The figures in table 18 are in sharp contrast to those of 1879 in table 19.

Table 19
Total number examined in Irish

Junior	Boys Middle	Senior	Junior	Girls Middle	Senior
13	6	0	—	—	—
		Number who passed			
Junior	Middle	Senior	Junior	Middle	Senior
9	3	—	—	—	—

When Dr Hallinan made the reference to 'secular knowledge' which has been quoted, he was scarcely unaware of the influence of Catholic schools and Catholic clerics on the range of subjects available to the pupils. It must be borne in mind that a subject sometimes appeared on the curriculum of a school simply because a teacher of that subject was on the staff, and, as the number of priests in the country increased, so did the number of possible teachers of Latin and, to a lesser extent, Greek. Even in diocesan colleges, few pupils reached a stage when they derived real benefit from a study of these languages since many, as we have seen, did not remain to complete Senior Grade and, in addition, the oral command of Latin, developed in the hedge schools, died as the results of teaching came to be tested by written examinations.

Educational needs and examination needs were not to be confused, and the great variety of subjects offered by the grinding establishments and academies of the 1870s gradually gave way to a small group of extensively studied subjects, all carrying high marks. This change was hastened by the spread of the schools of the Christian Brothers who had a keen sense of the scholastic needs of their pupils and who prepared them thoroughly if within severely restricted limits. The list of subjects on the curriculum showed little change over the forty-year period of the Board's life, but the subjects in which candidates presented for examination were a far truer index to what was on offer within the schools. For instance, in 1921, out of 12,419 candidates who presented for examination, over 10,000 took each of the following subjects: English, arithmetic, algebra, history and historical geography. And, as we have seen in an earlier chapter, according as the examination requirements of such outside bodies as the universities came to approximate to those of the Board, the range of subjects studied narrowed.

Recognition by the universities was important for the Board, who saw in it a justification of their own standards. This was crucial in a system of education which based its monetary payments to the schools on the results of examinations. Linking the two was a dangerous experiment even if, in the case of Ireland, a necessary one. And, while it cannot be considered as one of the great administrative inventions, it did inject money into education and win popular support for State examinations at a time when teaching conditions were chaotic and every school a law unto itself. If Keenan's rights to the exclusive parentage of the system can be challenged, he was undeniably proud of the offspring, as his speech at the Social Study Congress of 1881 shows. 'The function of education is', he said on that occasion, 'to discover methods of instruction; the function of Governments is to discover tests of efficiency. In respect of the latter function, the great discovery of modern times is the system of payment for ascertained results.' But if it had its admirers there were also those who, like Archbishop Walsh of Dublin, were prepared to say that 'instead of helping on the work of *education*, it encourages a system merely of successful preparation for competitive examinations'.[13] This preoccupation with examinations deflected public attention from grave inadequacies in the system; the payment of teachers, their training and qualifications, the content of the curriculum, the equipment of schools, the uneven distribution of schools — problems which were only beginning to receive attention at the end of the Board's life. During its lifetime little was done to restructure education on a more democratic basis, nor was any more worthwhile aim proposed to teacher and pupil than a bleak insistence on examination success.

The modest prospects of many teachers may have reconciled them to such a modest aim. It is certainly true that when the Intermediate Commissioners began their work, the teacher was not too far removed, in terms of pay, from Goldsmith's schoolmaster who was forced to make do on £40 a year. Writing on 'Intermediate Education in Ireland' in 1878, W. G. Hubard said that 'the service of public instruction in Ireland is about the worst mode of obtaining a livelihood open to a man of intelligence and education'.[14] Twenty years later, if we are to judge by evidence given before the Commission of 1898, the position had changed but little. E. J. Hughes Dowling, who could claim twenty-five years' teaching experience, stated:

> The Irish teacher is often learned, sometimes experienced, but never trained. He is badly paid and worse respected; he has duties but no rights. His social position is nondescript and anomalous; in education and learning the equal of the local attorney and doctor, owing to the fact that his average salary, without board and lodging, is £100 a year, he is in social position and influence below the petty shopkeeper.

A profession in which the practitioners were, even as late as 1911, largely without training, without contract of employment, without security of tenure, without provision for gratuities or pension, meant that, as Dr Starkie said in that year, 'any man or woman, no matter how incompetent, may be appointed in a secondary school'.

The religious who controlled most of the schools must accept much of the blame for the lowly state of the teaching profession. They did little to raise the teacher in public esteem, rather did they appear to disparage his services and encourage the belief that his was a subordinate role. The answer of the Provincial of the Irish Jesuits to a request from Father Delany of Tullabeg for permission to appoint extern, i.e. lay, teachers is revelatory:

> I positively forbid you to put the names of those extern masters on any tableau in the college on which are to be found the names of our people. We must respect ourselves if we wish to be respected by others. I request also that no extra money be given to those extern masters. Let them get their wages — what they are entitled to — nothing more.[15]

The depressed state of the profession also meant that for much of the lifetime of the Board individual teachers had neither the authority nor the resolution to recommend changes in the system. At the outset of his career, the teacher may have been grateful for an examination system which limited what he had to study and transmit to the pupil, but, inevitably, it served to lower the standard of his work when continued over a period of years. Gradually, however, the image of the teacher as 'discontented, shabby and half-starved' changed and, after 1909, with the establishment of the Association of Secondary Teachers (Ireland), the lay secondary teachers began to identify their needs and seek means by which to satisfy them. The setting up, a few years later, of the Registration Council, changed the vertical grouping of educational forces with Church and State at the apex and introduced a third force, the teachers, who soon became strong enough to effect some degree of stratification.

One problem which the Board, because of the statutory restrictions placed upon it, could not attempt to resolve was that of the uneven distribution of schools (this has been referred to in Chapter 8, dealing with the Report of Messrs Dale and Stephens). However, even if differences in educational provision between the provinces still existed, they had lost something of their sharpness of outline. The Report for 1921 lists those schools which 'consented to inspection', and we find that there were thirty-three in Connacht, one hundred and thirty-six in Leinster, ninety-six in Munster and ninety-one in Ulster. Dale and Stephens had suggested that 'loans might be given to managers; local Technical Committees encouraged to assist schools in their areas, and that advanced departments might be established in national schools'. This was never done because political thought at the time was totally opposed to giving any direct aid for the building of schools on denominational lines.

Yet such aid was almost written into the Act of 1878 if we are to judge by an undated document found in the correspondence of Cardinal Cullen. It sets out in some detail plans for 'The building of new Intermediate Schools and Accommodation for teachers, or the improvement of existing schools,' which were 'to be encouraged by loans made by the Board on the plan sanctioned by the National Teachers Residence Act of 1875'. The emphasis was to be on the provision of day-schools and no loan was to be made for boarding accommodation, and the Board 'was to satisfy itself that there was a necessity for the erection of the school'. To safeguard itself against any accusation of religious discrimination, the Board stipulated:

the schools thus aided, if day-schools, to be subject to the same regulations as to religious instruction and religious emblems as are embodied in the rules of the National Board of Education: If both boarding and day-schools the Board to modify such rules so as to ensure that they shall only apply to the room or rooms used for the joint instruction of boarders and day scholars, and shall not extend to that part of the building and used for the accommodation of boarders.

The proviso that followed showed that examinations were never far from the mind of the planners; it may even indicate that some element of compulsion was thought desirable to ensure support for the examinations. It stated:

All schools thus aided to undertake to send up either the whole, or a certain proportion to be fixed by the Board, of their students of proper age for whom school accommodation is provided by the loan, to the examination held annually by the Board. Half the annual instalments in repayment of such loans to be allowed to the borrowers by the Board, on the certificate of their Secretary or other person deputed by the Board with the approval of the Lord Lieutenant, that these conditions have been complied with during the year, and that a proportion, to be fixed by the Board, of the students submitted for examination, had passed in at least three courses.[16]

This document is of value in indicating the trend of the Cardinal's thoughts on an important aspect of education. It was almost certainly written shortly before the passing of the Act. He was dead in the year it became law.

CHAPTER 16

THE COMMISSIONERS:
THEIR POWER AND LIMITATIONS

An historical graph of Ireland's educational advance would show an alternation between the principle of State insistence on statutory rights and that of Church insistence on a measure of clerical control. Unfortunately for the proposals that were in the forefront of the Chief Secretary's mind when he outlined a possible scheme of loans for school building, the legal restrictions on the Board of Intermediate Education imposed a severe rein on its activities. Not only could it not establish intermediate schools where they were needed, but it could give no direct financial assistance to schools in need of it for such purposes as maintenance and renovation. Section 6 of the Intermediate Education (Ireland) Act empowered the Commissioners to propose or amend rules relating to the operation and conduct of the examinations, but it did not empower them to propose or make changes in the principles or structure of the scheme itself. Such changes had to have the prior approval of Parliament and so, despite the impressive title given to the Commissioners, they were little more than an administrative body whose duties were to supervise a system of public examinations and distribute public money on the results of these examinations. As one writer said: 'Treasury minutes lay down, with the calmest impertinence, their views as to what should or should not be done with Education by so-called independent boards in Ireland, which are there responsible for it.'[1] Yet, in the course of time, the Commissioners came to be considered 'as autocratic a department in reality and in the last resort as any of the other Castle Boards with which our country has been afflicted'.[2] Nor was the country ill-equipped in respect of such Boards. A paper by Arnold F. Graves read to the Statistical and Social Inquiry Society of Ireland in 1882 lists no less than nine! They were:

> The National Board, the Intermediate Board, the Endowed Schools' Board, Erasmus Smith's Schools' Board, the Incorporated Society, the Commissioners of Charitable Donations and Bequests, the Science and Art Department of the Committee of Council of Education, the University of Dublin, and the Royal University.[3]

One of the most important characteristics of these Boards was their irresponsibility, using the word in the sense that the members were *responsible* neither to electors nor to Parliament. Added to this was the fact that few if any of the members, while concerned for educa tion, were dependent on the educational system for their livelihood. Had they been paid and had they been chosen because of their educa tional background or attainments, education might have benefited. As it was, John Redmond could say of them in 1916, that 'for the last ten years, no member of the Board has had any personal experience whatever of secondary education in Ireland'.[4] They did not have to have such experience; their work was unsupervised and they were responsible to Parliament only to the extent of having to produce an annual report for Parliament's benefit. Their totally unprofessional approach to the running of their business may be judged from the fact that they attended at the office only on meeting days and anyone wishing to see them on other occasions had to make an appointment at their homes. In the eyes of Graves, they were 'shifting bodies of men, whose energies are devoted to other pursuits, who cannot attend regularly, who have nothing to gain by dis charging their duties, nothing to lose by neglecting them, and who are therefore practically irresponsible'. Dr Walsh, Archbishop of Dublin, made the same point when he rejected the label 'Castle Boards' as applied to the two Education Boards over whom it, the 'Castle', 'had no more authority than the Tsar of Russia has in this country to order either Board to do anything'. As defined by itself in a letter to the Treasury, the Intermediate Education Board,

> a body corporate, was established by an Act of Parliament, derives its original funds from Parliament, and has statutory authority for the appointment and superannuation of its own Officers (except that the Assistant Commissioners are appointed by the Lord Lieutenant and hold office at his pleasure).

This independence was a source of strength but it also left them open to attack from organisations such as the Gaelic League which looked upon the Board as 'one that would be impossible if the nation had any voice at all in the appointments'. And, looking at the names of those who composed the Board, it is true to say that they repre sented a segment of society which was itself unrepresentative of the people whose children followed the school programme which they administered. Nor did the character of the Board change greatly in the course of its life since a certain continuity of policy was assured by replacing a Commissioner who died or resigned with someone of the same religion and, often, of the same profession. When Balfour introduced the amending Act of 1900, increasing the number of Commissioners to twelve, two of the original members, Baron Palles and the O'Conor Don, were still acting on the Board, and three of those acting as Commissioners in 1911, i.e. Rev. T. Finlay, Rev. M. Sheehan and T. P. Gill, were still members in 1921.

The day-to-day business was dealt with by the Assistant Commissioners and, again, in the case of these officials, there was the same suggestion of well-bred amateurishness. They were not civil servants who had secured their appointments through competitive examination but, instead, 'had got their appointments through the nomination of their particular friends in the Tory party'. Yet, whether nominated by Tories or Liberals, it was they who, acting on behalf of the Commissioners, each year set in motion the machinery which controlled the examinations and it was with them that the school authorities conducted all official correspondence. Yet they were doubtless made aware that they could not at any time exceed their limited duties and when, in 1897, they sought an alteration of the examination dates in consequence of Queen Victoria's jubilee, they were informed, one would imagine with a certain sharpness, that 'the examinations should proceed as in the timetable'.

For the first twenty-two years of the Board's life the number of members did not exceed seven, and the proportion of four Protestants and three Catholics had been resolutely maintained from the outset. This, to at least one member of Parliament, appeared strange when they were administering education to pupils 'the overwhelming majority of whom were Catholics'. It was on the proposal of Mr Tim Healy, M.P., that the number of Commissioners appointed to act on the Intermediate Education Board was, in 1900, increased by 'five additional members, who shall be nominated by the Lord Lieutenant'. Changes in the personnel of the Board rarely exceeded one or two in the year so that members came to share their collective grievances; their Annual Report was characterised by a certain sober restraint, even in the dissatisfaction they at some times found themselves compelled to express. Those appointed were rarely young men and, in general, their unwillingness to seek reappointment was due to age. The 'composition' of the Board remained constant, i.e. Protestant replaced Protestant and Catholic replaced Catholic, an aspect of education administration which drew scathing comment from the President of the University College, Cork, Sir Bertram Windle. To him, the whole arrangement of education in Ireland resembled 'an army going out to fight with separate commanders, wholly unconnected with one another, and totally ignorant of one another's plans, but, perhaps, a little scornful of them'.[5]

Reading the Minute Books of the Commissioners is entirely disappointing for anyone seeking some insight into individual attitudes towards the educational questions of the day. It may of course be that, as in the minutes of any organisation, many of the antagonisms revealed and many of the opinions expressed were not recorded in the final abstract of the proceedings of the meeting. All the trivia are recorded — dates for receipt of examination entries, petty cash account, purchase of stationery — but no even brief record is given of their deliberations on any educational topics. It was as though the Commissioners went on from year to year exercising their power regardless of the high winds of controversy and, sometimes, disfavour that blew about them. This exercise of power was what made John Dillon refer to them as 'irresponsible' because, although they were represented in the House by the Chief Secretary, they were not responsible to anybody. 'I have raised this question over and over again', he complained on one occasion,

> and the answer of the Chief Secretary has been 'I cannot control the Board. I am the mouthpiece of the Board in this House, still I am not responsible.' The only way the Irish office can control the Board of Education is by dismissing them all — a very Draconian method and one which no Chief Secretary has yet seen fit to adopt.[6]

He went on to damn with very faint praise the members of the Board, to whom he referred as a very respectable body,

> and I do not want to say anything offensive to them, but the Board is mostly composed of men who have no experience and no special knowledge of education, and who are engaged in the occupations of life. They come down and sit once a month or once a week, I forget which, and conduct their operations in secret, and are responsible to no one.

Clearly he found it difficult to understand the paradox of a loose collection of individuals, differing in religion and traditions, holding the reins of educational power in a society with its own urgent problems of cohesion, and he ended by saying, 'I think I am absolutely on solid ground when I say there is no other civilised country in the world which has an educational system controlled in such a manner.'

The Chief Secretary, in his answer quoted by John Dillon, would appear to have underestimated his power. As administrative head of the British government in Ireland he was, in theory, subject to the authority of the Lord Lieutenant but, throughout most of the period 1870-1920, the administration of educational affairs was left almost entirely in the hands of the Chief Secretary. At an early stage in the life of the Board the then Chief Secretary, James Lowther, gave it as his opinion that his was the responsibility and his the power when he said:

> ... the Chief Secretary is responsible to this House for the Education of Ireland and, for the matter of that, no Secretary would wish, nor do I think any hon. Gentleman would desire, that he should get rid of that responsibility. Responsibility must be accompanied with power to some extent; and therefore I may state that I am responsible for the Education of Ireland, and I also feel that I ought to have, as I have, some power over its management.[7]

As his power and responsibility increased, his capacity to deal effectively with the business of the State was affected and, in an effort to make someone, in addition to the Chief Secretary, answerable for Irish affairs, Mr O'Shaughnessy, M.P., proposed a motion: 'That it is desirable that the Irish Law Officers, or one of them, having seats in this House, should represent in this House one or more of the numerous Departments now represented by the Chief Secretary.'[8] The motion found no support.

Rules made by the Commissioners were transmitted by the Chief Secretary to the Lord Lieutenant for his approval. Once they had received his approval they acquired the force of the Act of Parliament in accordance with which they were framed. When a minor crisis arose, as it did in 1906 when the House of Commons refused to sanction the rules of the Intermediate Board, the manner in which it was resolved did little to define where authority in education lay. On 21 May 1906 certain resolutions affecting education were passed in the House of Commons, the most important of which was that moved in the name of Thomas O'Donnell, M.P. for West Kerry:

> That the Rules of the Intermediate Education Board for Ireland for the year 1906-7 be not sanctioned by Parliament till they are amended in the following particular: Rule 34 (B), page 20, line 4, to leave out the words 'If only one language is taken it must be either Latin, French or German'.

The House also agreed on the insertion of the words 'in Irish' at the beginning of Rule 61, on page 26, line 1. This would appear to have been the end of the matter when a largely indifferent House agreed to admit the Irish language to a place of honour among other tongues. The Board, however, at its meeting on 31 May, feeling that the time allowed for consideration of the change involved, i.e. the placing of Irish on a level with the other languages, was too short, refused to include it in their Rules and Programme. On 20 June Mr O'Donnell asked if the Board had laid their Rules and Programme on the table of the House. He was told that 'they find it impossible to prepare a new set of rules in time to enable them to be approved by the Lord Lieutenant and lie forty days on the table of both Houses before August'. John Redmond pursued the matter when, a week later, he asked if it was true 'that after this House unanimously passed a Resolution altering these rules the Board of Intermediate Education passed a Resolution refusing to alter them?' The Chief Secretary, Mr Bryce, gave a rather evasive reply, saying that there had been correspondence between the Board and the Irish government.

What the debate did expose was the helplessness of the Chief Secretary which he admitted when he said:

> The hon. Member who moved the Resolution was mistaken in supposing he had any authority over the Intermediate Education Board. It was an independent Board and he had no power to suggest what rules it should make. The Board made rules for itself and stood apart from the Irish Government.

Though the government, in the person of the Lord Lieutenant, had already sanctioned the Rules for 1906-1907, the attitude of the House forced the Board to retain the old Rules, i.e. those for 1905-1906, for a further year. The Board did so, without conceding ground on the legal issue, but, to quote their own words, out of regard not only 'to the interests of secondary education in Ireland, but also to the express wishes of his Excellency on the reference to the resolution of the House of Commons'.[9] It was 1908 before O'Donnell's resolution was implemented and, in that year, the Modern Literary Course was divided into two parts and, in one, Irish, together with French and German, was one of the 'main subjects'.

Nominally then, at least, supreme authority lay with the Lord Lieutenant who stood at the apex of the educational pyramid, but real power resided with the Lords of the Treasury and their concern with education was slight. Lord Randolph Churchill put it bluntly when he said that it was a perfect farce discussing Irish Educational Estimates with no one to take part in the discussion from the Government Bench but the Secretary of the Treasury, for it is plain from his defence that he is hopelessly ignorant of the whole subject of Irish affairs from beginning to end.[10]

More conclusive evidence of Treasury attitudes to Ireland is this extract from a letter to the Chief Secretary from the Under-Secretary of State, Sir Antony MacDonnell, in which he accuses the Treasury not just of being ill-informed on 'Irish affairs', but of being ill-disposed to any claims made on her behalf: 'The Treasury is anti-pathetic to Irish demands; and while the present oppressive financial relations exist between the two countries there is no hope that argument or remonstrance from this side will avail.'[11]

Had the income of the Commissioners been based on a Treasury grant to be voted each year, then their affairs would have been subject to budgetary debate. Their income, however, was a statutory one and as such was not discussed, whereas in England and Scotland 'the whole educational system of the country has been brought up for review every year, yet in Ireland where the system is infinitely worse and owing to many causes is starved, we are not allowed to discuss it'. So it was, too, that when Birrell introduced special grants for intermediate education, the rules governing such grants were statutory rules which, after a period of forty days, had the effect of an Act of Parliament. He himself summed up the position in words which showed that the unique position of Ireland was not lost on him:

> I have already explained that Secondary education does not count in these Votes at all. Nothing is given in this House. Secondary education in Ireland lives like a gentleman on its means. It has the interest of £1,000,000 of the Church fund, and it has now a stereotyped amount in place of what it used to receive in Whisky money.[12]

The 'gentleman' living on his means was to find himself during his later years in very reduced circumstances as money declined in value and as costs of administration increased.

Why was it that, unlike England, where the Education Act of 1902 authorised local authorities to strike a rate for educational purposes, Ireland was to go on to the end living on its increasingly slender means? The operational strains, the sense of insecurity, the doctrinal tensions must have made the life of the Commissioners one saturated with anxieties, and yet never once did they appeal to have education 'put on the rates'. That they did not do so and that 'we have never been able to have recourse to the rates to aid education' was, in the opinion of John Dillon, nothing less than 'a great national misfortune'. However, the explanation which he went on to give is hardly the entire truth. To him,

> it was due to the fact, as the Chief Secretary for Ireland well knows, and every Chief Secretary has learnt to know, that the Irish people never had control over their own education. It is a foreign system controlled without reference to the people, and consequently no Chief Secretary has ever had the courage to propose that the rates should be made to contribute.[13]

He must have known that the striking of a local rate with its concomitant of local control would have been strongly opposed by the Catholic Church and so, significantly, his Party did nothing.

It is all too easy to condemn the Commissioners for a certain political inertia, a willingness to accept the rule of those on top. They had little choice: they accepted office to administer a system in which inconvenient dissent would have meant paralysis. They were appointed to administer an Act of Parliament and it is as administrators they should be judged. They were at a disadvantage from the outset in that there was no prototype, no previously tested system, no examination machinery on which to base their work and methods. They were amateurs dealing with professional problems; middle and upper-class for the most part, who, we may assume, valued moderation, tradition and a sense of continuity. If at times they settled for compromise it is difficult to blame them and, when disparagement has had its say, it was, perhaps, entirely fitting that a tribute should be paid their work by a member of the Dáil in one of the first debates on education by that body. In the course of a lengthy speech Professor W. Magennis said of them:

> The public who criticise the Intermediate Board with such asperity, knowing very little of its productive work would, I think, be surprised to know that the Intermediate Board was opposed to the Chinese system of examination and the paying of teachers on the results of a paper examination, and had advocated and advocated very strenuously the substitution of inspection, and on one occasion the Commissioners arranged to resign in a body unless their demand for a body of permanent inspectors was complied with by the British Treasury.[14]

CHAPTER 17

CHURCH AND STATE DEFEND THEIR POSITIONS

Seen historically, the system of education in Ireland is the product of decrees that have come from outside rather than of any impulsion from within. It has been much less a history of educational ideas and principles than the history of a power struggle between Church and State. The unifying element had gone out of education with the entry of proselytism; it was never to return. The cohesive link was destroyed and with the expansion of education to all classes of the community, a vacuum was created. This the State sought to fill but, inevitably, it clashed with a Church then only beginning to turn from purely missionary aims to the serving of the social needs of her followers.

These were seen as being primarily educational, an extension of the apostolate in the serving of human needs, and the people, with the bitter memories of penal deprivation in their minds, welcomed the new schools which the religious orders began to establish. The mixed school as well as the lay school was doomed in a society which saw in the Church school a reassertion and reaffirmation of its faith. The Church placed its wealth and unpaid resources at the disposal of education and, in the nineteenth century, with the State doing nothing to build new schools or maintain existing ones, secondary education came to be almost a Church monopoly. Only the religious orders, with their unpaid resources of teachers drawn from their own members and their access to credit, could hope to build schools, equip them and pay for them. They did build schools, showing such evangelical fervour that no less than twenty-seven secondary schools were built in the post-Famine period before 1870. But, by doing so, they helped to make absolute the division between schools of different denominations so that, to the social barriers that separated Catholic and Protestant in nineteenth century Ireland, was added a formidable educational barrier. This barrier was not erected by accident; it owed its existence to the belief of the Catholic hierarchy that undenominational education would displace it from its dominant position of control.

In deciding to seek control of the social and educational development of the people, the Church may have appeared to have ignored the political evolution of the nation. This was not so. The strategy of the Church was to see to it that the Irish members of Parliament and the leaders of public opinion considered all legislation from a Catholic standpoint and not just from that of Catholics who were also members of Parliament and leaders of public opinion. This distinction was important as it ensured that the Church exercised a more general control over society, independently of the individual parties. As Emmet Larkin says in *The Roman Catholic Church and the Creation of the Modern Irish State*, 'as far as the bishops were concerned they understood they had an explicit undertaking on the part of the party that the intiative with regard to the education question on all its levels would remain with them'.[1]

The hierarchy, acting through the members of their flock, had the requisite power to insist that such an understanding should be respected. A striking illustration of this was the fate which befell Gladstone's University Bill, which the Church opposed. Thirty five Irish M.P.s voted against it thus ensuring its rejection and their action was, in the opinion of Gladstone, influenced by the hierarchy. In the general election which followed, every Irish member who supported Gladstone's bill directly or indirectly was defeated. Reading the editorial in the *Freeman's Journal* one could almost believe that, in the opinion of the writer, the wrath of God had been visited upon them. Commenting on their defeat, he said: 'To this general rule of exclusion for desertion of the Irish race, by aiding to enforce a system of education hostile to their consciences and their judgment, there is not a solitary exception.'[2] The Irish bishops have often since had to face not dissimilar dilemmas when sectarian and political issues refused to be separated; Cardinal Newman may have been expressing a perennial truth when he wrote: 'I must not say that they were Irishmen first and Catholics afterwards, but I do say that in such a demand they spoke not simply as Catholic Bishops but as the Bishops of a Catholic nation.'[3]

There always had been links of a sort between the hierarchy and the government ever since the establishment of Maynooth in 1794, each seeking to establish its authority on the basis of respect either for religion or government. Cardinal Cullen had been one of the first to see the advantages to the Church of recognition by the government of the role of education in upholding authority and we find him writing to Monsignor Kirby, Rector of the Irish College in Rome, after the 1867 Rising and saying, 'education without religious control is well calculated to promote revolution'.[4] These words were not intended only for Kirby and much later Dr Woodlock drew them to the attention of Hicks-Beach in a letter dated 23 November 1878, in the course of which he said: 'You may remember how strongly his

Eminence expressed his conviction that only through religious educa tion would Fenianism or any other kind of revolutionary organisa tion be checked in Ireland.'[5] Successive British governments accepted this truth and realised that by helping to extend the influence of the priest in the field of education it was, at the same time, increasing its own influence over the products of that system.

The system was, therefore, above all else conservative and, in return for a certain peaceful inertia induced especially by the unchanging rhythm of examinations, the government was happy enough to concede ground when faced with Church insistence. On the various fronts on which it engaged in conflict between the years 1870 and 1921 the Church invariably emerged successful. It opposed 'direct' compulsory attendance at school as an infringement of parental rights and while a School Attendance Act was passed in 1892, it remained ineffective. It successfully resisted co-education, meeting any move in that direction 'with the most determined opposi tion', believing that 'the mixing of boys and girls in the same school is injurious to the delicacy of feeling, reserve and modesty of demeanour that should characterise young girls'. It held up the application of the Birrell Grant which sought to specify the propor tion of lay teachers to be employed in schools controlled by religious. But, most of all, it showed its teeth when the question of local control of education was broached. It effectively killed the 1907 Bill and, later, the MacPherson Bill of 1919. Of the two, the latter was of vital importance, given the nearness of Home Rule, and Miller points out that whereas the Church could rely on the representatives of the people to defend Church control of schools once '*de facto* sovereignty' had been achieved, 'It would be much more difficult to get rid of popular control, however, if it were already in operation when *de facto* sovereignty was attained.'[6]

The question of control still remains at the core of all educational debate and, seen in retrospect, it is doubtful if any British govern ment could have pushed through a measure based on popular control. In the years following the Famine, power had come too rapidly to the Church to allow for the development of the tolerances which the democratic use of power requires. What is unfortunate is that the struggle for educational control never became a nationally unifying issue. Had it become so, then, once the land question was resolved, education might in time have come to replace it as the single most important social question of the century. Religious antagonisms ran too deep and a militant Catholic Church, conscious of its rising power, was in no mood to give ground to rivals — religious or lay.

Today, after the lapse of more than half a century, one can see more clearly some of the secondary results of that seizure of control: the stifling of lay initiative in education, a certain anti-clericalism among teachers generally, and the delayed emergence of a Catholic laity prepared to debate and, if necessary, defend the tenets of their Church.

So unchallenged was Church control that, when the change of government came, there was not even a ripple of dissent when it was seen that education, in defiance of the historical trend almost every where else in Europe, was more firmly in the control of the Church in 1921 than in 1878.

Yet, whether one approves or disapproves of Church influence in education, it is part of the totality and reflects both the strength and weakness of our society. If in the years of this account it turned its energies towards serving the social needs of the Catholic bourgeois, it did so because that new middle-class wished to be prepared for competition in terms of the requirements of a mercantile empire. And, while some may sigh after such a system as that of Germany with its clearer lines of authority, or that of France with its administrative orderliness, one can at least be grateful that it did extend education to far greater numbers than seemed possible before the Act of 1878 became law, that it did give schools a framework within which to operate and that, at the end, pupils and, to an extent, teachers, the two elements in education which matter most, were better off. As for the Commissioners, their epitaph might well be words they wrote in their first-ever Report when they said: 'good schools and successful students are not the peculiar possession of any religious denomination'. To emphasise the truth of that statement, they had devoted themselves unselfishly to the service of the Irish nation for forty three years.

APPENDIX 1

Final Recommendations of the Intermediate Education (Ireland)
Commission 1899

1. That a public general examination should be retained as the basis of the calculation of the school grant, but that this examination should not be competitive.
2. That the papers set at this examination should be of such a character as (a) to test true educational work, as distinct from the mere overloading of the memory, and (b) to be within the capacity of a well-taught pupil of average ability.
3. That the programme of the Board should prescribe at least two distinct courses — (i) the Grammar School Course, and (ii) the Modern Course in either of which a student may present for examination.
4. That the school grant should be a capitation grant paid on the 'Intermediate School Roll', ascertained in the manner which we have already explained.
5. That in order to receive a grant at the minimum rate, a school should be required to pass a fair proportion of the total number of pupils on the 'Intermediate School Roll', as defined above.
6. That a school possessing the prescribed percentage of the total number of pupils on the roll as defined above should receive a grant at a certain rate; and that the percentage should be graduated according to the proportion of passes until a defined maximum rate is reached. The capitation grant payable to a school, thus ascertained, may be called 'the Normal School Grant'.
7. That in order to encourage schools of more than average efficiency the 'Normal School Grant' payable to a school should be increased by the addition of bonuses, at rates to be prescribed by the Board, as for instance
   (a) By the addition of a bonus, or bonuses, if the average marks gained by its pupils, in all grades, amount to a certain percentage of the maximum marks attainable at the public general examination.
   (b) By an additional bonus, if the number of its passes in the Middle Grade be not less than prescribed percentage of the number of its passes in Junior Grade.
   (c) By an additional bonus, if the number of its passes in the

Senior Grade be not less than a prescribed percentage of the number of its passes in Junior Grade.

    (d) By an additional bonus as a result of inspection, subject to the limitations stated in the body of our report.

8. That the 'Normal School Grant' should be reduced by a prescribed percentage in the case of a school the number of whose passes in the Junior Grade does not bear a fair proportion to the number of its passes in the Preparatory Grade.

9. That, to guard against the inconvenience otherwise likely to result from sudden changes in the amount of the yearly school grant, the grant should be given each year, not upon the results of the examination in one year only, but upon an average taken on a triennial period.

10. That, to enable a school to have, before breaking up for the summer vacation, an exact knowledge of its financial position as affected by the grant from the Board, the three years preceding each current year should be taken as a triennial period.

11. That, in subjects which cannot be adequately tested by written examination, the Board shall adopt means to satisfy itself of the efficiency of the teaching, by the visit of an inspector, or by *viva voce* examination in the school or at a common centre.

12. That the Board should satisfy itself as to the sufficiency of the teaching staff; the sanitary conditions of the school; and the reasonableness of the arrangements as to school hours.

13. That the Board should satisfy itself that, in schools where Natural and Experimental Sciences are taught, proper equipment and appliances have been provided and used for teaching these subjects.

14. That submission to the requirements of the Board in the matters mentioned in 11, 12 and 13 should be a condition precedent to a school obtaining any grant from the Board.

15. That an honour examination should be held each year immediately after the pass examination, and that the Board should continue to allocate in each year a portion of the funds under its control for exhibitions and prizes, subject as regards the mode of distribution, to any modification which may take place under the suggestion contained in Part IX of the Report.

16. That the Board should be authorised to stipulate with managers presenting pupils for examination in the Natural and Experimental Sciences, that a certain proportion of the school grant should be applied to the proper equipment and appliances for the practical teaching of these sciences.

Appendix 1

17. That the Board should be empowered to advance to managers of schools upon appropriate security, to enable them to provide proper equipment and appliances for the teaching of Practical Science, or for similar purpose approved by the Board.

Source: *Intermediate Education (Ireland) Commission, 1899. Final Report* (C. 9511), XII, pp. 23-4.

APPENDIX 2

The First Registration Council

Very Rev. Canon Barrett
John Thompson
Brother J. P. Hennessy
W. J. Williams
Miss Elizabeth Steele
Miss H. M. White
W. J. M. Starkie
Justice Madden
Sir Samuel Dill
Justice Molony
Most Rev. T. O'Dea
T. P. Gill
Professor E. R. Cuverwell
Dr D. J. Coffey
Professor R. M. Henry

Source: Minutes of the Proceedings of the Commissioners of Intermediate Education, 15 November 1915.

APPENDIX 3

Table showing number and percentage of candidates presenting in each grade

Year	Junior	Middle	Senior
1880	2,929 boys (71.19)	773 boys (18.78)	412 boys (10.01)
	1,030 girls (71.18)	298 girls (20.56)	119 girls (8.22)
	3,959 (71.19)	1,071 (19.25)	531 (9.54)
1890	3,164 boys (72.88)	549 boys (12.64)	230 boys (5.29)
	933 girls (65.33)	237 girls (16.59)	123 girls (8.33)
	4,097 (71.01)	786 (13.62)	353 (6.10)
1900	3,081 boys (54.91)	843 boys (15.02)	309 boys (5.50)
	1,148 girls (57.48)	317 girls (15.87)	156 girls (7.81)
	4,229 (55.58)	1,160 (15.24)	465 (6.11)
1910	3,094 boys (38.83)	1,716 boys (21.54)	550 boys (6.90)
	1,749 girls (44.43)	817 girls (20.77)	259 girls (6.58)
	4,843 (40.69)	2,533 (21.28)	809 (6.79)
1920	4.346 boys (58.19)	1,989 boys (26.63)	1,133 boys (15.27)
	3,402 girls (64.18)	1,308 girls (24.68)	590 girls (11.13)
	7,748 (60.68)	3,297 (25.82)	1,723 (13.49)

N.B. These figures indicate that while the overall figure for those attending intermediate schools might appear reasonably satisfactory, in fact the great majority benefited only at the early stages.

Sources: Reports of the Intermediate Education Board for Ireland.
   1880   C.2919 XXXIV   p. 25.
   1890   C.6324 XXVIII pp. 22-3.
   1900   Cd.5173 XXV   p. 53.
   1910   Cd.5768 XXI   p. 64.
   1920 Cmd.1398 XI   p. 402.

APPENDIX 4

Table showing total number of students presenting for examination in
each year and the percentage of students passed

Year	Number of students	Percentage passed
1879	3,954	60
1880	5,561	72
1881	6,953	67.2
1882	6,614	60.4
1883	6,162	60.7
1884	5,504	69.7
1885	5,181	61.2
1886	3,510	63.3
1887	5,931	60
1888	6,058	67.5
1889	6,533	61.5
1890	5,236	59.2
1891	5,156	59.6
1892	5,759	57.7
1893	6,974	59
1894	7,682	58.9
1895	8,323	59.8
1896	8,711	57
1897	8,877	62.4
1898	9,073	62.1
1899	7,768	68.3
1900	7,618	69.8
1901	8,117	65.7
1902	8,379	58.9
1903	7,909	62.1
1904	8,530	63.3
1905	9,677	68.9
1906	10,967	63
1907	11,821	57.5
1908	11,383	61.2
1909	11,332	55.3
1910	11,900	53.7
1911	12,105	54.3
1912	12,481	55.7
1913	9,706	55.6
1914	10,176	59.4
1915	11,525	62.4
1916	12,426	57.7
1917	12,604	60.1
1918	12,025	55.7
1919	12,119	50.8
1920	6,328	49.6
1921	12,419	47.6
1922	10,114	49.4
1923	9,230	58.9

Sources: Reports of the Intermediate Education Board for Ireland, 1879-1923.

APPENDIX 5

Table showing the numbers who presented themselves in the various subjects at the first examination held under the Rules of the Intermediate Education Board in 1879 and at last (for all Ireland) in 1921

	1879	1921	
Drawing	754	2,421	
English	3,759	12,354	
French	2,079	8,030	
German	187	687	
Irish (Celtic)	19	8,275	
Italian	66	14	
Greek	1,219	1,186	
Latin	2,194	5,810	
Music	645	79	
Natural Philosophy	900	6,223	Physical Science
Chemistry	430	348	Natural Science
Botany	219	944	Domestic Economy
Physical Geography	669	11,450	History and
and Geology	51		Historical Geography

N.B. In 1879 3,954 students presented themselves for examination.
In 1921 12,419 students presented themselves for examination.

Sources: *Report of the Intermediate Education Board for Ireland, 1879*, p. 10.
Report of the Intermediate Education Board for Ireland, 1921, p. xxvii.

APPENDIX 6

Number of candidates who presented themselves (a) in 1879, (b) in
1921

1879	3,954	candidates presented themselves
	3,218	boys
	736	girls
	2,327	candidates passed
	1,845	boys
	482	girls
1921	12,419	candidates presented themselves
	7,299	boys
	5,120	girls
	5,907	candidates passed
	3,502	boys
	2,405	girls

Sources: *Report of the Intermediate Education Board for Ireland, 1879* (C.2600),
XXIII, p. 4. *Report of the Intermediate Education Board for Ireland, 1921*, p. xi.

APPENDIX 7

'Superior Schools' in Ireland, according to the Census Returns

Year	Schools	Pupils
1871	574	21,225
1881	488	20,405
1892	474	24,271
1901	490	35,373
1911	489	41,157
1921	274	20,776

N.B.
(i)   'Superior School' is defined as one in which a foreign language is taught, at least to an appreciable extent.

(ii)   Some authorities give slightly higher figures for the early years when students taking first university examinations in schools and colleges affiliated to the Catholic University were included.

(iii) The figures for 1921 refer only to the Irish Free State.

(iv) Generally, the classification in the Census Reports is by type of school and not by type of education given. In fact in 1911 for the whole Thirty-two Counties there were 4717 pupils in Primary Schools who were classified as receiving 'Superior Education'. On the other hand, 14,496 pupils in Superior Schools and Colleges were classified as receiving 'Primary Education only'.

Sources: Census Returns.

APPENDIX 8

List of Convent Schools that withdrew from the intermediate system
between 1880 and 1889

Loretto Convent, Rathfarnham
     North Great George's Street
     Bray
     Fermoy

Convent of Mercy, Baggot Street
     Golden Bridge
     Crumlin Road, Belfast
     Sussex Place, Belfast
     Mount St Vincent, Limerick
     Sligo
     Kells
     Carlow
     Dundalk
     Dungarvan
     Galway
     Tullamore
     Enniskillen
     Londonderry
     Strabane
     Killarney
     Ballinasloe
     Rathdrum

Presentation Convent, Lucan
     Midleton
     Kilkenny
     Galway
     Killarney

King's Inn Street School (Irish Sisters of Charity)

Sienna Convent, Drogheda

Carrigtwohill Convent

French Convent, Castleknock

Source: *Intermediate Education (Ireland) Commission 1899, Minutes of Evidence* (C.9512), p. 76.

APPENDIX 9

Table showing the number of pupils attending schools in Ireland
exclusive of the Six Counties

Year	Attending primary schools	Attending secondary schools
1871	470,165	19,420
1881	520,682	18,828
1891	516,230	21,748
1901	459,262	31,560
1911	467,676	35,771
1926	522,090*	47,112**

*Numbers on roll on last day of school-year, 1925-6, in national schools, excluding industrial and reform schools.

**Pupils in Secondary Schools at the beginning of the school-year, 1926-7, aged between 12 and 20 together with 22,336 pupils attending Technical Schools. The previous figures included such establishments as universities, Maynooth College, etc.

Sources: 1871 to 1811, Census of Population Reports.
1926 *Dept. of Education Report, 1925-27.*

NOTES

CHAPTER 1

1. *Census Report, 1871,* Pt 1, Vol. 1 (1876), p. 1173, fn.

2. Adolphe Perraud, *Études sur l'Irlande Contemporaine,* translated as 'Ireland under English Rule' (Dublin: 1863), Tome II, p. 413.

3. 'The curriculum of the Secondary School' in *Report of the Council of Education* (Dublin: 1962), p. 44, par. 80.

4. *Royal Commission of Inquiry into Primary Education (Ireland) 1870,* Pt I, Vol. I (1870), p. 504.

5. *Synge Street Centenary Record 1864-1964* (Dublin: 1964), pp. 29-30.

6. F. S. L. Lyons, *Ireland since the Famine* (London: 1971), p. 79.

7. Donald H. Akenson, *The Irish Education Experiment* (London: 1970), p. 389.

8. *The Endowed Schools Commission, Appendix 1881* (C. 2831), Vol. I, p. 238.

9. Emmet Larkin, *The Roman Catholic Church and the Creation of the Modern Irish State, 1878-1886* (Dublin: 1975), p. 11.

10. Letter to Dr Kirby, Rector of the Irish College in Rome, quoted by Larkin, p. 11.

11. James J. Auchmuty, *Irish Education* (Dublin and London: 1977), p. 151.

12. An t-Athair Mac Suibhne, 'Early History of Carlow College' in *Irish Ecclesiastical Record,* 5th Ser., Vol. LXII (October 1943), p. 21.

13. Rev. T. Cunningham and Rev. T. Gallogly, *St. Patrick's College, Cavan. A Centenary History* (Cavan: 1974), p. 60.

14. Maurice C. Hime, *Home Education or Irish versus English Grammar Schools for Irish Boys* (London: 1887), p. 2.

15. *Education Endowments (Ireland) Commission 1888-89* (C. 5766), Vol. XXX, pp. 68, 70.

16. R. B. O'Brien, *Fifty Years of Concessions to Ireland* (London: 1883), Vol. II, pp. 322-3.

17. *Report of the President of the Queen's College, Cork, for the year 1886-7* (C. 5203), pp. 44-5.

18. House Status, 1877, in *Historia Colegii Tulliolani* at Tullabeg. Jesuit Archives.

19. William Graham Brooke, 'Educational Endowments and their application to the Middle Class and Higher Education of Girls and Women' in *Journal of the Statistical and Social Inquiry Society of Ireland,* Vol. 6 (February 1872), p. 118.

20. *The French College, Blackrock. Distribution of Premiums for the Academical Year 1877* (Dublin: 1877), back cover.

21. *The Capuchin Annual* (1960), p. 334.

22. *The Clongownian* (1914), p. 251.

23. Ibid., p. 21.

24. R. Lee Cole, *A History of Wesley College* (Dublin: 1963), p. 13.

25. Michael Quane, 'Drogheda Grammar School' in *Journal of the Royal Society of Antiquaries of Ireland,* Vol. XV, No. 3 (1963), p. 243.

26. *The Irish Catholic Directory* (1870), p. 31.

27. Lord Randolph Churchill to Sir J. Bernard Burke, December 1877 (1878), p. 14.

28. *St. Vincent's College, Castleknock Centenary Record* (Dublin: 1935), p. 109.

29. T. J. Morrissey, S.J., Some Jesuit Contributions to Irish Education with special reference to the 16th and 19th centuries (unpublished Ph.D. thesis, University of Cork, 1977), Vol. 1, p. 354.

30. Evidence of Stephen de Vere before *Powis Commission,* Pt 1, Vol. XXVIII (1870), p. 507.

31. Michael Quane, 'Dundalk Grammar School' in *County Louth Archaeological Journal,* Vol. XVI, No. 10 (1966), p. 100.

32. *The Endowed Schools (Ireland) Commission, 1870* (C. 6111), Pt IV, q. 25793.

33. 'The Standard of Education in the New School' in *Synge Street Centenary Record 1864-1964,* p. 29.

34. Henry Mangan, 'Clio in Ireland' in *O'Connell Centenary Record* (Dublin: 1928), p. 61.

35. R. Marshall, *Methodist College, Belfast. The First Hundred Years 1868-1968* (Belfast: 1968), pp. 55-6.

36. R. D. Altik, *The English Common Reader: A Social History of the Mass Reading Public* (Chicago: 1957), p. 184.

36. *Catholic Education. Report of a Meeting of the Catholics of the Diocese of Dublin* (Dublin: 1872), p. 57.

38. R. D. Lyons, *Supply and Demand for an enlarged system of Irish University Education* (London: 1873), pp. viii-ix.

39. W. K. Sullivan to Lord Emly, undated. N.L.I., Monsell MS. 8317.

40. Rev. Dr Walter McDonald, *Reminiscences of a Maynooth Professor* (London: 1925), pp. 24-5.

CHAPTER 2

1. Rev. James MacCaffrey, *History of the Catholic Church in the Nineteenth Century* (Dublin: 1909), p. 233.

2. George F. Shaw, 'How to improve School Education in Ireland' in *Journal of the Statistical and Social Inquiry Society of Ireland,* Vol. 3 (January 1861), p. 368.

3. *The Blackrock College Annual* (Centenary Edition, 1960), p. 82.

4. Cardinal Newman's Letters, No. 1, 26 May 1872. Given in Appendix to the *Memorial sent to the Chief Secretary,* Hicks-Beach, in 1875.

5. Cullen to Gladstone, 25 February 1872, Gladstone Papers, B.M., Add. MS. 44433, f. 237.

6. *Hansard.* 3rd Ser., Vol. 214 (1873), p. 379.

7. Ibid.

8. Graham Balfour, *Educational Systems of Great Britain and Ireland* (Oxford: 1903), p. 264.

9. Lady Victoria Hicks-Beach, *Life of Sir Michael Hicks-Beach* (London: 1932), Vol. I, pp. 46-7.

10. Disraeli to Hicks-Beach, 17 December 1874. St Aldwyn MSS. PCC/75.

11. *The Times,* 2 February 1875.

12. Keenan to Lord Emly, 5 May 1874. N.L.I., Larcom MS. 8317.

13. Ibid., 8 July 1875.

14. Ibid.

15. Ibid., 2 December 1876.

16. Ibid., 17 December 1876.

17. Ibid.

18. Bishop Conroy to the Earl of Granard, 7 February 1876. St Aldwyn MSS. PCC/52.

19. Ibid.

20. Ibid.

21. Bishop Conroy to Hicks-Beach, 20 February 1876. St Aldwyn MSS. PCC/64.

22. Ibid., 12 February 1877.

23. Keenan to Lord Emly, 12 March 1877. N.L.I., Larcom MS. 8317.

24. Keenan to Hicks-Beach, April 1877. Quoted in *The Life of Sir Michael Hicks-Beach*, Vol. I, p. 54.

25. Bishop Conroy to Hicks-Beach. Quoted in *The Life of Sir Michael Hicks-Beach*, Vol. I, p. 54.

26. Keenan to Lord Emly, 13 January 1878. N.L.I., Larcom MS. 8317.

27. Letter dated 7 February 1878 in Cardinal Cullen's correspondence at the Holy Cross College, Clonliffe, Dublin.

28. Hicks-Beach to Cardinal Cullen, January 1878. St Aldwyn MSS. PCC/64.

29. Dr Porter to Hicks-Beach, 18 July 1878. St Aldwyn MSS. PCC/54.

30. Cardinal Cullen to Hicks-Beach, 7 February 1878.

31. Hicks-Beach to Disraeli, 12 March 1877. Disraeli MS. Cited in David Thornley, *Isaac Butt and Home Rule* (London; 1964), p. 353.

32. Bishop Conroy to Hicks-Beach, 9 March 1877. St Aldwyn MSS. PCC/64.

33. Dr Porter to Hicks-Beach, 15 March 1877. St Aldwyn MSS. PCC/64.

34. Undated letter from 'Bishop's House, Newtownforbes, Co. Longford' (the residence to Dr Conroy), in Cardinal Cullen's correspondence.

35. Bishop Conroy to Hicks-Beach, 9 March 1878. St Aldwyn MSS. PCC/64.

CHAPTER 3

1. A Christian Brother, *Edmund Ignatius Rice and the Christian Brothers* (Dublin: 1926), p. 481.

2. Fitzgibbon to Cassidy, Commissioner of Intermediate Education, 22 June 1878. Delany Papers, Jesuit Archives.

3. Keenan to Lord Emly, 3 February 1878. N. L. I., Larcom MS. 8317.

4. Ibid.

5. Ibid., 24 March 1878.

6. *Hansard*, 3rd Ser., Vol. 240 (1878), p. 1228.

7. R. R. James, *Lord Randolph Churchill* (London: 1959), p. 64.

8. *Hansard*, 3rd Ser., Vol. 240 (1878), p. 1235.

9. *Hansard*, 3rd Ser., Vol. 241 (1878), p. 7.

10. Letter to Dr M. F. Ward, M.P., published in *The Nation*, 29 June 1878.

11. *Hansard*, 3rd Ser., Vol. 241 (1878), p. 1523.

12. *Freeman's Journal*, 22 June 1878.

13. *The Times*, 22 June 1878.

14. *The Nation*, 29 June 1878.

15. Keenan to Lord Emly, 25 June 1878. N.L.I., Larcom MS. 8317.

16. *Hansard*, 3rd Ser., Vol. 241 (1878), p. 423.

17. Ibid., p. 434-5.

18. Ibid., p. 441.

19. Keenan to Lord Emly, 30 June 1878. N.L.I., Larcom MS. 8317.

20. Butt to Hicks-Beach, 18 June 1878. St Aldwyn MSS. PCC/56.

21. F. H. O'Donnell, *The Irish Parliamentary Party* (London: 1910), Vol. 1, p. 299.

22. *Hansard*, 3rd Ser., Vol. 241 (1878), p. 1487.

23. *Hansard*, 3rd Ser., Vol. 242 (1878), pp. 316-17.

24. *Hansard*, 3rd Ser., Vol. 241 (1878), p. 1495.

25. Woodlock to Hicks-Beach, 29 June 1878. St Aldwyn MSS. PCC/64, and ibid., 17 July 1878.

CHAPTER 4

1. Patrick J. Walsh, *William J. Walsh, Archbishop of Dublin* (Dublin: 1928), p. 75.

2. *Irish Times*, 5 July 1879.

3. Unsigned article, 'The Great Tradition of O'Connell School' in *The O'Connell School Centenary Record* (Dublin: 1928), p. 23.

4. Rev. M.O'Riordan, *Catholicity and Progress in Ireland* (London: 1905), p. 464.

5. Cit. *Blackrock College Annual*, p. 70. Speech delivered by Dr William Walsh at Blackrock College, December 1896.

6. *Cork Daily Herald*, 18 September 1879.

7. *Report of the Intermediate Education Board*. 1880 (C. 2919), p. 5.

8. Ibid., 1881 (C. 3176), p. 6.

9. Ibid., 1882 (C. 3580), p. 6.

10. *Freeman's Journal*, 28 January 1882.

11. Letter signed William J. Walsh, Chairman of the Standing Committee, dated 3 March 1882.

12. Minutes of the Meeting of the Schoolmasters' Association, 29 June 1883.

13. William J. Walsh, *Statement of the Chief Grievances of Irish Catholics* (Dublin: 1890), p. 233.

14. *Irish Times*, 16 May 1891.

15. R. Dudley Edwards, 'The Beginnings of the Irish Intermediate System, 1878-1883' in *Catholic University School Centenary Record* (1967), p. 54.

16. Dr. Nulty, Bishop of Meath, *The Relations existing between Convent Schools and the Systems of Intermediate and Primary National Education* (Dublin: 1884), p. 20.

17. J. P. Mahaffy, quoted in article 'Mr. Mahaffy on Irish Intermediate Education' by Rev. L. Healy in *Irish Ecclesiastical Record*, Vol. IV (1898), p. 542.

18. *Hansard*, 4th Ser., Vol. 95 (1901), p. 1416.

19. Mahaffy Autographs, T.C.D., MS. 2075, No. 33.

CHAPTER 5

1. J. L. Hammond, *Gladstone and the Irish Nation* (London: 1938), p. 26.

2. Letter of Dr Croke, Archbishop of Cashel, to Archbishop Walsh, 11 January 1886, quoted in Walsh, *William J. Walsh, Archbishop of Dublin*, p. 510.

3. *Freeman's Journal*, 8 October 1885.

4. T. M. Healy, *Letters and Leaders of my Day* (London: 1928), Vol. 2, p. 436.

5. Ibid.

6. Mary Colum, *Life and the Dream* (New York: 1958), p. 23.

7. James M. Meenan, 'The Student Body' in *Struggle with Fortune* (Dublin: 1954), p. 105.

CHAPTER 6

1. *Minutes of the Proceedings of the Commissioners of Intermediate Education, 1898-9*, p. 278.

2. *Hansard*, 4th Ser., Vol. 129 (1904), p. 207.

3. Denis Gwynn, *The Irish Free State* (London: 1928), p. 384.

4. *Census of Ireland for the year 1911*, p. 256.

5. *Intermediate Education (Ireland) Commission, 1899. Miscellaneous Documents* (C. 9513), p. 365.

6. *Intermediate Education (Ireland) Commission. Final Report* (C. 9512), p. 56.

7. Maurice C. Hime, *Irish Schools for Irish Boys* (London: 1887), p. 2.

8. W. J. M. Starkie, 'Recent Reforms in Irish Education' (an address to the British Association in Belfast, 11 September 1902, printed as a pamphlet), p. 2.

9. Cunningham and Gallogly, *St. Patrick's College, Cavan. A Centenary History*, p. 66.

10. *Intermediate Education (Ireland) Commission. Miscellaneous Documents Pt II. Memorandum on Inspection,* p. 289.
11. *Commission on University Education, 1902. Minutes of Evidence* (Cd. 286), p. 24.

CHAPTER 7

1. 'Report of the General Meeting of the Catholic Headmasters' Association and the Convent Intermediate Schools' in *The Irish Educational Review,* Vol. III (October 1909), p. 56.
2. *Vice-Regal Committee on Intermediate Education (Ireland)* (Cmd. 66, 1919), p. 14.

CHAPTER 8

1. W. J. M. Starkie, 'The History of Irish Primary and Secondary Education during the Last Decade' (inaugural address in Queen's University, Belfast, 3 July 1911; printed as a pamphlet), p. 26.
2. State Paper Office, CSO RP (1904), 10032.
3. Ibid.
4. A paper by Mahaffy, entitled 'The New Scheme for Sizarships' in *The Report of Messrs. Dale & Stephens, 1905* (Cd. 2546), p. 37.
5. *Report of Dale & Stephens,* p. 16. (N.B. The Appendix to Volume 2 of the Commission of 1899 gives but eighteen schools to supply the educational needs of the six counties west of the Shannon.)
6. *Royal Commission on University Education in Ireland 1903. Minutes of Evidence* (Cd. 826), p. 21.
7. Hanna Sheehy Skeffington, 'Irish Secondary Teachers' in *The Irish Review,* Vol. 2 (October 1912), p. 394.
8. Association of Secondary Teachers, *Secondary Education in Ireland* (Dublin: 1904), p. 4.
9. MS. V. Mun. 42, 1. Trinity College, Dublin.
10. Ibid.
11. Kenneth Bailey, *The History of Trinity College* (Dublin: 1947), p. 9.
12. Graham Balfour, *Educational Systems of Great Britain and Ireland* (Oxford: 1903), p. 209.
13. T. W. Moody and J. C. Beckett, *Queen's University 1845-1949* (London: 1959), Vol. I, p. 317.
14. Letter from the Hon. Sec. given in the agenda for the meeting of the Commissioners, 26 May 1904.

CHAPTER 9

1. Draft letter from the Irisn Office in London received in Dublin Castle 20 December 1902. State Paper Office, CSO RP (1904), 10032.
2. David W. Miller, *Church, State and Nation in Ireland, 1898-1921* (Dublin: 1973), p. 122.
3. *Freeman's Journal,* 22 January 1906.
4. *An Claidheamh Soluis,* Vol. IX, No. 9 (1907), p. 7.
5. *Irish Times,* 8 May 1907.
6. *Freeman's Journal,* 13 May 1907.
7. Miller, *Church, State and Nation,* p. 186.
8. Dillon to Redmond, 11 May 1907. N.L.I., MS. 15182.

9. Denis Gwynn, *The Life of John Redmond* (London: 1932), p. 143.
10. *Hansard*, 4th Ser., Vol. 174 (1907), p. 121.
11. Gwynn, *The Life of John Redmond*, p. 148.
12. *Hansard*, 4th Ser., Vol. 175 (1907), p. 337.
13. *Church of Ireland Gazette*, 24 May 1907.
14. Emil Strauss, *Irish Nationality and British Democracy* (London: 1951), pp. 214-5.
15. Ibid.

CHAPTER 10

1. S. Rosenbaum (ed.), *Against Home Rule* (London: 1912), pp. 278-9.
2. *Hansard*, 4th Ser., Vol. 29 (1895), p. 244.
3. Arthur W. Samuels, K.C., 'Some Features in Recent Irish Finance' in *Journal of the Social and Statistical Inquiry Society of Ireland*, Vol. 12 (1906), p. 24.
4. Rosenbaum (ed.), *Against Home Rule*, p. 280.
5. Ibid.
6. 29 December 1908.
7. Rev. M. O'Riordan, *Catholicity and Progress in Ireland* (London: 1905), p. 475.
8. *Hansard*, 5th Ser., Vol. 21 (1911), p. 1648.
9. F. H. O'Donnell, *The Irish Parliamentary Party* (London: 1910), Vol. 1, p. 309.
10. Hanna Sheehy Skeffington, 'Irish Secondary Teachers' in *The Irish Review*, Vol. 2 (October 1912).
11. Statement of the Catholic Headmasters' Association, 5 September 1912.
12. *Irish Educational Review*, Vol. V, No. 1 (1912), p. 752.
13. Ibid., Vol. VI, No. 1 (1913), p. 48.
14. Dr O'Dwyer, Bishop of Limerick, quoted in the *Irish Times*, 19 December 1913.

CHAPTER 11

1. *Dáil Debates*. Vol. I (1925), p. 2595.
2. *Security of Tenure, 1909-1934*, published by the A.S.T.I. (December 1934).
3. Minutes of Meeting of the Senate of the National University, 20 December 1910.
4. Minutes of Meeting of the Senate of Queen's University, 14 December 1913.
5. Rev. Daniel Coghlan, *Trinity College and the Trinity Commission* (Dublin: 1908), p. 53.
6. *Report of the Intermediate Education Board for Ireland, 1918* (C.323), p. viii.

CHAPTER 13

1. T. L. Jarman, *Landmarks in the History of Education* (London: 1951), p. 294.
2. Miller, *Church, State and Nation*, p. 437.
3. Ibid., p. 442.
4. T. J. O'Connell, *A History of the I.N.T.O.* (Dublin: 1968), p. 306.
5. *Irish Times*, 13 March 1920.
6. *The Hibernian Journal*, April 1920.
7. *Times Educational Supplement*, 5 March 1920.
8. McDonald, *Reminiscences of a Maynooth Professor*, p. 193.

9. *Belfast Newsletter*, 19 November 1919.
10. *Irish Independent*, 19 December 1919.
11. *Hansard*, 5th Ser., Vol. 129 (1920), p. 1734.

CHAPTER 14

1. *Hansard*, 5th Ser., Vol. 138 (1921), p. 1118.
2. P. H. Pearse, *The Murder Machine* (Dublin: 1912), pp. 43-4.

CHAPTER 15

1. M. Tierney, *Education in a Free Ireland* (Dublin: 1920), p. 30.
2. Ibid.
3. *Hansard*, 4th Ser., Vol. 157 (1906), p. 1070.
4. F. H. O'Donnell, The Ruin of Education in Ireland (London: 1902), p. 151.
5. *Intermediate Education Board for Ireland. Reports of Inspectors*, Vol. 2 (2 May 1910).
6. Lyons, *Ireland since the Famine*, p. 81.
7. Starkie, 'The History of Irish Primary and Secondary Education during the last decade', op. cit.
8. Gwynn, *The Irish Free State*, p. 384.
9. J. P. Mahaffy, 'How to circumvent "cramming" in Irish Secondary Education' in *The Nineteenth Century* (November 1898), p. 867.
10. James Comerton, 'Reform in Irish Education' in *The New Ireland Review*, Vol. 2 (September 1894 — February 1895), pp. 718-19.
11. Rev. Dr. W. Delany, S.J., *Irish University Education* (Dublin: 1904), p. 37.
12. Rev. E. Cahill, S.J., 'Secondary Education for Rural Ireland' in *Studies* (January 1916).
13. Walsh, *Chief Grievances of Irish Catholics*, p. 233.
14. W. G. Hubard, 'Intermediate Education in Ireland' in *Frazer's Magazine* (March 1878), pp. 378-9.
15. Tuite to Delany, 31 August 1880. Delany Papers, Jesuit Archives.
16. Correspondence of Cardinal Cullen in the archives of Clonliffe College, Dublin.

CHAPTER 16

1. Major Gerald Dease, *A Plea for Educational Reform* (pamphlet, Dublin: 1917), p. 33.
2. John Dillon in a speech later printed as a pamphlet (Dublin: 1904).
3. Arnold F. Graves, 'The Reorganisation of Irish Education Departments' in *Journal of the Statistical and Social Inquiry Society of Ireland*, Vol. 8 (1882), p. 350.
4. *Hansard*, 5th Ser., Vol. 86 (1916), p. 490.
5. Sir Bertram Windle, 'The Prospects of Education in Ireland Today' (presidential address to the Technical Instruction Congress of 1917; printed as a pamphlet), p. 6.
6. *Hansard*, 5th Ser., Vol. 96 (1917), p. 836.
7. *Hansard*, 3rd Ser., Vol. 252 (1880), p. 1514.
8. Ibid., p. 1506.
9. R. B. McDowell, *The Irish Administration* (London: 1960), p. 241.
10. *Hansard*, 3rd Ser., Vol. 291 (1884), p. 1856.
11. State Paper Office. CSO RP (1904), 10032.

12. *Hansard*, 5th Ser., Vol. 41 (1912), p. 2174.
13. *Hansard*, 5th Ser., Vol. 25 (1911), p. 2059.
14. *Dáil Debates*, 1 December 1922.

CHAPTER 17

1. Larkin, *The Roman Catholic Church and the Creation of the Modern Irish State*, p. 395.
2. *Freeman's Journal*, 18 February 1874.
3. Cardinal Newman, from 'Introductory Remarks', *Difficulty of Anglicans II, A Letter to the Duke of Norfolk*, p. 185.
4. Cullen to Kirby, No. 86, 12 March 1867. Kirby Papers.
5. Woodlock to Hicks-Beach, 23 November 1878. St Aldwyn MSS. PCC/64.
6. Miller, *Church, State and Nation*, p. 439.

SOURCES AND BIBLIOGRAPHY

MANUSCRIPT SOURCES

National Library of Ireland
  Gill, T. P., MS 13,478-13, 526.
  Larcom, T. A., MS 7659. Pamphlets and news-cuttings relating to the Endowed
    Schools Commission and Intermediate Commission, 1858-78.
  Monsell of Tervoe papers, MS 20,685. Letters to William Monsell from P. J.
    Keenan, 1867-1888.
    MS 8317-8315, Letters to William Monsell and miscellaneous documents
      dealing mainly with religious and educational affairs.
  MS 13,903 (Jan. 1882). Petition signed by a number of teachers and others to
    the Board of Intermediate Education against a proposal to institute separate
    examinations for boys and girls.
  MS 17,984. Dr Michael Quane papers, c. 1900-1930.
  MS 15,182 and MS 15,243. Redmond papers. Letters mainly to John Dillon on
    political and educational matters.
  MS 15,356. Three letters to M. J. Synott, Naas, Co. Kildare, 1917-1919, on
    educational topics, with a few associated documents.

Dublin University (Trinity College)
  MS 964 (1.4.30). Copies of letters of the Rev. B. Woodlock on education in
    Ireland, 1871.
  MSS 5225-5679 and MSS 5680-5859. The Archives, relating to the Schools of
    the Incorporated Society in Dublin for Promoting Protestant (English)
    schools in Ireland, to 1894.
  MS V. Mun. 42,1., 42,2., 42,3. Regulations of Examinations for Women,
    University of Dublin.

Department of Education (Library), Dublin
  Minutes of the Meetings of the Commissioners of Intermediate Education, 1
    November 1878 to April 1883; 1893-1899; 1900-1920 (printed).
  Selections from the Reports of the Temporary Inspectors of Intermediate
    Schools, 1901-1902.

Holy Cross College, Clonliffe
  Cullen papers. The sorting and numbering of these has been begun and there are
    many letters and documents of relevance dealing with educational matters.

State Paper Office, Dublin Castle
  Chief Secretary's Office, Registered Papers: 114/1870; 12782/1873;
    1869/1877.

Public Record Office
  Papers of the Commissioners of Intermediate Education, 1890-1918.
  MS 5866. Prospectuses of Girls' schools in Dublin.

St Vincent's College, Castleknock
  Records of the Catholic Managers' Association in the possession of the
    President.

Record Office, County Hall, Gloucester
  MSS 2455 et al. PCC/52, PCC/53, PCC/54, PCC/56, PCC/64.
  St Aldwyn papers. All the correspondence of a non-personal nature belonging to

Sir Michael Hicks-Beach has been deposited in the Record Office by his grandson, Lord St Aldwyn.

UNPUBLISHED THESES

Coolahan, John 'A Study of Curricular Policy in the National and Secondary Schools of Ireland. 1900-1935.' Ph.D. thesis, University College, Dublin, 1975. 'The Payment by Results Policy in Irish Education.' M.Ed. thesis, Trinity College, Dublin, 1974.
Henderson, Elspeth A. 'The Schoolmasters' Association.' In partial fulfilment of requirements for the degree of M.Ed. at Trinity College, Dublin.
McGough, William 'Secondary Education in Ireland and the Intermediate Education Act.' M.A. thesis, University College, Dublin, 1954.
Murphy, John C. 'The Erasmus Smith School Endowment.' M.A. thesis, University College, Cork, 1963.
O'Connor, Daniel C. 'Secondary Education in Ireland, 1878-1968.' M.A. thesis, Maynooth College, 1971.
Sexton, Peter F. 'The Lay Teachers' Struggle for Status in Catholic Secondary Schools in Ireland between 1878 and 1937.' In partial fulfilment of requirements for the degree of M.Ed. at the University of Birmingham, 1972.
Stevenson, George 'A Critical Survey of the Development of Secondary Education in Ireland, 1871-1880.' M.A. thesis, Queen's University, Belfast, 1957.

PRINTED SOURCES

BOOKS

A Christian Brother *A Century of Catholic Education* (Dublin: 1916).
A Christian Brother *Edmund Ignatius Rice and the Christian Brothers* (Dublin: 1926).
Atkinson, Norman *Irish Education* (Dublin: 1969).
Archbishop of Dublin *Statement of the Chief Grievances of Irish Catholics in the Matter of Education* (Dublin: 1890).
Armour, W. S. *Armour of Ballymoney* (London: 1934).
Auchmuty, J. J. *Irish Education — A Historical Survey* (Dublin: 1937).
Balfour, Graham *The Educational Systems of Great Britain and Ireland* (Oxford: 1903).
Barkley, J. M. *Short History of the Presbyterian Church in Ireland* (Belfast: 1959).
Birch, P. *St Kieran's College, Kilkenny* (Dublin: 1951).
Cole, R. Lee *Wesley College, Dublin* (Dublin: 1963).
Committee of Irish Catholics *Intermediate and University Education in Ireland, Part I. Intermediate Education* (Dublin: 1872).
Corcoran, Timothy *Education Systems in Ireland from the close of the Middle Ages* (Dublin: 1928).
Cardinal Cullen *Pastoral Letters of* Moran (ed.) (Dublin: 1882).
Delany, V. T. H. *Christopher Palles* (Dublin: 1960).
Dowling, P. J. *The hedge schools of Ireland* (London: 1935).
Dowling, P. J. *A History of Irish Education. A Study in Conflicting Loyalties* (Cork: 1971).
Dubois, L. Paul *Contemporary Ireland* (Dublin: 1908).
Fitzpatrick, J. D. *Edmund Rice, founder and first superior general of the brothers of the christian schools in Ireland* (Dublin: 1945).
Freeman, T. W. *Ireland; its physical, historical, social and economic geography* (London: 1950).

Gallagher, Anthony M. *Education in Ireland* (Washington, D.C.: 1948).

Grimshaw, T. W. *Facts and Figures about Ireland. Part I* (Dublin: 1893).

Gwynn, D. *John Redmond* (London: 1932).

Gwynn, D. *A Hundred Years of Catholic Emancipation 1829-1929* (London: 1929).

Gwynn, Stephen *The History of Ireland* (London: 1928).

Hammond, J. L. *Gladstone and the Irish nation* (London: 1938).

Hime, Maurice C. *Home Education. Irish Schools for Irish Boys* (London: 1887).

Healy, T. M. *Letters and Leaders of my day* Vols I & II (London: 1928).

Howley, Edward *The Universities and Secondary Schools of Ireland, with Proposals for their Improvement* (Dublin: 1871).

Lampson, C. Locker *A Consideration of the State of Ireland in the Nineteenth Century* (London: 1907).

Larkin, Emmet *The Roman Catholic Church and the Creation of the Modern Irish State, 1878-1886* (U.S. and Dublin: 1975).

Lyons, F. S. L. *Ireland since the Famine* (London: 1971).

MacCaffrey, L. J. *History of the Catholic Church in the Nineteenth Century, 1789-1908* Vols I & II (Dublin: 1909).

McCarthy, Michael *Five Years in Ireland, 1895-1900* (London & Dublin: 1901).

McDonald, Walter *Reminiscences of a Maynooth Professor* (London: 1925).

McDowell, R. B. *Public Opinion and Government Policy in Ireland* (London: 1952).

MacSuibhne, P. *Cardinal Cullen (Paul Cullen and his contemporaries, with their letters)* (Naas: 1962).

Mansergh, N. *Ireland in the age of Reform and Revolution* (London: 1940).

Marshall, Ronald *Methodist College, Belfast* (Belfast: 1968).

Mescal, John *Religion in the Irish System of Education* (Dublin: 1957).

Moody, T. W. and Beckett, J. C. *Ulster since 1800: A Social survey* (London: 1958).

Norman, E. R. *The Catholic Church and Ireland in the age of rebellion* (London: 1965).

O'Brien, R. Barry *Fifty years of concessions to Ireland, 1831-1881* (London: 1885).

O Broin, Leon *The Chief Secretary, Augustine Birrell in Ireland* (London: 1969).

O'Connell, Phillip *Schools and Scholars of Breifne* (Dublin: 1942).

O'Connell, T. J. *History of the Irish National Teachers' Organisation, 1868-1968* (Dublin: 1968).

O'Donnell, F. H. *A History of the Irish Parliamentary Party* Vols I & II (London: 1910).

O'Donnell, F. H. *The Ruin of Education in Ireland* (London: 1902).

O'Hagan, John *Occasional Papers and Addresses* (London: 1884).

O'Riordan, M. *Catholicity and Progress in Ireland* (London: 1905).

Sadler, Michael (ed.) *Special reports on education subjects, 1896-1897* (London: 1897).

Strauss, E. *Irish nationalism and British democracy* (London: 1951).

Thornley, David *Isaac Butt* (London: 1964).

Tierney, Michael *Education in a Free Ireland* (Dublin: 1920).

Walsh, P. J. *William J. Walsh, Archbishop of Dublin* (Dublin & Cork: 1920).

Whiteside, Lesley *A History of the King's Hospital* (Dublin: 1975).

GOVERNMENT PUBLICATIONS

Parliamentary Papers

Report upon the State of Education in the Island of Trinidad, P.P. 1870 (450), L. 655.

Report of the Commission on Primary Education in Ireland, P.P. Vol. 28. (Parts I-VIII). Powis Report. 1870.

Report of Commission appointed by the Lord Lieutenant to inquire into Endowments Fund and Condition of all Endowed Schools in Ireland, 1881. P.P. Vol. 35 (C. 2831).

Reports of the Intermediate Education (Ireland) Board, 1879 to 1921.

Report of the Endowed Schools (Ireland) Commission, 1886-1894.

Intermediate Education (Ireland) Commission, 1898. First Report and Appendix; Minutes of Evidence: Miscellaneous Documents; Final Report.

Report of Messrs. F. H. Dale and T. A. Stephens, His Majesty's inspectors of schools, Board of Education, on intermediate education in Ireland, 1905. H. C. XXVIII (Cd. 2546).

Report of the Intermediate Education Board for Ireland under the Intermediate Education (Ireland) Act, 1914, as to the application of the Teachers' Salaries Grant, 1917-18. H.C.XI (Cd. 8724).

Report of the Vice-Regal Committee on the conditions of service and remuneration of teachers in intermediate schools, and on the distribution of grants from public funds for intermediate education in Ireland, 1919. P.P. XXI (Cmd. 66).

Statutes

Intermediate Education (Ireland) Act, 1878 (41 & 42 Vic., c. 66).
Intermediate Education (Ireland) Act, 1882 (45 & 46 Vic., c. 69).
Educational Endowments (Ireland) Act, 1885 (48 and 49 Vic., c. 78) and Schemes framed under this Act.
Local Taxation (Customs and Excise) Act, 1890 (53 & 54 Vic., c. 60).
Agriculture and Technical Instruction (Ireland) Act, 1899, (62 & 63 Vic., c. 43).
Intermediate Education (Ireland) Act, 1900 (63 & 64 Vic., c. 43).
Intermediate Education (Ireland) Act, 1913 (3 & 4 Geo. V., c. 29).
Intermediate Education (Ireland) Act, 1914 (4 & 5 Geo. V., c. 29).

Census Reports

Census of Ireland for the year 1871. General Report. LXXXI (C. 1377).
Census of Ireland for the year 1881. General Report. LXXVI (C. 3365).
Census of Ireland for the year 1891. General Report. XC. I (C. 6780).
Census of Ireland for the year 1901. General Report. C. XXIX (Cd. 1190).
Census of Ireland for the year 1911. General Report. CXVIII.I (Cd. 6663).

NEWSPAPERS, JOURNALS, YEAR-BOOKS AND ALMANACS

Belfast Newsletter
Cork Constitution
Cork Examiner
Daily Express
Freeman's Journal
Irish Times
The Times (London)

An Claidheamh Soluis
An Múinteoir Náisiúnta
Church of Ireland Gazette
Hibernian Journal
Irish Ecclesiastical Record
Irish Educational Review
Irish Journal of Education

Nation
Nineteenth Century (London)
Studies
Times Educational Supplement (London)

Battersby's Catholic Directory
Belfast Almanack and Ulster Directory, 1878
Cork Directory, 1877-78
Eason's Almanac and Handbook, 1879
Ellis's Irish Educational Directory and Scholastic Guide, 1888
Galway Year-Book and Directory, 1907
Irish Educational Almanac, 1881
Irish Educational Directory, 1887-1888
Irish Educational Year Book, 1879-1885
Limerick Directory, 1870-1877

PAMPHLETS

Association of Irish Schoolmistresses. Two papers read during the session 1889.
Catholic Headmasters of Ireland: *Memorial to the Board of Intermediate Education*, 1879.
Corish, Rev. Patrick (ed.) *A History of Irish Catholicism*, Vol. 5, Catholic Education, 1971.
Dease, Major Gerald *A Plea for Educational Reform*, 1918.
Education Reform Association: *Secular Control of secular education*, 1904.
'Educationist' *The Irish Intermediate Education Act of 1878; with an explanatory introduction*, 1878.
Gaelic League Pamphlets, No. 12 *The Irish Language and Intermediate Education*, 1901.
Gill, T. P. *Science in Secondary Schools; the Department's Programme*, 1902.
Humphreys, Rev. David *The Erasmus Smith Endowment*, 1895.
Lyons, R. D. *Supply and Demand for an enlarged system of Irish University Education*, 1873.
MacCaffrey, L. J. *The home rule party and Irish nationalist opinion, 1874-1876*. Reprint from *The Catholic Historical Review*, Vol. XLIII, No. 2, 1957.
McCarthy, M. J. F. *An Address on 'Education in Ireland'*, 1901.
Miller, J. D. H. *Clericalised Education in Ireland: A Plea for popular control*, Part 1, 1907.
Security of Tenure, 1909-1934. A pamphlet compiled by the Standing Committee of the A.S.T.I., December 1934.

INDEX

Aberdeen, Earl of, 83
Alexandra College, 9, 58, 96
Ancient Order of Hibernians, 103, 135-6
Asquith, H. H., 106
Association of Intermediate and
    University Teachers, 70-1, 93, 96
Association of Secondary Teachers
    (Ireland), 115, 118, 125, 128, 133,
    139-40, 158

Balfour, Arthur, 79, 162
Balfour Education Act, 100-1, 166
Balfour, Graham, 19
Ballymena Academy, 85
Ball, J. T., 40
Belfast Newsletter, 137
Belmore, Earl of, 40
Biggar, Joseph, 24, 34
Birrell, Augustine, 55, 100, 102, 104,
    109-17, 124, 166
Birrell Grant, *see* Teachers' Salaries
    Grant
Blackrock College, 10-11, 17
Bodkin, Fr (Castleknock), 75
Bonar Law, Andrew, 136
Boyd, Elisabeth, 66-7, 72
Brugha, Cathal, 145
Bryce Commission, 64
Bryce, James, 165
Burnham Scale, 141
Butler, W. F., 141, 144
Butt, Isaac, 32-3, 36
Byers, Mrs, 72

Cadogan, Earl of, 81
Cairns, Lord, 32-3, 38, 40, 49
Cahill, Fr E., 153
Campbell College, 86
Campbell-Bannerman, Sir Henry, 103-4
Carlow College, 5
Carrigy, Fr (St Patrick's, Armagh), 75
Carson, Sir Edward, 122-3, 137-8
Catholic Church, and secondary
    education, 2-4, 6, 16, 18-9, 22-4,
    26-9, 33-6, 52-4, 56-7, 77-8, 83-4,
    94, 109, 112-8, 127-8, 155, 157-8,
    167-71; *see also* Irish Councils Bill;
    MacPherson Bill
Catholic Clerical School Managers, 132
Catholic Headmasters' Association, 41,
    49-50, 83-4, 85, 112, 115, 125,
    139-40
Catholic University, 20, 23, 62-3
Central Association of Irish
    Schoolmistresses, 75, 125, 133

Charleville C.B.S., 149-50
Christian Brothers, 2, 4, 12-3, 50-2, 68-
    70, 91-2, 95, 106-8, 139, 152, 156
Church of Ireland Gazette, 103
Church of Ireland Training College, 60
Churchill, Lord Randolph, 11, 26, 31-2,
    165-6
Civil Service examinations, 14, 23, 34-5
Claidheamh Soluis, An, 101, 147, 154
Clongowes Wood College, 9, 119
Colum, Mary, 61
Comerton, James, 73
Commissioners of Education in Ireland,
    60, 144
Conroy, Bishop, 22-4
Convent schools, 2, 9, 71-2, 84-5
Convent Schools' Committee, 85, 112
Corcoran, Fr T., 127
Cork Daily Herald, 46
Corry, James P., 38, 40
County Councils' General Council,
    111-2, 136
Croke, Archbishop, 36, 56
Cullen, Cardinal Paul, 18-9, 26, 33, 57,
    158-9, 169-70

Dale and Stephens Report, 87-94, 105,
    121, 158
Davitt, Michael, 99
de Vere, Stephen, 11-2
Delaney, Fr William, 11, 30, 36, 53-4,
    157
Devitt, Fr (Clongowes), 74-5
Dillon, John, 102, 109, 163
Diocesan colleges, 1, 3-4, 5-6, 15, 21,
    92, 155
Disraeli, Benjamin, 20
Doherty, Dr J. J., 74
Dolan, Charles, 148
Dominican Convent (Eccles St), 9, 96
Dorrian, Bishop, 34
Dougherty, Rev. J. B., 56, 59
Dowling, E. J., 74, 157
Dundalk Educational Institute, 12
Dunsany, Lord, 35

Education Acts, *see* Balfour Education
    Act; Intermediate Education Acts
Education Bill (1919), *see* Macpherson
    Bill
Education Commission (1858), 25
Educational Endowments' Commission,
    38, 54, 56-60
Emly, Lord, 14, 20, 22, 26, 31, 34

Endowed Schools Commission, 32, 90
Endowments and endowed schools, 3, 18-9, 25-7, 31-2, 91; *see also* Educational Endowments' Commission
England, Professor John, 67-8
Ennis C.B.S., 85
Erasmus Smith schools, 11, 58-9

Female education, 8-9, 26-8, 38-9, 40, 43, 53-4, 71-2, 149; *see also* Convent schools
Finlay, Rev. T., 162
Fisher, H. A. L., 131-2
Fitzgibbon, Gerald, 30
Fitzgibbon, Lord Chief Justice, 56, 59
Fogarty, Bishop, 135
Foley, Bishop, 73, 101, 134-5
Forster, W. E., 49
Freeman's Journal, 26, 33, 169

Gaelic League, 5, 145, 154, 161
Gibson, Edward, 30
Gill, T. P., 162
Gladstone, W. E., 19-20, 37-8, 169
Gorst, Sir John, 98-9
Government of Ireland Act (1920), 138, 140-1
Granville, Earl, 38
Graves, Arnold, 71, 160-1
Greenwood, Sir Hamar, 140-1
Gwynn, Denis, 152

Hallinan, Bishop, 153, 155
Healy, Tim, 59, 162
Hedge schools, 4, 152
Henry, R. M., 127
Hicks-Beach, Sir Michael, 20-31, 36, 39, 169
High School (Dublin), 86
Hime, Maurice C., 6-7, 70
Houston, W. A., 141, 144
Houston, Dr (Coleraine Academical), 67-8
Howley, Edward, 16-8
Hubard, W. G., 157
Hyde, Douglas, 147, 154

Incorporated Association of Assistant Teachers, 122, 125, 140
Incorporated Society for the Promotion of the Protestant Faith in Ireland, 1, 12, 58
Inspection of schools, 23, 35-6, 73-7, 79-85, 87, 96
Intermediate Education Acts: (1878), 2, 25-6, 30-40, 158-9; 'conscience clause', 28-9, 33-6, 45; (1900), 76-7, 79, 162; (1914), 116-8, 123.
Intermediate Education Board, 10, 12-3, 22-9, 39-41, 43-4, 46-55, 60-3, 73, 79-85, 105-11, 118-20, 124-6, 139-44, 147-67; *see also* Dale and Stephens Report; Intermediate Education Commission
Intermediate Education Commission (1898), 64-79, 112
Irish Catholic Directory, 9, 11
Irish Councils Bill, 100-4, 170
Irish Ecclesiastical Record, 53
Irish Educational Review, 115-6
Irish Journal of Education, 115-6
Irish language, 37-8, 145, 147-8, 154-5, 164-5
Irish National Teachers Organisation, 132-3, 140
Irish Parliamentary Party, 33-4, 36, 100, 102-3, 134-6, 138, 167
Irish Times, 44-5
Irish University Commission, 92
Irish Universities Act, *see* Universities Act

Jesuits, 11, 157

Keenan, Patrick, 1, 17, 20-4, 26, 30-1, 33-4, 156
Kelly, Bishop, 71-2, 148
Kennedy, Professor (St Kieran's), 70
Kildare Place Society, 60
Killanin Commission, 131, 147
Kilmore, Bishop of, 5

Ladies' General Educational Institute, 38
Laffan, Bishop, 67
Lewis, Charles, 36-7, 39
Logue, Cardinal, 136
Longford convent school, 2
Lowther, James, 30-2, 39, 164
Lyons, R. D., 14

McCabe, Cardinal, 53
MacDonald, Dr Walter, 15, 137
MacDonnell, Sir Antony, 89, 102, 166
McEvilly, Rev. John, 4
McHugh, Annie, 127
Macken, James, 72
McKenna, Sir Joseph, 39
MacKillip, Misses, 72
McNeill, Hugh, 73
MacPherson Bill (1919), 131-9, 147, 170

Madame de Prins College (Limerick), 86
Magennis, William, 117-8, 167
Mahaffy, J. P., 3, 48, 54-5, 75, 152-4
Maxwell, Bro. Richard A., 51
Mechanics Institutes, 153
Methodist College (Belfast), 13, 68
Middleton, Viscount, 35
Model Schools, 23-4, 29
Molony Report, *see* Vice-Regal
    Committee
Molloy, Dr (Asst. Commissioner), 40,
    49, 70
Molloy, Fr Gerald, 56, 59
Monsell, William, *see* Emly, Lord
Morley, John, 106
Mungret College, 10, 62, 88
Murder Machine, The, 146
Murphy, Fr Andrew, 68
Murphy, Fr (Headmasters' Assoc.), 115

Naish, John, 56, 58
Nanetti, J. P., 98
Nation, The, 33
National Board of Education, 24-5, 28,
    60, 89, 91, 110, 144, 151
National schools, 1-3, 6, 8, 22-4, 68-9,
    89
Newman, Cardinal, 17-8, 20, 169
Nulty, Bishop, 54

O'Brien, Justice, 58-9
O'Ceallaigh, Sean, 145
O'Connor, T. P., 99
O'Conor Don, The, 37-8, 40, 49, 52,
    154, 162
O'Donnell, Frank Hugh, 36, 149
O'Donnell, Thomas, 164-5
O'Dwyer, Bishop, 78, 92, 100-1
O'Hagan, Lord, 34-6, 40
Omagh convent school, 9
Oranmore and Browne, Lord, 35

Palles, Baron Christopher, 40, 71, 79,
    162
Parnell, Charles Stewart, 34, 36
Pearse, Patrick, 144, 146-7
Primary schools, *see* National schools
Portarlington School, 6
Porter, Dr J. L., 27-9, 48
Power, John O'Conor, 37
Powis Report, 1-2, 11-2
Protestants and secondary education, 1,
    3, 6-7, 11, 28-9, 36, 39-40, 46, 54-
    7, 86, 90, 92, 114-5, 123, 136, 140-
    1, 154; *see also* Endowments and
    endowed schools; Schoolmasters'
    Association.

Queen's University, Belfast, 95-6, 120

Ratoath national school, 1
Redmond, John, 64-5, 99, 102-3, 161,
    165
Registration Council, 116, 119, 158
Rice, Edmund Ignatius, 91
Rockwell College, 68
Royal Belfast Academical Institution,
    86
Royal Schools, 1, 11, 57-60
Royal University, 62, 72, 92, 95

Sadler, Michael, 74
St Columba's College, 11
St Enda's, 147
St Joseph's Convent (Charleville), 88
St Joseph's Seminary (Galway), 85
St Kieran's College (Kilkenny), 5, 15
St Mary's College (Knockbeg), 5
St Munchin's College, 68
St Patrick's College (Cavan), 73
St Patrick's Seminary (Tullow), 10
St Peter's College (Wexford), 9
St Stanislaus College, *see* Tullabeg
    College
Salmon, Dr George, 40
Samuel, (Solicitor-General), 123-4
Samuels, Arthur, 106
School Attendance Act (1892), 150,
    170
Schoolmasters' Association, 21, 41, 49-
    50, 75, 80, 84, 110, 121, 125, 133
Seminaries, *see* Diocesan colleges
Shaw, George F., 16
Sheehan, Rev. M., 162
Sheehy Skeffington, Hanna, 93, 114
Sinn Fein, 133-4
Society for the Preservation of the Irish
    Language, 154
Society for the Promotion of Protestant
    Schools, 90
Starkie, Dr Walter, 71, 77, 87, 93, 152-
    3, 157
Sullivan, W. K. (President, Q.C.C.), 7,
    14-5, 48, 68
Synge Street C.B.S., 69

Teachers, 7-8, 60, 72-3, 85-7, 91-6,
    108-10, 112-9, 122-3, 126-8, 139-
    40, 147, 157-8, 171
Teachers' Guild of Great Britain and
    Ireland, 73
Teachers' Salaries Grant, 112-5, 117-8,
    122-4, 170
Technical Instruction Act (1850), 153

Thompson, J., 140
Thompson, John, 73
Tierney, Professor Michael, 147-8
Times Educational Supplement, 137
Times, The, 21, 33
Traill, Dr, 8, 56, 58
Treasury, 76-7, 81-3, 101, 107, 109,
    111, 119, 141, 160, 165-7
Trinity College, Dublin, 90, 95, 108,
    120-1
Tullabeg College, 8, 10-11

United Irish League, 102-3
Universities, and school system, 14, 47-8,

    90-3, 95-6, 111-2, 120-1, 153-6
Universities Act (1908), 108, 111
Universities Bill (1872), 19, 169
Ursuline Convent (Waterford), 9, 96

Vice-Regal Committee, 86, 125-31

Walsh, Archbishop William, 41, 46, 73,
    82, 156, 161
Williams, W. J., 127
Windle, Sir Bertram, 162-3
Woodlock, Dr B., 20, 31, 39, 170
Wyndham, George, 54-5, 87, 89, 98-9